The American Myth of Success

THE

AMERICAN

MYTH

OF

SUCCESS

From Horatio Alger
to Norman Vincent Peale

Richard Weiss

UNIVERSITY OF ILLINOIS PRESS

Urbana and Chicago

Illini Books edition, 1988
© 1969 by Richard Weiss
Manufactured in the United States of America
P 5 4 3 2 1

This book is printed on acid-free paper.

Library of Congress Cataloging-in-Publication Data
Weiss, Richard, 1934-
    The American myth of success : from Horatio Alger to Norman
Vincent Peale / Richard Weiss. — Illini Books ed.
        p. cm.
    Reprint. Originally published: New York : Basic Books, ©1969.
    Bibliography: p.
    Includes index.
    ISBN 0-252-06043-1 (pbk. : alk. paper)
    1. United States — Social conditions.   2. Success — United States.
3. Success in literature.   I. Title.
HN57.W45 1988
306'.0973 — dc19   88-18720
                                                                     CIP

For my sons, Daniel and Jonathan

Acknowledgments

Many people have aided and advised me in the course of writing this book. The President's Office of Columbia University and the Academic Senate of the University of California at Los Angeles provided funds and released time which hastened the completion of my work.

Two of my former teachers and colleagues at Columbia University, Walter Metzger and Robert Cross, read an early draft of the manuscript and gave me valuable criticism. Robert Dallek, Frederic Jaher, and Lawrence Levine generously took time from their own work to give the manuscript a searching reading. Their suggestions were very helpful. Richard Hofstadter, whose imaginativeness and freshness of mind have inspired a generation of students, provided much wise counsel.

Contents

Introduction   3

Chapter 1   *The Emergence of an Ideal*   16

Chapter 2   *Horatio Alger, Jr., and the Gilded Age*   48

Chapter 3   *The Christian Novel and the Success Myth*   64

Chapter 4   *How to Succeed: Conduct-of-Life Literature in the Industrial Era*   97

Chapter 5   *The Revival of the Transcendentalist Dogma:* PART I—*The Defense of Idealism*   128

Chapter 6   *The Revival of the Transcendentalist Dogma:* PART II—*The Religion of Optimism*   154

Chapter 7   *The American Mystique of the Mind*   195

Selected Bibliography   241

Index   265

The American Myth of Success

Introduction

Tradition has it that every American child receives, as part of his birthright, the freedom to mold his own life. There are, to be sure, many dissenters from this aspect of the national folklore. Social critics have long insisted on the limitations that circumstances impose on life patterns, and historians have raised serious questions about the nature and extent of social mobility in American society. Despite such skepticism, however, the idea that ours is an open society, where birth, family, and class do not significantly circumscribe individual possibilities, has a strong hold on the popular imagination. The belief that all men, in accordance with certain rules, but exclusively by their own efforts, can make of their lives what they will has been widely popularized for well over a century. The cluster of ideas surrounding this conviction makes up the American myth of success.

Many myths born in the nineteenth century have withered and disappeared; the myth of success, however, continues to flourish. Conveyed in a massive literature, it stands as one of the most enduring expressions of American popular ideals. I do not use the word "myth" to imply something entirely false. Rather, I mean it to connote a complex of profoundly held attitudes and values which condition the way men view the world and understand their experience. However inaccurate as a description of American society, the success myth reflects what millions believe that society is or ought to be. The degree to which opportunity has or has not been available in our society is a subject for empirical investigation. It rests within the realm of verifiable fact. The *belief* that opportunity exists for all is a subject for intellectual analysis and rests within the realm of ideology. This latter dimension of the success myth is the primary focus of this book.

II

Though the success myth did not become crystallized until the second third of the nineteenth century, its roots are found in early American Puritanism. Success literature bears much resemblance to the prescriptive writings of the divines of seventeenth-century New England. These Puritan guides gave advice on the achievement of material success, but always in the context of a larger framework of values. More than lists of commercial maxims, these writings were essays on the general conduct of life. This comprehensiveness of concern also characterizes the later literature of self-help which provides the main focus of this book. The habit of telling people how to live properly did not die with the Puritans. It reappears in the writings of Benjamin Franklin, in the "rags-to-riches" literature of the nineteenth century, and in the inspirational writings of the twentieth. The more closely one looks into this success literature, the more apparent it becomes that "climbing life's ladder" is only one of its concerns, and by no means the most important one. Surrounding the notion of mobility are beliefs, implicit and explicit, which reveal the deeper meanings that the ideal of open opportunity holds for American society.

It is important, therefore, to distinguish between the urge to material accumulation, unhampered by formal ethical goals and restraints, and the more variegated complex of ideas which make up the ideology of self-help. To be sure, success writers always tender the promise of material rewards. Observers of American culture, however, have attached too literal a significance to this fact. Tradition has it that we are a materialistic people, lovers of money and things, the more the better. Yet the American's desire for the creature comforts does not much distinguish him from the rest of mankind. While the United States may be unique in its achievement of material well-being, it is hardly so in its desire for it. Wealth, material goods, a decent standard of living, are coveted well-nigh universally. What does distinguish the American's pursuit of success is the particular significance he attaches to its achievement. My aim is to enlarge our insight into what this is and how it relates to the broader fabric of our civilization.

III

The "rags-to-riches" tradition in the nineteenth century centered around the ethical maxims of industry, frugality, and prudence—in short, around the behavioral patterns enjoined by the Protestant ethic. Men living by these rules were likely to be successful; men living in violation of them were certain to fail. But the Puritan legacy to the self-help tradition extended further. The theology of the Puritans stressed pre-destination, but, at the same time, their idea of the covenant introduced an element of reasonableness into the relationship between God and man. God's governance was conceived of as rational. The idea of contract implied a mutuality of obligation. Reason dictated that God would reciprocate if man fulfilled his terms of the covenant. In this way, man acquired some role in determining the outcome of his life. As Perry Miller wrote: "With the notion of a covenant to assist them, theologians could give reasons for what physicists could but lamely assert, that in a universe governed by God's providence and sustained by His concurrence, the will of man remains free." [1]

This aspect of the Puritan legacy gained force as American society became less elitist and more egalitarian. It was incorporated into the success mythology as the ideal that each man should find rewards commensurate with his merit, an ideal congenial to the ethos of a democratic nation. By the Jacksonian period, when the notion of the self-made man began to gain broad currency, the assumptions underlying this ideal were so generally accepted they existed below the level of open discussion. "Rags-to-riches" writers explicitly linked virtue with success and sin with failure. They rarely stated the premises on which this view rested, namely, that justice must reign in a universe governed by moral law and that in such a universe man's freedom to sin or not to sin gave him power to govern his own destiny. The belief that all men could achieve material success by living according to certain ethical rules of conduct was a kind of secular transmutation of the covenant theory. As the Puritan viewed material well-being coupled with piety as a sign of grace, so the nineteenth-century American viewed success coupled with morality as a sign of freedom. The mobility ideology, then, was inextricably bound up with a supernaturalistic cosmology. While the success myth's symbols were material, its impulse was idealistic.

IV

The relation of the success myth to American capitalism has been an ambivalent one. On the one hand, as many historians have noted, the "rags-to-riches" tradition, by creating an illusion of opportunity, served as a social pacifier inimical to reform. Furthermore, by equating failure with sin and personal inadequacy, self-help popularizers obscured the objective causes of social injustice. The beneficiaries of this misplaced emphasis, so this argument runs, were the corporations and the wealthy. While this viewpoint is illuminating, I find it ascribes too monolithic a function to ideas that found adherents among progressives and conservatives alike. The belief that anyone can succeed is a two-edged sword. Taken as a description of what is, it encourages complacency; taken as a prescription for what ought to be, it encourages the impulse to reform. Historically and in the present, the commitment to open opportunity was and is an important weapon in the reformer's ideological arsenal.

Other aspects of the success myth also placed it into an ambivalent relationship to American capitalism. This was particularly true after the Civil War when the United States industrialized with such rapidity. Success writers were extremely critical of the unfettered impulse toward acquisition. Here it is important to remember that the success myth was forged when the United States was still a nation of yeomen and artisans. The conception of riches expressed in success literature was very moderate by comparison with the wealth achieved by the magnates of industry. To sensibilities formed prior to industrialization, the sheer size of those new fortunes was jarring. Also "rags-to-riches" literature in the post-bellum period retained a strong rural bias, long after its social context had begun to disappear. While millions flocked to mushrooming urban centers in search of better lives, the apostles of opportunity looked upon the expanding metropolis with a kind of horror. Most often, they advised their readers to stay home on the farm. Cities were the citadels of wealth, but the chances for a decent life were much greater in rural settings away from such lures of Satan as the theater and the saloon. Similarly, the behavioral patterns enjoined in success tracts were more congenial to the counting-house than the factory. The caution and prudence, so central to the Protestant ethic, better reflected the merchant-agrarian capitalism of the early nineteenth century than the innovative spirit which characterized the newly emerging industrial order. Other earmarks of the Gilded Age—the conspicuous leisure of the rich, the degraded condition of the poor, the grimness of industrial conflict—were all viewed as corruptions of the natural order. Post-bellum America, labeled an "age of excess," was stamped by unprecedented social conflict; the ideal world described by success cultists was a harmonious one, marked by moderation in all things. By and large, then, the values embodied in the myth of success conflicted with the day-to-day practices of a rapidly industrializing society. This clash lent the myth a reformist tendency.

Indeed, the reform movement of the early twentieth century can be interpreted as an attempt to translate the "rags-to-riches" tradition into social realities. This applies, particularly, to the emphasis which success writers gave to the idea of the autonomous individual. From one perspective, the era of the robber barons appears to mark the quintessence of self-made manhood. This view, however, is akin to the proverbial "missing the forest for the trees." While a handful of men achieved remarkable wealth and power, the structure of the new economy threatened to eradicate irrevocably the basis of economic individualism for society as a whole. Progressive reformers were much alarmed by this threat. By the turn of the century, the builders of corporate capitalism candidly acknowledged that traditional entrepreneurial individualism was gone forever. John D. Rockefeller knew of what he spoke, when he pronounced: "The day of combination is here to stay. Individualism has gone, never to return." [2] Reformers, however, refused to give up the ghost, and one stream of Progressivism was devoted to revivifying this aspect of American tradition. Corporations were seen as the arch-enemies of individualistic enterprise; its defenders were in the party of reform. The success myth, with its commitment to individual economic independence and open opportunity, provided a value base for criticizing the new industrial order.

V

Beliefs, however, have a personal as well as a social relevance. The challenge which industrialization presented to the ideology of self-help created a major psychic crisis that was acutely felt on the individual level. The traditional association of virtue and success came under increasing ridicule during the Gilded Age. The inequities that characterized the period—the enormous accumulation of wealth by a few, on the one hand, and the poverty of the masses of men, on the other—strained the faith of even the most credulous. It became increasingly difficult to relate success and failure to the virtue or vice of the individuals involved. The fact clearly was that venality, in both the political and economic spheres, often paid off handsomely. Such occurrences, while not new, did become more troubling after the Civil War, simply because they took place on a larger scale than ever before. The spectacle of sharp dealers garnering riches and power did not merely outrage the sense of justice; it threatned to shatter an entire *weltanschauung*. The assault on the moral equation of the success ideology brought the whole range of assumptions on which it rested into the open. Just as the supporting structure of an edifice remains concealed until its façade is torn away, so the ideological underpinnings of the success myth remained protectively submerged until its superstructure began to crumble. The breakdown of the moral equation was so profoundly unsettling because it brought into question the most fundamental beliefs Americans held about the nature of man and the universe.

New intellectual currents intensified the sense of crisis. The higher criticism of the Bible, studies in comparative religion, naturalism in science, and positivism in philosophy, all combined to weaken the supernaturalistic beliefs to which the psychic stability of Americans was anchored. At the same time, Darwinism dealt the human ego the greatest blow it had sustained since the Copernican revolution three and a half centuries earlier. Changes, mundane and intellectual, shook the whole structure of the American world-view to its very foundations. As a consequence, confidence, security, all sense of certainty, began to waver. Reverend Josiah Strong, recalling his own bewilderment at changes in post-bellum

America, described what must have been a common experience of the time.

> My . . . views felt the shock of great changes, theological and social, which have taken place during the past generation. Broken loose from their ancient moorings, men seemed to me to be drifting. New views fostered by science were believed to be hostile to religion, paralyzing to faith, and demoralizing to conduct. Impatience of restraint rather than love of truth seemed to inspire the attacks on many beliefs which the fathers held sacred.
>
> When would these changes cease? How much of the old structure of society and belief would they leave standing? Were there any great certainties left? [3]

The outpouring of conventional success tracts during the Gilded Age was an attempt to prove that there were. As the pace of change increased, the defenders of traditional values multiplied. Their writings reflect the craving for stability in a society in the throes of transformation.

VI

In the context of the new America, the "rags-to-riches" myth became increasingly anachronistic. As the achievement of economic independence, in the traditional sense, became less possible, its function as a symbol of man's freedom was undermined. The belief in the autonomous individual remained but within a new framework of supporting ideas. These emerged by the end of the nineteenth century. Their appearance is marked by the publication of Ralph Waldo

Trine's *In Tune With the Infinite* (1897), which became one of the greatest nonfiction best-sellers of the twentieth century. The new inspiration stressed psychological techniques of self-manipulation as the means to achievement. Its keynote was "mind-power." For a time, both schools of self-help flourished side by side. After the First World War, however, the older tradition declined while the newer continues to be widely propagated, most notably in the writings on "positive thinking" by Norman Vincent Peale.

Early mind-power advocates sought to counteract the growing impact of "materialism" and "determinism" on the popular consciousness. These "isms" cast doubt on the supernaturalistic assumptions implicit in the success ideology. Sensing this threat, "rags-to-riches" writers had responded with reassertions of traditional morality. The proponents of mind-power developed a new and different argument more in line with the ethos of a modern industrialized society. They confronted many of the basic questions around which much of the intellectual debate of the twentieth century, on all levels, revolved: Is man free or is man determined by forces beyond his control? Is man responsible or merely a helpless and therefore blameless object in the hands of a capricious fate? These seemingly abstruse questions had, by the turn of the century, penetrated deeply into the popular mind. Mind-power advocates "answered" them, and therein lay their appeal. Never too subtle, they combined simplicity with certitude. Denying determinism, they exalted the individual. Man was free; the universe was governed by law; man was the center of creation and possessed an element of divinity. Learn the laws of the universe, and there was no limit to what individuals might accomplish. It would be difficult to overstate the importance of the idea of individual power in the new success cult. The words "mastery," "power," "control," dominate its literature.

Despite this, mind-power writings have a tone of plaintiveness. They lack the ring of full conviction, somewhat in the manner of an individual trying to believe in spite of himself. This suggests the extent to which the belief in the autonomous individual was shaken by the revolution in both the techniques and organization of production after the Civil War. The sense of self-direction enjoyed by the independent entrepreneur did not come naturally to the white-collar member of a corporation bureaucracy. Yet the commitment to individualism was so central a tenet of the American faith that to surrender it was tantamount to a kind of treason. As I have noted, certain reformers tried to keep economic individualism alive. Their attempts, however, could have only the most limited success. The demands of modern production and distribution could not be fulfilled by small-scale, individually owned businesses. While such enterprises continued to exist, even to flourish, they became increasingly marginal to the economy as a whole. Ever-increasing numbers of people were destined to spend their careers within complex organizational structures. The stability of the new order required some means of reconciling the ideal of individual freedom with the realities of a society patterned along corporate lines. This is precisely what the new success myth accomplished. It provided an ideological construct which enabled members of a mass society to preserve at least an illusion of independence.

In defending the notion of man as free, mind-power advocates developed a kind of neo-idealism. Their thought was eclectic, drawn from thinkers as different as Emerson and Hegel, and from disciplines as diverse as physics and psychology. At first glance, their writings seem an indecipherable confusion of unrelated ideas. Upon more careful examination, however, they display a logic of their own. Granting their premises, their conclusions, if unwarranted, are at least comprehensible. God, in the mentalistic self-help tradition, is defined in Emersonian terms, as a Universal Intelligence or Over-Soul. The individual is held to be a partial incarnation of this cosmic force. The locus of divinity in man is his mind which relates him, in a manner of speaking, to the Universal Mind and gives him access to its power. Translated into the popular idiom, this provides the ideological basis for the conviction that all men can "think" their way to success. In promulgating this notion, mind-power advocates became heir to the earlier "rags-to-riches" tradition. Their inspirational literature is probably the single greatest conveyor of the success ideology in the twentieth century.

Like the earlier success myth, the cult of mind-power embodies a world-view. Its advocates equate mind with soul, and a sound mind is conceived in much the same way as a regenerate spirit. This merging of entities formerly regarded as quite separate from one another is one of the distinctive moral creations of our time. Virtue, in this cosmology, is identified with health rather than the classic behavioral patterns of industry, frugality, and prudence. Sin is sickness, and sickness is incompatible with success, just as laziness, let us say, was in the earlier mythology. The presuppositions underlying this new moral equation, however, are by no means confined to success writers. They have entered the mainstream of American religion and are found among psychologists and psychoanalysts as well. Indeed, mentalism, in its various forms, is one of those pervasive phenomena that permeate culture as a whole. The use of mind to support an idealistic conception of man and the universe forms one of the central elements in the ideological climate of twentieth-century America.

VII

Any student of the success myth encounters the seemingly insoluble dilemma of finding any consistent definition of success. At different times, it seems to mean virtue, money, happiness, or a combination of all three. Furthermore, the means for achieving success suggested by self-help popularizers are markedly different in the nineteenth and twentieth centuries. Mind-power advocates de-emphasize the ascetic virtues of the Protestant ethic, and extol ease, relaxation, and comfort. These differences reflect important changes in American values. On another level, however, there are lines which connect the two traditions and link them both to the heritage of the seventeenth century. The success myth has always joined the promise of material rewards to a supernaturalistic cosmology and remains rooted in the belief that in a universe of reason and of law, man is free to decide his own fate. These continuities may be likened to a single thread—winding, and of many colors—stretching across the whole of the American experience.

NOTES

1. Perry Miller, *The New England Mind, From Colony to Province* (Cambridge, Mass.: Harvard University Press, 1962), p. 402.
2. Quoted in Allan Nevins, *Study in Power, John D. Rockefeller* (New York: Charles Scribner's Sons, 1953), I, p. 402.
3. Josiah Strong, *The Times and Young Men* (New York: The Baker and Taylor Co., 1901), pp. 13–14.

Chapter 1

The Emergence of an Ideal

I

American guides to living continue a long tradition, beginning early in the sixteenth century with the appearance of Count Baldassare Castiglione's *Il Cortegiano* (The Courtier). Translated into English in 1561, it was followed by a shower of books, pamphlets, and sermons on learning, manners, and daily conduct.[1] Sixteenth-century England, in transition from a Catholic, feudal, manorial society to a Protestant, centralized, and commercial nation contained a variety of classes and interests, often in conflict, each with its own set of problems, aspirations, and beliefs. Guide books were part of the running dialogue of this civilization, represented at one end of the spectrum by *The Courtier*'s defense of the knightly virtues—military prowess, leisure, and elegance—and, at the other, by the growing number of sermons preaching work, simplicity, and service to God.

In the great expansion of that civilization to the North American continent in the seventeenth century, the dialogue changed. In the new setting one voice—the voice of the knight, the lord of the manor, the nobleman—thinned and almost disappeared. The talk was now carried on chiefly by the minister, the merchant, and the yeoman. Time, distance, and natural conditions lessened the force of aristocratic tradition; conflict and diversity remained, but within the more limited context of what was, from its beginnings, a Protestant, middle-class civilization.[2]

Protestantism, in its Puritan variant, forms one of the cornerstones of American culture, and the prescriptive literature it produced is one of the richest sources of what Weber called the Protestant ethic. While Weber confined his conclusions to the relationship between this ethic and incipient capitalism in the seventeenth and eighteenth centuries, American scholars have applied them to the nineteenth century as well. The Talcott Parsons English translation of *The Protestant Ethic and the Spirit of Capitalism* appeared in 1930. The first full-length study of the American success myth was completed four years later.[3] This and later works on the subject are all informed by the "spirit of Weber." In using the Weber thesis to explain the significance of guides to self-help, success tracts, and the "rags-to-riches" myth—the purveyors of the Protestant ethic in the nineteenth century—students have related the Puritan virtues to a never-ending desire for material acquisition. These virtues, they argue, served as a continuing endorsement of the get-ahead values of the business community, as a standing rationalization for the growing American plutocracy, and as a form of social control hostile to the reform movements seeking to curb the excesses of industrialism.[4]

This particular application (or misapplication) of Weber's ideas is not without a certain irony. Weber emphasized the effect of belief on economic behavior, rather than vice versa. His work was a running argument against the historical materialism of Marx, which stressed the derivative nature of ideas. In evaluating the importance of the Protestant ethic in the nineteenth century, students of the success myth have, whether wittingly or no, supported the materialist viewpoint. The ethic is not seen as causal so much as re-enforcing an established economic system. Thus Weber's ideas are used to support an interpretation of history diametrically opposed to his own. In essence, what has been taken from the Weber thesis is simply that Protestantism is congenial to capitalism. This congeniality is deemed constant in spite of changing historical circumstances. The inevitable conflict between the Protestant ethic and the values fostered by capitalism—a collision Weber was at pains to demonstrate—is largely ignored. Some examination of Weber's work may be helpful in understanding the problems raised by its later application.

II

Weber, in his *Protestant Ethic and the Spirit of Capitalism*, sought the answer to an obvious but troublesome question. Arguing that capitalistic enterprise in its inception required a value structure which disciplined individuals in accordance with its needs, he asked where such a structure originated.

Weber maintained that, before modern times, economic activity—whether on a large or small scale—had been pursued only for what it could bring to the individual in the way of sustenance, comfort, or power. It was a means to life. He argued that in the sixteenth and seventeenth centuries, in certain areas of western Europe, this traditional attitude changed. Economic pursuits became ends in themselves. Work became a reason for living rather than the reverse. As such, economic activity, in all its phases, was subject to a uniquely rational discipline. This discipline formed the "spirit of capitalism" in the West, and distinguished it not only from other forms of economic organization, but from earlier forms of capitalism as well.

In seeking the origins of this *geist* and the behavior patterns it fostered, Weber observed that in the past "the magical and religious forces, and the ethical ideas of duty based on them . . . [were] always among the most important formative influences on conduct," [5] and chose to concentrate his investigation on these forces. His concern was with the ethical maxims which fostered early capitalism and not with the means by which a mature capitalism preserved itself. He denied, for example:

> that a conscious acceptance of these ethical maxims on the part of the individuals, entrepreneurs, or labourers, in modern capitalistic enterprises, is a condition of the further existence of present-day capitalism. The capitalistic economy of the present day is an immense cosmos into which the individual is born, and which presents itself to him, at least as an individual, as an unalterable order of things in which he must live. It forces the individual, in so far as he is involved in the system of market relationships, to conform to capitalistic rules of action. [6]

An economic order, once established, compels individuals to act in a certain way. Originally a consequence of the practical effects of certain values, it creates its own and, like any offspring, frequently encourages behavior quite antagonistic to the values of its parents. But, Weber continues: "In order that a manner of life so well adapted to the peculiarities of capitalism . . . should come to dominate others, it had to originate somewhere . . . as a way of life common to whole groups of men. This origin is what really needs explanation." [7] He found this explanation in the practical ethics of the ascetic branches of Protestantism. Asceticism flourished in many places but it had developed, in Western monasticism, a rational character, lacking elsewhere, which was adopted by Protestant adherents to the ascetic principle. Weber contended:

> It [monasticism] had developed a systematic method of rational conduct . . . to free man from the power of irrational impulses and his dependence on the world and on nature. It attempted to subject man to the supremacy of a purposeful will, to bring his actions under constant self-control. . . . Thus it trained the monk, objectively, as a worker in the service of the Kingdom of God. . . . This active self-control, which formed the end . . . of the rational monastic virtues everywhere, was also the most important practical ideal of Puritanism.[8]

Unlike Catholics, however, the Puritans selected no special group for God's service. They made no monks and built no monasteries, but imposed the obligation of service equally on all men. The callings, or occupations, which God assigned to men, were to be performed with the same commitment and fervor which had attached to the obligations of the cloister. The most mundane tasks became devotional. Each man—be he mechanic, merchant, or magistrate—had to perform his job as a religious duty.

> Sebastian Franck struck the central characteristic of this type of religion when he saw the significance of the Reformation in

the fact that now every Christian had to be a monk all his life . . . and those passionately spiritual natures which formerly supplied the highest type of monk were now forced to pursue their ascetic ideals within mundane occupations.[9]

For the Lutheran this meant resigned acceptance of the lot which God had assigned to him. For the Calvinist it meant that and more. Resignation had to be accompanied by the *methodical* performance of duty. In this way, the rational asceticism of the monastery was transferred to the whole gamut of worldly occupations, and provided the ethical impulse for the rationalization of economic activity. The methodical pursuit of economic interest was not only tolerated but enjoined, so long as the transcendant motivation remained a conscious performance of God's work. One of the chief consequences of this ethic was the making of money. At the same time the Puritan condemned foolish and extravagant expenditure. The urge to make money complemented by restrictions on spending resulted in the accumulations of capital essential to furthering capitalistic enterprise. In this way, the ascetic branches of Protestantism provided those "magical and religious forces" which encouraged a manner of life congenial to the development of capitalism. They did so not by specifically encouraging material acquisition but by preaching the subjection of life to a rational discipline. Work, diligence, and frugality were not upheld as economic virtues but as ethical maxims for the conduct of life. In its broadest sense, the Protestant ethic demanded order, moderation, and service. It permitted recreation, in so far as it was necessary to keep one balanced, healthy, and efficient, but condemned spontaneous enjoyment, or pleasure for pleasure's sake.

Yet, as leaders of ascetic movements themselves observed,

asceticism was subject to the workings of a cruel dialectic. The practice of the ascetic virtues produced wealth but could not survive its influence. This had been true in the monastic movements of the Middle Ages and had stimulated periodic attempts at reform. It continued to be true when the ascetic ideal was extended to worldly affairs. From the religious point of view, nothing caused failure so much as success. John Wesley, the founder of English Methodism, stated the paradox perfectly:

> I fear, wherever riches have increased, the essence of religion has decreased in the same proportion. Therefore I do not see how it is possible, in the nature of things, for any revival of true religion to continue long. For religion must necessarily produce both industry and frugality, and these cannot but produce riches. But as riches increase so will pride, anger, and love of the world in all its branches. . . . So, although the form of religion remains, the spirit is swiftly vanishing away. Is there no way to prevent this—this continual decay of pure religion?[10]

This question obsessed the minds of the American Puritan divines. The more their holy experiment thrived, the less holy it became. In 1679, the Boston Synod of Churches declared that an "insatiable desire after land and worldly accommodations" was causing men to forsake the church. "Farms and Merchandisings have been preferred before the things of God." [11] Ministers preached jeremiads decrying the sins which brought affliction upon the colony. Merchants had to be reminded not to substitute their own purposes for God's. Mechanics were warned that ambition for self was sinful. Matrons were cautioned against fancy dress and frippery, for such worldly concerns undermined religious life. An errant people were warned to reform themselves lest

God rain down his wrath.[12] Thus, even in early New England the Protestant ethic was preached to restrain the capitalistic spirit.

III

A substantial body of criticism has arisen around the Weber thesis. Recently, the Swedish economic historian, Kurt Samuelsson, has argued persuasively that no causal connection between Protestantism and capitalism exists.[13] I am not concerned here with a general evaluation of the Weber thesis but only with certain of its applications to the American scene. Even granting that some aspects of American Puritanism helped forge a character congenial to capitalism, it is important to realize that other aspects of the same phenomenon did not. In the Puritan conception, economic activity was subject to both moral and social considerations. The founders of the Bay Colony never assumed an inevitable harmony between the pursuit of self-interest and the well-being of the community as a whole. On the contrary, they believed that government could and should supervise individual economic activity and make it conform to the commonweal. Economic liberalism advanced only with the decline of the influence of the clergy. The loosening of economic controls marked the waning of religious orthodoxy.[14] Thus, at best, the Protestant ethic bore an ambivalent relation to the rapid economic development of New England.

Secondly, any attempt to apply the Weber thesis to the situation in early New England must be qualified by an awareness of the differences between the American setting and that of Europe. The Protestant Reformation and the consequent extension of the ascetic principle to worldly affairs occurred against the backdrop of a seignorial civilization. In general, the secular values which prevailed in western Europe before the modern period were the values of the landed nobility. These included, first of all, military prowess. The education of the noble, if he had any at all, was intended to prepare him to perform on the field of battle. The high Middle Ages added the courtly virtues of charm, wit, and elegance. The life of the noble was marked by conspicuous learning, conspicuous manners, and conspicuous dress, or what Thorstein Veblen defined more generally, at a later day, as the marks of the leisure class.[15] The soil of aristocratic values—reverence for leisure and contempt for productive labor—was uncongenial to the growth of the capitalistic spirit; by contrast, assuming the validity of the Weber thesis, the values of the ascetic branches of Protestantism were. To some degree, however, the revolutionary economic potential of Protestantism derived from this conflict of value systems.

On the American continent such a conflict never existed. There was no feudal class and no substantial repository of aristocratic values. In England, the dissenting minister and the merchant might join forces against the aristocrat, the common enemy of both. In New England, the minister and merchant frequently found in each other the greatest obstacle to their respective interests. In England, the Puritan clergy resisted the establishment; in New England, they were the establishment and resisted change.

Massachusetts Bay was founded with the intention of creating a perfect commonwealth, strictly disciplined in the service of God. Soon, however, personal ambition began subverting the original purpose. Many sermons of the late seventeenth century were angry warnings to a drifting populace. These jeremiads were among the first chords of reform struck on the American continent. Rapid development encouraged secular ways of life and undermined the values of the pious. Any attempt to preserve those values assumed the quality of a demand for reform. From this time onward, whenever the pursuit of personal gain seemed to endanger the larger moral aims of society, the Protestant ethic was invoked to remind men of their obligations. When expressed in writing, it became the conscience literature of America.

IV

A prototype of the Puritan guides to the conduct of life is Cotton Mather's *Bonifacius: Essays to Do Good.* It was written to teach the ways of doing God's will on earth. "There needs abundance to be done," wrote Mather, "that the *Evil Manners* of the World, by which men are *drowned in Perdition,* may be Reformed; and mankind rescued from the Epidemical Corruption and Slavery which has overwhelmed it." [16] Interpreting the doctrine of election rather loosely, Mather linked good works to salvation and insisted that men "Consider Good Works, as the *Way* to, yea, as a Part of, the Great Salvation, which is Purchased and Intended . . . [them], by . . . [their] Blessed Saviour. Without an Holy Heart," he went on, "you can't be fit for an *Holy Heaven. . . .* But an *Holy Heart* will cause a man to do *Good Works* with all his Heart." [17] Thus, in its largest sense, the good life was offered as a sign of grace which was coveted above all things.

The will to do good could be demonstrated in all callings

and all human relationships. Aid to the widowed and orphaned drew praise; the poor were the responsibility of the entire community. Doctors were especially blessed "with Opportunities, to help the *Poor,* and heal them for Nothing." [18] Sounding a note which was to echo loudly in the twentieth century, Mather counseled the doctor not to confine his healing skills to the body. To help the patient he should "raise in him as *Bright Thoughts* as may be, and Scatter the *Clouds,* remove the Leads, which his Mind is perplexed withal: Especially, by Representing and Magnifying the *Mercy* of GOD IN CHRIST unto him." [19]

Another calling offering unique possibilities for service was the ministry. The minister might lack "Wordly *Riches*" and the means of acquiring them, but was amply compensated by "*the Opportunities to Do Good*" which came to him more often than to others. These opportunities were riches enough and should be prized "above any Farms, or Bags, or Whatever Temporal Possessions." [20]

Those men whom God had put in the way of large fortunes were advised to follow ". . . the Example of some Eminent Merchants, who have set their Estate at a Moderate and Competent Elevation, and Resolved, they would never be any Richer than *that.* They have carried on a Great and Quick Trade; but what ever Gain carried their Estates beyond the Set Sum, they Devoted it all to Pious uses." [21]

In a similar vein Mather provided wisdom for wives, husbands, children, and servants. Goodness could and should govern all the manifold activities of living.

Bonifacius stands at the beginning of a literary tradition that spans two centuries. The huge outcroppings of success literature in the nineteenth century belong to this genre, and, with rare exceptions, can be classed as "essays to do good."

Discussions of wealth occupy an important place in this

literature. The Puritan viewed material success as a sign of the diligent performance of the callings which God assigned all men, but also feared it as a temptation to sin. Riches were considered so corrupting that their acquisition and expenditure were hedged with all kinds of conditions. Men were besought to do their jobs well but not with a view toward leaving the station in life in which Providence had placed them. Yet the opportunities presented by a virgin continent were an invitation to restlessness and ambition. Men who felled the forests and cleared the fields were quick to sense the possibilities of rising in the world and were prone to disregard moral restraints that might bar the way. Ministers cautioned against this get-ahead mentality. One tract, written by an Englishman but widely circulated in America, reminded the ambitious that "The wise Governor of the universe . . . appointed to every one his *proper place* and work . . . [and would] rather reprove than reward those who . . . [acted] out of their own sphere." [22] Contentment was preached as an antidote to ambition. Diligence was necessary, "but when persons endeavor to grasp at all the business in their own callings, or to invade those of others, merely to increase their riches; it is too plain an indication of a covetous disposition." This admonition admitted some exceptions. "In some cases, indeed, it may be allowable for one person to engage in two or three callings; but then a just necessity, and not an avaricious desire of wealth, must oblige you to it." [23] Pursuit of material self-interest might become the hallmark of the American, but the continued assertion of the values of the Protestant ethic indicate that this quest was never free of a certain amount of guilt and ambivalence.

V

The guides of Benjamin Franklin serve to link the inspirational writings of the seventeenth and nineteenth centuries. In his classic contribution to success literature, "The Way to Wealth," Franklin espouses Industry, Frugality, and Prudence, the great trinity of the Protestant ethic. He also warns that these virtues may be "blasted without the Blessing of Heaven" and advises men to "ask that Blessing humbly. . . ." [24] Despite this deference to the Almighty, Franklin is essentially earthbound. He and Mather preached many of the same virtues, but in radically different contexts. This world rather than the next was Franklin's central concern. Work was a social necessity and a means for improving one's station in life, but not the fulfillment of divine commandment. This secularization of the Protestant virtues also had a utilitarian aspect. Proper behavior, Franklin assured his audience, brought rewards. His was not, however, a narrow conception of self-interest, nor was his idea of success simply financial. Virtue was the means to the good life, in a full humanistic sense, for both the individual and the community. [25] Beyond this, methods useful to achieving success were ethical maxims of behavior, and constituted values in themselves. Franklin was more moralist than pragmatist, a quality shared by most later success writers. "Poor Richard" helps us mark the change from the awesome piety of the Puritan to the moralism of the nineteenth-century inspirationalist.

Franklin also differed from earlier authors of guides to living in his advocacy of a fluid social structure. The Puritans clung to the medieval notion of man as born into a fixed social sphere. Ambition, or the desire to leave one's appointed station in life, was sinful. Franklin, on the other hand, encouraged the wish to advance in the social hierarchy. Elites in the new republic were to be of worth rather than wealth or family.[26] Though the phrase "self-made man" did not become current in American folk culture till some decades after Franklin's death, he—the boy of modest circumstances who grew up to share the company of kings—became its first archetype. He not only popularized the ideal of social mobility but became its first symbolic representative.

By the 1830's, conduct-of-life literature begins to reflect a certain concern over the threat which changing patterns of American life posed for traditional values. Until that time, the United States, to all appearances, was developing a society chiefly of industrious yeomen of middling circumstances, and therefore untroubled by extreme inequalities of wealth, a nation the latter-day Puritan might approve. The triumph of Jackson introduced a disturbing element into this picture. The ordered liberty so precious to the heirs of Puritan moderation was being relegated to oblivion by marauders who styled themselves "natural" men. The religion of the Puritans had dictated a social as well as an individual ideal.[27] The disciplined subjection of natural impulses was the chief function of civil society. Just as individual moral precepts regulated and controlled the life of the individual, so government implemented regulation and control in society as a whole. Civil liberty and natural liberty were seen as distinct phenomena, and there was a certain apprehension that the former might not fare well unless the latter were restrained.[28]

Jackson's victory over Adams struck a blow at the traditional authority which the losers—spiritual descendants of the Puritans—hoped would govern the nation's development.[29]

The principle of orderly, regulated development gave way to a "natural," unsystematic, uncontrolled unleashing of the nation's energies. Jackson symbolized this freedom from control. The face of the country was changing, and in a way which caused apprehensions. The numbers engaged in manufacturing increased at a faster rate than those laboring on farms; cities grew in size and population and began showing the sores of slums and poverty.[30] Speculation raged, the promoter became a very important figure in the economy, and the corporation began to replace the private business association. These transformations gave men "a feeling of deep misgiving which was less an economic or political than a moral protest. . . ."[31]

Although the protest took many forms, it is clearly evident in the large body of children's literature written at the time. These books were designed "not so directly to communicate knowledge as . . . to develop the moral and intellectual powers,—to cultivate habits of discrimination and correct reasoning, and to establish sound principles of moral conduct."[32] As a rule, these books taught that a life governed by the Christian virtues was crowned with worldly success. However, while un-Christian conduct always drew punishment, it was not the sole cause of hardship. The identification of poverty with depravity was never absolute. Many of the boys who "made good" in these stories came from fine families which were nevertheless poor.[33] These books invariably treated the indigent with kindness and extolled charity as an obligation as well as a good.[34] While the attitude toward poverty was compassionate, the position on wealth was frequently hostile. In children's fiction of the Jacksonian period, a "mean" banker or mill owner who treats the hero badly is a common figure. Even more common is the portrayal of the wealthy man's son as a weak, wicked, and generally unpleasant character. The virtuous hero usually ends up somewhat better off financially than when he started, but nowhere is there endorsement of acquisition for its own sake.

The books were generally religious in tone, as, for example, were the works of Jacob Abbott, author of the widely read Caleb stories. Something of the religiosity of the literature can be seen in the following incident in *Caleb in the Country*. A young boy hurts another without reason. Scolded, he promises never to do it again. But this is not enough. His grandmother admonishes him further:

> Children don't know how deeply seated their sins and sinful tendencies are, and I want you to understand it, so that you may go to work in the right way. Now, this feeling of malice and ill-will, which begins to show itself in all children very soon, is very sinful, it is true; but then as to the injury it does, in childhood, it is not of much consequence. . . . It is what these wicked feelings will finally grow into, unless they are thoroughly changed, that makes me so anxious about it. Your determination will help you in not indulging the bad feelings; but I want to have your heart changed, so that you could not possibly *have* such feelings. . . . I hope that God will give you a benevolent and tender heart, so that there shall be no *tendency* in you to do wrong. He will change yours, if you pray to Him to do it.[35]

This distinction between action and motivation, between doing and feeling, is a rather subtle one for children, but then children in the 1830's were expected to perform adult roles at a much earlier age than today.[36] The teaching of ethics was very pronounced in books for the young. Morality, in this literature, was not only to guide one's actions, but pervade one's entire consciousness, and morality extended beyond the economic virtues of industry, frugality, and prudence. While these elicited praise, they were but part of a spectrum of values that included piety, devotion to family, and usefulness to the community.

VI

The children's texts of William H. McGuffey were among the most widely read guides to behavior. It is fitting that McGuffey, destined to become one of the most influential moralizers of the century, was born and raised in a strict Presbyterian household of Scotch-Irish descent. He was educated for the ministry and ordained in 1830. Preferring the classroom to the pulpit, he spent most of his active career teaching at various universities. His greatest impact, however, was felt through his texts. The first of these "readers" appeared in 1836, with others following in the immediately succeeding years.[37] All of them went through numerous reprintings for the remainder of the century. On the whole, these books expressed a philosophy of life derived from Protestant middle-class ideas of morality, piety, and religious orthodoxy. Closer in spirit to the Protestantism of seventeenth-century New England than to the rationalism of Jefferson, they reflect the eclipse of Enlightenment values in nineteenth-century America.[38]

Historians generally agree that these books belong to the literature popularizing the "cult of the successful self-made man." [39] Students of this cult have emphasized that it helped maintain "the existing order of private property, competitive enterprise, and corporate wealth." [40] This thesis, however, does not explain the presence in the ranks of self-help writers of Margaret Fuller, Lyman Abbott, Washington Gladden, and others associated with American reform. To do so we must qualify the equation of capitalism and ideas of self-help and examine the whole system of values of which these were only a part.

McGuffey's readers were certainly among the earliest and most widely read books of the self-help genre. Like writers of most self-help literature, however, he never confined himself to problems of getting ahead in the world. Even in this area, though, the values he preached are different from those which dominated American enterprise.

He did advance the notion that opportunity existed for everybody. The following is typical of his advice to youngsters:

> The road to wealth, to honor, to usefulness, and happiness, is open to all, and all who will, may enter upon it with the almost certain prospect of success. In this free community, there are no privileged orders. Every man finds his level. If he has talents, he will be known and estimated, and rise in the respect and confidence of society.[41]

Opportunity, however, is not synonymous with capitalism, and when the latter did produce a "privileged order" the role of self-help ideas in supporting this elite is questionable. Furthermore, where business success and morality conflicted, the latter was always considered more important. For example, one of the readers directly raised the question as to whether success required a lax standard of morals. It admitted that rules of conduct could be a hindrance in the scramble for money.

> Possibly, your neighbor, by being less scrupulous than yourself, may invent a more expeditious way of acquiring a for-

tune. If he is willing to violate the dictates of conscience, to lie and cheat, and trample on the rules of justice and honesty, he may, indeed, get the start of you, and rise suddenly to wealth and distinction.

Unable to deny the occasional rewards of sharp dealing, inspirationalists assured their readers that in the long run men paid a high price for easy money. "Sudden wealth, especially when obtained by dishonest means, rarely fails of bringing with it sudden ruin." Men "beggared in morals" are soon "beggared in property." Their riches are corrupted "and while they bring the curse of God on their immediate possessors, they usually entail misery and ruin upon their families." Such were the penalties awaiting those who disregarded divine precepts. So while "strict honesty is not always the shortest way to success" it is "the surest, the happiest and the best." Furthermore, though one might end up with less money, one was assured "a fair character, an approving conscience, and an approving God," prizes to be esteemed above all others.[42]

Such moralizing hardly reflects the spirit of American business in the three decades preceding the Civil War. Describing the ethos of this period, Bray Hammond has written: "People were led as they had not been before by visions of money-making. Liberty became transformed into *laissez faire*. A violent, aggressive, economic individualism became established." [43]

Unrestrained pursuit of economic interest characterized McGuffey's America, but more in violation than in accordance with his teachings. If anything, the "readers" resisted the "man on the make" psychology of the time, though perhaps ineffectively, and contained more idealism than ambition. The economic opportunities America offered could be its nemesis unless they were pursued with conscience and restraint. These books attempted to inculcate the discipline needed to keep the country's blessings from becoming its curse.

> We must educate! We must educate! or we must perish by our own prosperity. If we do not, short will be our race from the cradle to the grave. If in our haste to be rich and mighty, we outrun our literary and religious institutions, they will never overtake us; or only come up after the battle of liberty is fought and lost, as spoils to grace the victory, and as resources of inexorable despotism for the perpetuity of our bondage.[44]

Self-help writers tried to keep enterprise from running amok. This is not to say that guides to conduct opposed private property or preached revolution. But a belief in private property can exist quite comfortably within varied value systems. The yeoman may oppose communal ownership as much as the financier, but to conclude from this that the values of one support the actions of the other only blurs the very important distinctions between them. In the context of a choice between capitalism and socialism, self-help literature certainly would support the former. These, however, were not the alternatives Americans faced. Instead the choice was between the values of an old and traditional capitalism and those of a new and innovative one. These were the poles between which the argument progressed. Self-help writers were caught squarely in the middle of this conflict, and their books reflect the tension and ambivalence of the world around them. They attempted to reconcile the values of the old with the energies of the new at a time when the two were becoming hopelessly incompatible:

I acknowledge that luxury, and the blandishments of prosperity and wealth, are greatly to be feared; and if our softness and indulgences, and foreign fashions, must inevitably accomplish our seduction, and lead us away from the simplicity, honesty, sobriety, purity, and manly independence of our forefathers, most readily and fervently would I exclaim, Welcome back to the pure old times of the Puritans! . . . for infinitely better would be hard doctrines and dark brows, Jewish Sabbaths, strait garments, formal manners, and a harsh guardianship, than dissoluteness and effeminacy; than empty pleasures and shameless debauchery; than lolling ease, and pampered pride, and fluttering vanity; than unprincipled, faithless, corrupted rulers, and a people unworthy of a more exalted government. . . .

But is it necessary that we must be either gloomy or corrupt, either formal or profane, either extravagant in strictness, or extravagant in dissipation and levity? Can we not so order our habits, and so fix our principles, as not to suffer the luxuries of our days to choke, and strangle, with their rankness, the simple morality of our father's days?[45]

The question was not easily answered; but as it persisted, it continued to evoke a defense of the imagined morality of the past.

VII

Writers of guides to young men joined the chorus of protest. Stressing the dangers of running after money, which they labeled the obsession of the time, these guides offered those embarking on life advice on how to make a living and stay decent at the same time. The most prominent of these guides before the Civil War were written by Freeman Hunt of New York and Edwin Freedley of Philadelphia.

Hunt was aware of following in Franklin's footsteps. "Franklin," he wrote, "was the first . . . to bring together with some little attempt at system the rules of business conduct—the maxims of thrift. The influence of his writings, which were full of the true philosophy of business life, in giving tone and direction to the mercantile mind of America, and in a measure of Europe, has been marked and lasting." Since that time, however, "while the materials have immensely increased nothing has been done towards arranging and digesting them." [46]

Hunt rushed in to fill the gap. He titled his book *Worth and Wealth*, suggesting that the two were not identical, a distinction he maintains throughout.

Types of wealth fell into two broad categories: that acquired by honest labor and that acquired by shrewd speculation. The first was worth having; the second was a blemish to the possessor. Hunt cautioned men to "keep . . . to honest toil in a legitimate business, and . . . not [to] aspire to become a financier." [47] Money tied to work and gradually accumulated by the sweat of one's brow was deserved, but money amassed without commensurate labor was not; and what was not deserved was not kept for long. This was seen in that most people who entered business failed: a fact surprisingly stressed in success tracts.[48] Why the failures? Simply that most people entered business hoping to get out more than they put in. Wealth had to be matched by effort, and when it was not, justice balanced the scales. "The primary cause of half the failures," Hunt wrote, "was the haste to be rich . . . while a resort to speculation . . . [would] take the balance." [49] Only gradual gains were natural, and rapid accumulation was contrary to God's law. Extravagant spending was a corollary to quick money, and was equally bad. Industry and simplicity were "the most beautiful ornaments of successful merchants." [50] The easy come, easy go mentality violated the money principle at both ends.

Yet despite harangues about "the inordinate love of money being one of the most degrading vices," [51] inspirationalists persisted in teaching the ways to wealth. Freedley, for example, claimed to show "how fortunes have been made and can be made," [52] and in the next breath urged men to ask God to "give us neither poverty nor riches; feed us with food convenient for us, lest we be full and deny thee." [53] This divided attitude, so common in success guides, reflected a genuine ambivalence.

The passion for material accumulation ranks high in most commentaries on the American character. Guidebooks for the young, with their assurances of opportunities for everyone, appear to support and encourage ambition for wealth; so much so, that this has generally been regarded as the chief social impact they had. The Protestant ethic, so the argument goes, helped create capitalism, and, though somewhat altered, continued to aid it through the centuries. Yet capitalism and the ambition for material goods usually associated with it have survived the passage of this ethic. I doubt anyone would argue today that the American passion for material goods rests on religious foundations. Why, then, assume that it did a hundred years ago? Certainly by that time this passion seemed so general as to permeate the whole fabric of our civilization. Nobody, including inspirationalists, ever expressed the feeling that Americans were not ambitious enough. Ambition was observed as a fact of life, not as a characteristic which required bolstering. In a culture so dominated by the image of the hustler, the push given by self-help literature to the desire for accumulation must have been inconsequential.

Hunt, certainly one of the chief popularizers of the cult of self-help, ascribed the American lust for wealth to other causes. He explained:

> It is natural to man to create factitious distinctions in society. In every form of political society, except the republic, such distinctions exist by birth or in permanent civil and ecclesiastical orders. Pride is nurtured and vanity gratified by blood, or family, or title, or inherited rank. But such distinctions are precluded in a republic by its very constitution. Hence, there remains but one basis of social distinction, namely wealth. In limited circles, indeed, there may be an aristocracy of talent, of education and refinement, of literature or science, but in society at large, gradations of social position are measured by stock certificates, rent-rolls, and bank accounts. In the old world a patent of nobility holds good, though there is no income adequate to sustain it; and a penniless count stands higher in the social scale than the untitled millionaire. Here the appearance of wealth is the passport from circle to circle. . . . Here it creates rank; it gives social position, even without antecedent respectability or correct education; and hence pride and vanity, that in other countries have so many and various outlets, here crowd into this one channel. . . .[54]

In a society where money conferred social distinction as well as comfort, men tended to prize it above everything else. Fearing this national inclination, self-help writers exhorted: "It is folly supreme, nay madness, to make the acquiring of riches . . . the chief end of life."[55] Though optimistic about possibilities of rising in the social order, these writers were acutely conscious of the moral disintegration that surrounded them. Bemoaning the low level of the national character, they described their time as one of "failures in business, of cheating and awful delinquencies of moral character—an age of suicides, of maniacs and of murders."[56] They firmly believed improvement was possible, however, and vested their hopes for social regeneration in the young. Sharing the widespread conviction that moral men made a moral society, they directed their salvos toward men rather than conditions. Inculcating wholesome values seemed the best way of curing social ills.[57] Parents, they taught, might leave their children "a better patrimony than money." More valuable were "the worth of a good example, good habits, a religious faith, a true estimate of the desirable things of this life; and resources of mind and a heart which will shed sunshine on adversity, and give grace to prosperous fortune." [58]

Guidebooks uniformly gave virtue precedence over wealth. They all taught that young men must begin their careers with a determination to be good rather than to be rich. Freedley, for example, wrote: "It does not lie with the young man, when he begins life, to say whether or not he is to be *rich;* but whether or not he will make a mischievous *failure* is, in most cases, an affair that he can decide for himself." [59] Industry and frugality could usually be counted on to secure at least a competence, but, even moralists were forced to admit, there were exceptions to the rule. There was no denying that there were men "who possess every ennobling qualification; talented, intellectual, humane, brave and kind, that are beset by pecuniary difficulties and surrounded by poverty; while others, who are not fit to untie the latchets of their shoes, are rolling in wealth, like the hog in his mire." [60] Such cases, however, were atypical. The only consolation they could offer was that some time, in the next life if not in this, justice would be meted out.

The advice on money young men received was much the same as the advice they imbibed as children. The quest for money without regard to means was sordid. On the other hand:

If money be sought with moderation, by honorable means, and with a due regard to the public good, no employment affords exercise to higher or nobler powers of mind and heart. And such should be the character of the merchant. He should guard his heart against the seductive influence of money; he should carefully shield his mind against the narrow precepts of avarice. Money should be regarded as the agent and representative of the good it may be made to perform . . . in affording the means of promoting the public good.[61]

While honest commerce drew plaudits, the urban centers which it created did not. Inspirationalists discouraged men from flocking to the cities. But if they exaggerated the dangers of the city, they idealized the working of the soil. The myth of the yeoman was as much a part of the cult of self-help as the Protestant ethic. Charles Sumner, the Massachusetts Senator, said: "Cities are, to the dwellers in the country, very like what lights are to flies—brilliant and attractive, but certain ruin." [62] Besides, the life of trade was not always enviable. Freedley cited a sentiment that was common: "The lot of the merchant is one of great labor and anxiety, compared to that of the farmer. He labors harder, his life is shorter, and he is less sure of a competency in old age." [63] The ideal setting for the moral life for most men was thought to be the homestead, with its fresh air and proximity to nature.

This reveals another aspect of conduct-of-life literature—its generally nostalgic tone. The farm represented the past. The city presaged the future. Even the glorification of the merchant could not obscure the fact that his heyday had passed and the goodly master of the counting-house had receded into the romance of a golden age to which people looked back longingly. Hunt wrote: "In these days of mercantile degeneracy and mercantile recklessness, it is profitable for us to pause in our career, and look back to other days, to the period when mercantile honor existed in fact, as well as in name—when our merchants were above princes, and our traffickers [*sic*] the honorable of the earth." [64]

The superiority of the past extended beyond merchants to the public in general. Mayor James Watson Williams, in an address before the Young Men's Association of Utica, voiced a typical protest when he lamented the general decline in morals and accused the people of worshipping Mammon as the chief end of man. Sniping at the wealthy, he pointed out that often "the acquisition of great riches is . . . the result of sacrifices which no truly good man can conscientiously make. . . ." [65] The legitimate pursuit of moderate comfort was no sooner realized than men began to "grasp at opulence and luxury." [66] These were more to be avoided than even poverty itself. However degrading poverty might be, it often was a fertile ground for virtue. Luxury, on the other hand, was an unmitigated evil. It diverted wealth from its proper uses and invariably destroyed character.

He invoked the legacy of the past to sharpen his point:

> The pilgrims, when they landed from the Mayflower—a weary and comfortless group—had little to rely upon but God and their own severe virtues; those virtues which adorn freedom, no less than they become Christianity; which give life, vigor, and endurance to a republic. The first was *Industry*, without which it was impossible to render their conditions tolerable; in its train followed *Frugality*, the exercise of which, at all times desirable, was rendered imperious by circumstances; *Perseverance*, essential to the success of all human efforts. . . . On these virtues, next to Heaven, as on a foundation of rock, did they depend as the chief supports of their independence and prosperity. [67]

Instead of cherishing this legacy, Americans violated it in every important particular.

Were they contented with a moderate competence? We are greedy of more abounding riches. Were they frugal? We are running into a ruinous extravagance. Were they stable and persevering? We are ever varying our pursuits in the vain hope of realizing wealth in some different avocation from that to which we were educated. Like Atalanta, with whatever determination we at first set out in life, we hardly begin to run the race with energy before we are tempted aside by golden apples. We forsake our farms, our merchandise, our workshops, and our professions, and seek elsewhere that affluence which only perseverance can secure. Instead of cherishing those qualities which are vital in a republic, we are imitating the vices of monarchies where there are vast accumulations of hereditary wealth. It is time we should return to the ancestral virtues. They are the essential virtues which bless and adorn life, and become a plain and republican people.[68]

The message of those who instructed the young on how to conduct their lives and find their places in the world was all-inclusive. Their advice ran the gamut from how to treat mother to whom to marry. Rags-to-riches was only one theme among many, and the special emphasis it has received obscures the rest. Reading their books, one is impressed by how little space they gave to ways of making money and by how much they devoted to contentment, temperance, and duty to family and community.[69]

The victorious egalitarianism of Jackson's America—the breakdown of the caucus system in politics, the parceling out of the public domain, the substitution of general for specific laws of incorporation—fostered expansiveness at the expense of stability. Moralists tried to harness and direct this energy by fortifying traditional discipline. The disintegrating effect of expansion on family life and communal attachments was enormous,[70] and the need for personal control became more imperative as institutional restraints weakened.

The social and economic changes initiated in the Jackson period produced a mound of literature on the proper conduct of life. As these changes accelerated after the Civil War, the mound became a mountain. The number of guides increased as the need for guidance became more pronounced. The success myth throve more on complaint than opportunity. In a society of runners, moralists urged men to walk slowly, and offered men racing headlong into the future the corrective of a backward glance.

NOTES

1. See Louis B. Wright, *Middle-Class Culture in Elizabethan England* (Chapel Hill: University of North Carolina Press, 1935).

2. For an interesting discussion of the transmutation of certain English traditions in America, see William B. Hesseltine, "Four American Traditions," *Journal of Southern History*, XXVII (February 1961), 3–32.

3. Alfred Whitney Griswold, "The American Gospel of Success" (unpublished Ph.D. dissertation, Department of History, Yale University, 1934). The Weber classic first appeared in German in 1904–1905.

4. See particularly Irvin G. Wyllie, *The Self-Made Man in America: the Myth of Rags to Riches* (New Brunswick, N.J.: Rutgers University Press, 1954), and Richard M. Huber, "The Idea of Success in America, 1865–1929: A History of the Puritan Ethic" (unpublished Ph.D. dissertation, Department of History, Yale University, 1953).

5. Max Weber, *The Protestant Ethic and the Spirit of Capitalism*, trans. Talcott Parsons (New York: Charles Scribner's Sons, 1958), p. 27.

6. *Ibid.*, p. 54.

7. *Ibid.*, p. 55.

8. *Ibid.*, pp. 118–119.

9. *Ibid.*, p. 121.

10. Quoted in Weber, *ibid.*, p. 175.

11. Quoted in E. A. J. Johnson, *American Economic Thought in the Seventeenth Century* (New York: Russell & Russell, 1961), p. 99.

12. Perry Miller, *The New England Mind, From Colony to Province* (Cambridge, Mass.: Harvard University Press, 1962), pp. 27–39.

13. Kurt Samuelsson, *Religion and Economic Action, A Critique of Max Weber*, trans. E. Geoffrey French (New York: Harper and Row, 1964).

14. Johnson, *op. cit.*, pp. 119, 167.

15. See Thorstein Veblen, *The Theory of the Leisure Class* (New York: The New American Library, 1953).

16. Cotton Mather, *Bonifacius: Essays to Do Good* (Boston: B. Green, 1710), p. 19.

17. *Ibid.*, p. 38.

18. *Ibid.*, p. 129.

19. *Ibid.*, p. 133. For a further treatment of this theme see Cotton Mather, *The Angel of Bethesda Visiting the Invalids of a Miserable World . . . By a Fellow of the Royal Society* (New London: Timothy Green, 1722), pp. 12–13.

20. *Ibid.*, p. 89.

21. *Ibid.*, p. 142.

22. Richard Steele, *The Religious Tradesman* (Charlestown: Samuel Etheridge, 1804), p. 12. This was first published in London in 1684. See too Miller, *op. cit.*, pp. 40–52.

23. Steele, *op. cit.*, p. 175.

24. Benjamin Franklin, "The Way to Wealth," *The Writings of Benjamin Franklin*, ed. Albert Henry Smyth (New York: The Macmillan Co., 1905), III, 417–418. See too "Hints for Those That Would Be Rich," *ibid.*, II, 211–212, and "Advice to a Young Tradesman," *ibid.*, II, 370–372.

25. Carl Van Doren, *Benjamin Franklin* (New York: The Viking Press, 1938), pp. 73–115.

26. *Ibid.*, p. 774.

27. Miller, *op. cit.*, p. 416.

28. For a clear expression of this Puritan viewpoint, see John Winthrop, "Speech to the General Court, July 3, 1645," *The Puritans*, ed. Perry Miller and Thomas J. Johnson (New York: Harper and Row, 1963), I, 206–207.

29. See Samuel Flagg Bemis, *John Quincy Adams and the Union* (New York: Alfred A. Knopf, 1956), pp. 25, 60–65, 148–151.

30. Arthur M. Schlesinger, Jr., *The Age of Jackson* (Boston: Little, Brown and Co., 1953), pp. 8–12.

31. *Ibid.*, p. 334. See too Marvin Meyers, *The Jacksonian Persuasion* (New York: Vintage Books, 1960), pp. 11–12. For an example of the awareness of the need to control new conditions with traditional morality see Dorus Clarke, *Lectures to Young People in Manufacturing Villages* (Boston: Perkins and Marvin, 1836).

32. Jacob Abbott, *Caleb in the Country* (Boston: Crocker and Brewster, 1839), p. 3. For a general survey of children's literature, see Cornelia Meigs *et al.*, *A Critical History of Children's Literature* (New York: The Macmillan Co., 1953); see too Alice Jordan, *From Rollo to Tom Sawyer*

and other Papers (Boston: The Horn Book Co., 1948), and May Hill Arbuthnot, *Children and Books* (Chicago: Scott, Foresman and Co., 1957), pp. 49–50.

Children's fiction in the nineteenth century provides a better source for studying adult values than it does in the twentieth. This is because children were treated as adults in miniature and were not allowed a separate and distinct law of behavior. Also, the nineteenth-century literature was didactic; its chief purpose was to inculcate values rather than to provide entertainment.

33. This attitude was also expressed in literature for young adults. See, for example, John Frost, *The Young Merchant* (Philadelphia: R. W. Pomeroy, 1839), p. 131. "The rich man, who treats poverty with arrogance and contempt, tramples upon the ashes of his father or grandfather. . . ."

34. See, for example, John Todd, *The Young Man* (Northampton: Hopkins, Bridgman and Co., 1856), p. 273.

35. Abbott, *op. cit.*, p. 78.

36. For a more detailed discussion of attitudes toward children during this period, see Bernard Wishy, "Images of the American Child in the Nineteenth Century" (unpublished Ph.D. dissertation, Department of History, Columbia University, 1958).

37. For an over-all analysis of the McGuffey readers see Richard D. Mosier, *Making the American Mind: Social and Moral Ideas in the McGuffey Readers* (New York: King's Crown Press, 1947).

38. For this change of values in nineteenth-century America, see Henry Steele Commager, *The American Mind* (New Haven: Yale University Press, 1950), p. 86.

39. See Merle Curti, *The Growth of American Thought* (New York: Harper and Bros., 1951), p. 644. See too Wyllie, *op. cit.*, p. 126.

40. Curti, *op. cit.*, p. 645.

41. William Holmes McGuffey, *McGuffey's Newly Revised Eclectic Third Reader* (Cincinnati: Winthrop B. Smith, 1843), p. 175.

42. William Holmes McGuffey, *McGuffey's Newly Revised Eclectic Fourth Reader* (Cincinnati: Sargent, Wilson and Hinkle, 1853), p. 205. See too *Revised Third Reader, op. cit.*, p. 31.

43. Bray Hammond, *Banks and Politics in America* (Princeton: Princeton University Press, 1957), p. 327.

44. William Holmes McGuffey, *The Eclectic Fourth Reader* (Cincinnati: Truman and Smith, 1837), p. 57.

45. *Ibid.*, pp. 128–129.

46. Freeman Hunt, *Worth and Wealth: A Collection of Maxims, Morals and Miscellanies for Merchants and Men of Business* (New York: Stringer and Townsend, 1856), p. vii. For a discussion of the later use of Franklin,

see Louis B. Wright, "Franklin's Legacy to the Gilded Age," *The Virginia Quarterly Review*, XXII (1946), 268–279.

47. Hunt, *op. cit.*, p. 73.

48. Todd, *op. cit.*, p. 120.

49. Hunt, *op. cit.*, p. 80. See too T. S. Arthur, *Advice to Young Men* (Boston: N. C. Barton, 1849), p. 153. "Safe and sure beginnings are always small, and the growth gradual. Sudden inflations meet with as sudden collapses." Arthur is best remembered for his temperance tract, "Ten Nights in a Barroom," but also wrote several popular guides to conduct. See, for example, *Rising in the World: or a Tale for the Rich and Poor* (New York: Baker and Scribner, 1850), and *Lessons in Life* (Philadelphia: Lippincott, Grambo and Co., 1851).

50. Hunt, *op. cit.*, p. 77.

51. *Ibid.*, p. 105.

52. E. T. Freedley, *Opportunities for Industry and the Safe Investment of Capital or, A Thousand Chances to Make Money* (Philadelphia: J. B. Lippincott and Co., 1859), p. 13.

53. *Ibid.*, p. 54.

54. Hunt, *op. cit.*, p. 182.

55. W. H. Van Doren, *Mercantile Morals* (New York: Charles Scribner, 1852), p. 33.

56. Todd, *op. cit.*, p. 204.

57. Arthur, *Advice to Young Men*, pp. 163–164.

58. Hunt, *op. cit.*, p. 293.

59. Freedley, *op. cit.*, p. 235.

60. Hunt, *op. cit.*, p. 194.

61. *Ibid.*, p. 225.

62. Charles Sumner, quoted in *ibid.*, p. 233.

63. Quoted in Freedley, *op. cit.*, p. 213.

64. Hunt, *op. cit.*, p. 318.

65. James Watson Williams, *The Passion for Riches* (Utica: Eli Maynard, 1838), p. 5.

66. *Ibid.*, p. 8. See too Frost, *op. cit.*, p. 51.

67. Williams, *op. cit.*, pp. 16–17.

68. *Ibid.*, p. 18. For a discussion of nostalgia in America, see Arthur P. Dudden, "Nostalgia and the American," *Journal of the History of Ideas*, XXII (1961), 515–530. See too Edward M. Burns, *The American Idea of Mission: Concepts of National Purpose and Destiny* (New Brunswick: Rutgers University Press, 1957), viii. See too Meyers, *op. cit.*, pp. 16ff.

69. These themes are more fully examined in Chapter 4.

70. See Oscar and Mary Handlin, *Commonwealth, A Study of the Role of Government in the American Economy: Massachusetts, 1774–1861* (New York: New York University Press, 1947), p. 202.

Chapter 2

Horatio Alger, Jr., and the Gilded Age

I

Nations commonly use the names of important figures to designate particular periods in their history. France has its age of Louis XIX; England, its Victorian and Edwardian eras; and in the United States we hear much of the America of Jefferson, Jackson, Wilson, and F.D.R. Nonetheless, no president epitomizes the spectacular transformation of our country between the Civil War and 1900. Instead, the popular conception of this period is formed by the image of the millionaire. The use of the business titan to characterize a period marked by industrialization is understandable, even appropriate. The presence of a children's author among the representatives of this era is more curious. American weavers of juvenile tales comprise a long list, but only one has become a national symbol. This unique distinction belongs to Horatio Alger, Jr., whose name has entered the American vocabulary, though his books are scarcely read any longer.

This timid writer of children's stories somehow became identified with the golden age of American plutocracy. A later generation used his name to symbolize the spectacular

Reprinted with the permission of The Macmillan Company from *The Age of Industrialism in America*, F. C. Jaher, ed. Copyright © 1968 The Free Press of Glencoe, A Division of The Macmillan Company.

success that was possible in an era that seemed to spawn millionaires as salmon spawn roe.[1] Those who read the Alger stories with nostalgia envy their simplicity, a simplicity born of "the innocent, hopeful days before the turn of the century." [2] They idealize the certainties of a past time when wealth was regarded as "the direct consequence of honesty, thrift, self-reliance, industry, a cheerful whistle and an open, manly face," [3] and regret that they can no longer share Alger's benign view of the universe. They do not realize that if Alger was an innocent, he was an innocent in Babylon, and that like them he was a "communicant of a dying church" whose doctrine linked "sinlessness to solvency." [4] Correctly understood, Alger is not a representative of his time, but a nostalgic spokesman of a dying order. Of middle-class rural origins, he was always an alien in the industrially dominated society of his adulthood.

II

Born on January 15, 1832, during the heyday of Jacksonian democracy, Alger remained a truer spokesman of the era of his birth than that of his maturity.[5] The eldest of five children, he received special attention from his father. Horatio Alger, Sr., a Unitarian minister, wished his son to follow in his footsteps. He directly supervised Horatio's early education, and trained him rigorously. Discouraged from taking part in the frivolous activities of his peers, Alger, Jr., became so withdrawn that other youngsters dubbed him "Holy Horatio." His youth was spent with adults and his adulthood with children.

In 1844, when Alger was twelve years old, his father was

called to a church in Marlborough, Massachusetts, where Horatio attended Gates Academy. Marlborough, at this time:

> was embarking on a career as an industrial town with shoes as the principal business—made in small, isolated shops which employed in each maybe ten people. As this business prospered, larger shops were erected and attracted many Irish and French-Canadian immigrants. There were two small wool-fabric mills on waterpower of the Assabet River, and several saw and grist mills on lesser streams. . . . In general the town was engaged in agricultural pursuits, and there were large areas of forest, and swamp land.[6]

This was the atmosphere in which Alger passed his adolescence. He frequently used the setting of his youth as a background for his later stories. The pattern of New England life was changing, and it is probable that the shift from commerce to industry was not entirely to the liking of old families like the Algers. While industry increased the wealth of the community, it often placed power and prestige in new hands, upset established social patterns, and brought an influx of immigrants that threatened the homogeneity of the New England countryside.

In Alger's stories, the mill owner is frequently the villain of the piece. He is powerful and often dominates the better elements in the community. Industrial development was also threatening because it undermined the two mainstays of moral control, the farm and the family. Thus in his youth Alger saw in microcosm the industrial challenge to the rural New England way of life. His sympathies, in his writings, were always with the latter.

While Alger's family was well-to-do, the conditions of life were in many ways rather primitive. Roads were poor, and long-distance travel was by coach. The first railroad to Marlborough opened in 1850, after Alger had left the town. The facilities of Gates Academy, where he received his preparatory training, were meager indeed. There was only one classroom and one instructor. "The classroom was inadequately heated by a wood-burning stove during sessions, and the ink froze at night; it was inadequately lighted by a few windows which in the winter could not be opened for ventilaton; there was no artificial lighting; there was no plumbing—there was a well in the yard and also a 'privy.' " [7]

From Gates, Alger went on to Harvard. His background was typical of many who had been great figures in the affairs of the nation. Times, however, were changing. Harvard, so long a breeding-ground for the nation's leaders, was now producing what might be called the "alienated generation." Few groups in America before that time lived through as radical a change in the nation's social fabric as these men experienced in their adult years. The change produced shock that manifested itself in a variety of ways: in the indignation of the genteel reformers, the cynicism of Henry Adams, and the romantic nostalgia of Horatio Alger.

After graduating from Harvard in 1852, Alger spent most of the next five years teaching and writing. He enrolled in the Divinity School at Cambridge in 1857. Completing the three-year course, he left for Europe in the summer of 1860. When he came home in April of 1861, the nation was already at war. Alger tried to enlist in the Union army, but was rejected as physically unfit. He resumed tutoring and writing until he received an offer to fill a pulpit in Brewster, Massachusetts. The call came in the summer of 1865. For reasons that are not quite clear, Alger's pastorate in Brewster—his first and last—was not very successful. He left it after only eight months and went to New York, where he launched his career as a children's author in earnest. *Ragged Dick*, which appeared in book form in 1868, established him as a popular author, and from then on his reputation grew.[8] Alger's works do not rank high by literary standards, but they remain classic expressions of the rags-to-riches ideology in post-bellum America.

III

There was little magazine commentary on Alger at the time of his death (1899) and, interestingly, few articles appear until the 1920s, by which time his books were no longer read.[9] Commentary on Alger in the twenties and thirties was deprecatory. H. L. Mencken expressed a general belief when he denied that rural origins increased one's chances for success. "The notion that yokels always succeed in the cities," he remarked scathingly, "is a great delusion. The overwhelming majority of our rich men are city-born and city-bred. And the overwhelming majority of our elderly motormen, forlorn corner grocerymen, neighborhood carpenters and other such blank cartridges are country-bred." [10]

In 1932, the centenary of Alger's birth, the Children's Aid Society conducted a poll to determine his popularity among the younger generation. The results showed that the once-famous author had fallen into obscurity. "Less than 20 per cent of the seven thousand members of New York's juvenile proletariat had ever heard of the author of *Tom, the Bootblack;* only 14 per cent had read even one of his . . . published works. What will be even more alarming to some is the fact that a considerable number dismissed the theory of 'work and win' as a 'lot of bunk.' " [11] A nostalgia for Alger did develop after the Second World War, but no comparable children's literature has appeared.[12] The times have too much altered and American children are no longer receptive to Alger's message. Alger wrote 107 books, the sales of which have been estimated at seventeen million.[13]

IV

An examination of the Alger books belies the Alger myth. If his works reflect the spirit of a particular time, it was not the spirit of the Gilded Age.

Alger's preachments were largely in the classic mold. He urged his readers not to smoke or drink, not to stay up late, not to attend theaters or other places of entertainment. He reiterated the established litany of hard work, frugality, and prudence. Beyond possessing these traditional virtues, his heroes were kind and helpful to those they found in need. Often they were even generous to those who wronged them. These heroes, idealized as they are, lack a human dimension but exemplify a genuine decency.

In one significant way, however, Alger departed from the traditional formulation of the Protestant notion of success. That was in his repeated emphasis on luck, an element that the Protestant ethic did not admit. Either his heroes are left worthless lands which accrete in value, save rich men's sons or daughters and become wards of generous benefactors, or achieve wealth and comfort through other chance occurrences. They never make fortunes, they always find them. Alger himself admits that virtue does not always bring material rewards, though luck never comes to the wicked. Luck is always earned by those who have it, though it is not always had by those who have earned it. This resembles the Puritan notion of salvation: the saved are always virtuous, but the virtuous are not always saved. Alger's failures are not always wicked boys either. Lack of ambition, energy, or physical strength often retard the upward movement of his characters, who, while virtuous, will never "make it."

According to the author himself, his works had a twofold purpose: one was "to exert a salutary influence upon the class of whom he was writing, by setting before them inspiring examples of what energy, ambition, and an honest purpose may achieve"; the other was to bring to the attention of the public "the life and experiences of the friendless and vagrant children to be found in all our cities, numbering in New York alone over twelve thousand." [14] Notable as an example of the latter is *Phil, the Fiddler*, Alger's exposure of the *padrone* system in New York. In his preface to the book in 1872, he expressed the hope that "revealing for the first time to the American public the hardships and ill-treatment of these wandering musicians, shall excite an active sympathy in their behalf. . . ." [15] The padrones would purchase children, usually in southern Italy, and bring them to this country, where they would be sent about the streets playing and singing for money. They were poorly kept, brutally beaten, and often died before reaching adulthood. This ruthless exploitation Alger called "white slavery—for it merits no better name," and bemoaned the fact that it was "permitted by the law of two great nations," Italy and the United States. [16] At a time when Social Darwinism was being used to justify the elimination, however ruthless, of the unfit, Alger had a teacher in one of his books praise her class because their "sympathies are with the weak and oppressed." [17] Alger's reform work carried on something of a family tradition. His father had been an abolitionist and his sister, Olive Augusta, was active in the temperance and women's rights movements.

Alger's association with the Newsboys' Lodging House in New York was very close. He often lived there and found much of the material for his books in the lives of the newsboys. He took particular pride in the belief that his works were inclining the public toward a more sympathetic attitude to these homeless waifs. In 1879 he expressed gratification with "the warm reception accorded by the public" to his "pictures of humble life in a great metropolis." He was even more pleased that "his labors . . . awakened a philanthropic interest in the children whose struggles and privations" he described, and asked the public to contribute to the funds of the Children's Aid Society.[18] One receives the impression in reading his books that their inspirational quality springs more from a dread of despair than from a belief in opportunity. Confronted with the horrors of poverty, Alger attempted to give solace. Like other conscience-stricken members of his class, he was unable to view the consequences of industrialization with indifference. Most disturbing of these consequences was the plight of children. Youngsters surrounded by poverty and sickness needed something to sustain them in their early years. Deprived of virtually all material comforts, they must at least be given the hope of a better future. The popular tradition of mobility in American society provided a convenient means of doing so.

Both Alger's distaste for the results of industrialism and his assertion of the Protestant virtues are much more akin to the middle-class reform mentality of the period than to the naked acquisitiveness of the man-on-the-make. It is interesting to note that in terms of background, Alger fits the pattern of the genteel reformer rather well. He was born into a comfortable New England family, educated at Harvard, and was the son of a Unitarian minister.[19] He shared other characteristics of genteel reformers, among them a preference for Anglo-Saxons. Frequently, the ne'er-do-wells in his stories are "dark," like Jasper in *Tom, the Bootblack*, who is also "effeminate in appearance," "smooth, deceitful, and vain, running to dissipation, as far as he had opportunity." [20] This is inconsistent with his attitude toward Italian street urchins in *Phil, the Fiddler;* apparently his inherited bias sometimes conflicted with his humane inclination. For the most part, however, Alger's heroes are of rural American background, so the conflict is not often evident. Alger avoids dealing with the problem of the immigrants, who were not an important part of his public.

In some of his works there is an implicit belief in a kind of hereditary determinism, which is later found in the eugenics craze of the early twentieth century and receives expression in popular novels of the Progressive period. Again, this seems inconsistent with Alger's notions of mobility. A belief in mobility, however, was held at the same time and by the same Americans who believed that "blood will tell" and attached great importance to family. This inconsistency, though rather widespread, is especially striking in the "rags-to-riches" context. One of the best examples of this hereditary determinism appears in *Jed, the Poorhouse Boy*.[21] The hero, raised in a home for paupers and subject to all the degradations of such an upbringing, is a perfect gentleman. His manners would be the pride of any mother and his virtue in all things is beyond reproach. The mystery of a boy of such fine breeding, raised in such low circumstances, is finally dispelled by the revelation of his noble origins. Born into a family of high rank, he is shipped across the ocean as an infant by a wicked uncle who covets his title. The rest of the family think him dead. His innate nobility, however, survives all the years of pauperism and he is finally restored to his rightful estate. This belief in virtue transmitted through the blood provides one of the reasons that all of Alger's characters are orphaned. Poor boys are not likely to be the sons of good men who are alive. The absence of a father conveniently removes the problem of reconciling indigence with virtue.

V

Alger's settings are most often in the New York of the latter half of the nineteenth century, and his accurate descriptions of its streets, hotels, boarding houses, and restaurants made his books valuable as guides to those unfamiliar with the city. But his attitude toward the city he described so well was one of hostility. While the city was a place of opportunity, it also was a place of unspeakable corruption and moral turpitude. Virtue resided in the country. If the country boy could survive the city swindlers ready to prey on his innocence, his chances of success were greater than those of his city-bred peers. This was because he was usually stronger morally and had "been brought up to work, and work more earnestly than the city boys." [22] Country boys might come to the city to gain wealth, but city boys could well go to the country for moral regeneration. Alger also warned that "of the tens of thousands who come from the country to seek clerkships, but a very small proportion rise above a small income." [23] For the majority, it would be best to remain home. In fact, an attempt to relocate city waifs in country homes was fostered by Charles Loring Brace, who hoped in this way to lessen the pauperism resulting from the tremendous influx of people into the cities.[24]

Alger's ideal differs in other important respects from the realities of the time. His heroes are never the children of workers. They are generally impoverished through the death of their father, who was of the middle class. If their middle-class origins are not known, as in the case of Ragged Dick, their backgrounds are obscured altogether. One commentator has offered a Freudian interpretation of Alger's unvarying use of orphans in his novels.

> Alger, who was never freed from emotional bondage to his own father, found a sort of compensation in telling this one story over and over. In each of his novels he punished his father three times. He killed him before the story opened, by making the hero an orphan; he gave Horatio Sr.'s worst traits to the villainous squire; and finally he provided the hero with a new father to cherish him.[25]

The Freudian perspective might be more fruitfully applied from the cultural rather than the personal point of view. The use of the orphan in nineteenth-century literature is too widespread to be ascribed, in any one instance, to the psychic structure of a single individual. The orphan was a convenient fictional figure in a society eager to accept change but uneasy about losing its past. Eliminating the father, a symbol of tradition and authority, made the acceptance of change possible without requiring an explicit rejection of tradition. Seen in this light, the orphan reflects the tension between stability and movement that is expressed so frequently in literature with success themes.

This ambivalent attitude toward change is also revealed in Alger's choice of benefactors. They are, for the most part, engaged in mercantile rather than industrial enterprises. The idealization of the benevolent merchant is hardly an accurate reflection of an age in which industrial wealth was so predominant. It does, however, correspond to the widespread belief that the older form of enterprise honed finer character than the new.

None of Alger's heroes exhibits the aggressive acquisitiveness of the time. They are patient and virtuous, much more akin to the ideal bourgeois of ante-bellum time. The moderate fortunes his heroes accumulate are usually measured in five figures.[26] Alger shared the distaste and disdain of the genteel middle class for the "New Moguls," whose practice of "Wall Street speculation" was "more dangerous even than extravagant habits of living." [27] Alger never mentions the millionaire in his stories and never posits great wealth as a worthy goal. Henry A. Wallace correctly identified Alger's dream as a vision of America "not as a nation of propertyless workers but rather an America where all can become members of what has been called the 'middle class,' where all can share in the benefits which that class has enjoyed in the past." [28]

Others, less perceptive, made Alger a symbol of the Gilded Age. Implicit in Alger's own work is a critique of the post–Civil War period—of industrialization, urbanization, mammoth fortunes, and the general decline of morals. His stories bespeak a belief in a society where men reaped the fruits of their labor according to their merit. Nothing could have been more alien to Alger than the extremes of wealth and poverty that were characteristic of this period. The social conflict generated by the new order also disturbed him. Alger's work reflects an attempt to re-create the more harmonious society in which he was raised. His heroes come from another time, another society, another reality. Rather than extolling the dominant values of his day, he was reacting against them. His books exalted a time gone by when the middle class had played the major role in American life. It is interesting to note, in this connection, that Alger's greatest sales took place during the Progressive period when nostalgia for an imagined time of equal opportunity was running high.[29]

Straddling the worlds of the rural countryside and the urban metropolis, the Alger stories preserved the purity of the one while conveying the excitement of the other. In these stories, readers might find the reconciliation between different modes of life realities so harshly denied. People uprooted by the eddies of change found a kindred spirit in Alger, who, like them, was a stranger in a new society.

NOTES

1. See Thomas Meehan, "A Forgettable Centenary—Horatio Alger's," *New York Times Magazine*, June 28, 1964.

2. Henry F. Pringle and Katherine Pringle, "The Rebellious Parson," *The Saturday Evening Post*, CCXXIII (February 10, 1951), 30.

3. Clifton Fadiman, "Party of One," *Holiday*, XXI (February 1957), 6.

4. *Ibid.*

5. There has been some dispute as to the day of Alger's birth. Herbert Mayes in his biography of Alger, *Alger: A Biography without a Hero* (New York: Macy-Mesius, 1928), p. 13, states that Alger was born on Friday, January 13, 1832, pointing to the irony that the American apostle of success was born on an unlucky day. In fact, his birth certificate was procured by Ralph D. Gardner, a prominent Alger collector. See "Horatio Alger Books," *Hobbies* (April 1961), pp. 110–111. The January 15 birth date Gardner uncovered was confirmed in a letter to me from John A. Bigelow, town historian of Marlborough, Massachusetts, dated December 10, 1962.

The Mayes biography is open to question and gives no indication of where the sources of his material are. John Tebbel, in his biography of Alger, *From Rags to Riches: Horatio Alger, Jr. and the American Dream* (New York: The Macmillan Co., 1963) p. v., says: "It is a tribute to the research he [Mayes] did at twenty-eight to note that it can hardly be improved upon nearly four decades later," and offers his own book as a new interpretation of Alger's life based on the "facts" provided by Mayes. This interpretation consists of a good deal of parlor Freudianism centering on Alger's supposed sex life or lack of it.

The latest treatment of Alger's life is Ralph D. Gardner's *Horatio Alger, or the American Hero Era* (Mendota, Ill.: The Wayside Press, 1964). This book is written in the style of an Alger romance and suffers from the author's admittedly being "an unabashedly enthusiastic admirer" of Alger (p. 13). Mr. Gardner, does, however, provide an excellent and exhaustive bibliography.

6. For this description of the Marlborough of Alger's adolescence, I am indebted to John A. Bigelow in the letter cited above.

7. *Ibid.*

8. It was serialized in 1867 in *Student and Schoolmate*, a young people's magazine edited by William T. Adam (Oliver Optic). See Gardner, *op. cit.*, pp. 450–451.

9. For the decline of Alger in the twenties, see W. C. Crosby, "Acres of Diamonds," *The American Mercury*, XIV (May 1928), 104–113.

10. H. L. Mencken, *Prejudices: Second Series* (New York: Alfred A. Knopf, 1920), p. 223.

11. "The Cynical Youngest Generation," *The Nation* CXXXIV (Feb. 17, 1932), 186. See also, "A Forgotten Boy's Classic," *The Literary Digest*, CXII (Jan. 30, 1932), 20.

12. See above, notes 1 and 2. See also the following articles: "Up from Poverty," *The New Yorker*, XXIX (May 16, 1953), 23–24; Marshall Fishwick, "The Rise and Fall of Horatio Alger," *The Saturday Review* (November 17, 1956), p. 42; *Advertising Age*, December 1, 1947, pp. 18–19; Malcolm Cowley, "The Alger Story," *The New Republic* (September 10, 1945), pp. 319–320; and Frederick Lewis Allen, "Horatio Alger, Jr.," *Saturday Review of Literature*, XVIII (September 17, 1938), 3–4.

On the role of historians in perpetuating the myth of "rags to riches," see William Miller, "American Historians and the Business Elite," *Journal of Economic History* (November 1949), pp. 184–208.

For correspondence of some avid collectors of Algeriana see Alger collection at the Huntington Hartford Library.

13. For the number of Alger books, see Gardner, *op. cit.*, p. 356. After Alger's death, eleven more books bearing his name were written by Edward Stratemeyer, bringing the total number of books published under Alger's imprint to 118 (*ibid.*).

The estimate of Alger's sales is by Frank Luther Mott, *Golden Multitudes: the Story of Best Sellers in the United States* (New York: The Macmillan Co., 1947), p. 158.

14. Horatio Alger, Jr., *Fame and Fortune* (Boston: A. K. Loring, 1868), pp. vii–viii.

15. Horatio Alger, Jr., *Phil, the Fiddler* in *Struggling Upward and Other Works*, ed. Russel Crouse (New York: Crown Publishers, 1945), p. 282.

16. *Ibid.*, p. 311.

17. Horatio Alger, Jr., *Only an Irish Boy* (New York: Hurst and Co., n.d.), p. 94.

18. Horatio Alger, Jr., *The Telegraph Boy* (Boston: A. K. Loring, 1879), p. vii.

19. For an excellent description of the backgrounds of "genteel reformers," see James Stuart McLachlan, "The Genteel Reformers: 1865–1884" (unpublished Master's Thesis, Department of History, Columbia University, 1958), pp. 12–26.

20. Horatio Alger, Jr., *Tom, the Bootblack* (New York: New York Book Co., 1909), p. 122. See too *Wait and Hope* (New York: New York Book Co., 1908), p. 146, and *Chester Rand* (Philadelphia: John C. Winston Co., 1903), p. 254.

21. Horatio Alger, Jr., *Jed, the Poorhouse Boy*, in *Struggling Upward and Other Works*, pp. 401–566. See too *The Young Acrobat* (New York: American Publisher's Corp., 1890) and *A Cousin's Conspiracy* (Chicago: M. A. Donohue and Co., n.d.).

22. Horatio Alger, Jr., *Chester Rand*, p. 21.

23. Horatio Alger, Jr., *Bound to Rise* (Boston: A. K. Loring, 1873), p. 113.

24. Charles Loring Brace, *The Dangerous Classes of New York* (New York: Wynkoop and Hallenbeck, 1872), pp. 223–270. At the time the book was written, Brace noted (p. 241) that "between twenty and twenty-four thousand" children had been relocated.

25. "Holy Horatio," *Time*, XLVI (August 13, 1945), 98. See too John G. Cawelti, *Apostles of the Self-Made Man* (Chicago: University of Chicago Press, 1965), p. 123. Professor Cawelti's book, which appeared when the present study was largely completed, is perceptive in its treatment of Alger and other children's fiction writers of the nineteenth century.

26. See Horatio Alger, Jr., *Herbert Carter's Legacy* (New York: A. L. Burt, n.d.), p. 192.

27. Horatio Alger, Jr., *Struggling Upward*, pp. 79–80 (copy at Columbia University Library has no imprint). For a perceptive article on Alger's work, see Richard Wohl, "The 'Rags to Riches' Story: An Episode of Secular Idealism," *Class, Status, and Power*, ed. Reinhard Bendix and Seymour Lipset (Glencoe, Ill.: The Free Press, 1953), pp. 388–395.

28. Henry A. Wallace, *The Century of the Common Man* (New York: Reynal and Hitchcock, 1943), p. 56.

29. Mott, *op. cit.*, pp. 158–159. Mott estimates that by the first World War the aggregate sales of Alger books were over 16 million. Most of these sales came after Alger's death, at which time obituaries placed his total sales at about 800,000.

Chapter 3

The Christian Novel and the Success Myth

I

Popular taste in adult fiction from the Civil War to 1914 showed a marked preference for the inspirational novel. Among the most widely read books of this period were moralistic tales: sermons in fictional dress, similar in tone, in message, and often in plot line, to children's fiction of the Alger variety. The world presented in these novels was a simple one: good acts produced good results, evil behavior had evil consequences. Furthermore, the good were always rewarded and the evil punished. The forces of light were struggling successfully against the forces of darkness. Literature itself was a soldier on this battleground. As one student has noted, "fiction was meant to inspire, to exhort one to a fuller and finer life." [1]

This large body of inspirational fiction, ignored and forgotten by literary critics, contains a wealth of material for the student of popular attitudes. I shall examine the works of five representative writers. Two of them, Charles M. Sheldon and E. P. Roe, also wrote non-fiction success tracts. The others did not, but their work shares the didacticism of the non-fiction guides to life and helps sharpen our perception of the larger universe of values in which the success myth flourished. My designation of this genre as the Christian novel derives from its ministerial tone and its use as a conscious instrument in the cause of righteous living.

II

Augusta Jane Evans, the first southern woman to draw national attention in the field of American letters, was among the earliest writers of this genre. All her stories revolve around poor girls, though otherwise they conform to the classic "rags-to-riches" theme, and "argue that ambitious, Christian girls, whose virtue is attended by circumspection are justified in expecting material successes as comforting as their spiritual benefits." [2] In outline, Miss Evans' own life resembled that of her heroines. She was born into a well-to-do Georgia family, but her father went bankrupt when she was still very young and her childhood was spent in difficult circumstances. After the Civil War her novels brought her prosperity, though her marriage to a wealthy railroad manager in 1868 gave her financial security independent of her writings.

Like other success stories, her novels set forth general guidelines to living. Her biographer has written:

A careful reading of these stories will produce object lessons in a variety of situations—the proper treatment of aged parents by sons and daughters, the correct behavior of a young lady in a strange city, the benefits of good business and professional ethics, or the conduct of an actress who would avoid scandal—in fact, there is such an abundance of similar exhibits in the usefulness of decorous conduct and good morals that the social historian may consider these novels as textbooks in America's moral and social education.[3]

This estimate aptly applies to other Christian novels as well. They form part of the literature which popularized the success myth and, like most of that literature, they belong under the broader classification of guides to the proper conduct of life.

Miss Evans achieved her first national success with *St. Elmo*, published in 1867.[4] The heroine, Edna Earl, is an orphan living with her grandfather, to whom she is devoted. He is her only relative and her sole means of support. He dies when she is thirteen years old, leaving her alone, bereft of family and livelihood. Spurning charity, she leaves her country home to make her way in the world. As the story unfolds, the train she is on crashes and she is seriously injured. A wealthy matron in the community, Mrs. Murray, takes the injured girl into her own home and nurses her through her convalescence. She grows attached to Edna, and, after much coaxing, prevails upon her to remain after her recovery. Edna is persuaded to stay only when she realizes that her benefactress is acting not merely out of generosity but out of a need for companionship. Mrs. Murray, lonely and disconsolate over her errant son, treats Edna as a daughter. Edna in turn, more than fulfills her savior's expectations. She is intelligent, obedient, respectful, constant—altogether virtuous.

The perfect tranquility of the household is upset when the wicked son, St. Elmo, returns after a long absence. Now grown into a lovely and brilliant young woman, Edna is beginning her career as a writer. Repelled by St. Elmo's wickedness, she is irresistibly drawn to him. Failing in the struggle to control her emotions, she falls in love. Her intelligence and beauty attract many suitors and bring her several advantageous proposals of marriage. She rejects them all, however, and seems destined to spinsterhood, since his wickedness makes marriage to the man she loves unthinkable. St. Elmo is convinced that her virtue can be shattered and attempts every means of doing so. All his efforts, however, fail. Her perfection wins his heart and destroys his cynicism. He reforms, becomes a minister, and they marry. The classic ingredients of the literature of uplift are all there: the poor girl, the fortuitous encounter with a benefactor, the constant virtue, and the reward of material well-being.[5]

St. Elmo illustrates a number of themes characteristic of the Christian novel. Good always triumphs over evil, and the heroes and heroines live happily ever after. This association of virtue with happiness assures prizes in this world as well as the next. The need to end up with a moral frequently justifies the use of the most unlikely characters and situations. This genre resisted the developing literary realism of the period. Morality rather than reality was its chief concern, and the promise of rewards was clearly too great an incentive to virtue to be sacrificed. In this way, the "happy ending" became an essential part of the fictional defense of traditional morality.

III

An even more popular representative of the Christian novel than Augusta Evans was E. P. Roe, a minister turned author. His first literary success, *Barriers Burned Away*,[6] appeared in 1872. Its immediate inspiration was the Chicago fire, which provides the background for the final scenes of the novel. In plot, the book resembles the Alger stories. The hero, Denis Fleet, is an orphan who goes to Chicago to seek his fortune. Believing all labor worthy, if honestly and conscientiously performed, he takes a menial job in the establishment of a prominent art dealer. His industry and honesty soon bring him advancement. Fleet's life is complicated when he meets his employer's daughter and falls in love with her. The major problem is not his poor position, however. Rather —and here is *St. Elmo* in reverse—it is the girl's character. She is haughty, arrogant, and, worst of all, a religious skeptic. These characteristics place a seemingly insuperable barrier between them. Denis bears his unhappiness patiently and continues to live virtuously, helping all who cross his path. He also begins to develop as an artist, keeping in mind the axiom that "only the noble in deed and in truth can reach high and noble art." [7]

In the Chicago fire, the art gallery is destroyed and its owner dies. Denis, however, saves his beloved and teaches her courage through faith. She is converted, and, realizing the nobility of the boy she once held in contempt, accepts his love. Thus, the "barriers are burned away," and the two are finally united.

One reviewer caught the moral of the book perfectly. "The hero . . . is a young man who goes to Chicago, and, beginning at the bottom of the social ladder, as a porter and boot-black, rises to be a successful artist. The main lesson conveyed in his career is that of the virtue of a constant and complete communion with God in all the affairs of life, and this lesson is well conveyed. . . ." [8] Judging from the sales of Roe's books, the lesson was a popular one.[9] His popularity provides a measure of the appeal of traditionalism at a time when business was revolutionizing the country.

Roe himself had little concern for the literary merits of his work. He was content to know from his many readers that his books "were not only a source of pleasure, but also of help and benefit. . . ." [10] His popularity, however, did not save him from the barbs of literary critics. Unable to defend his writing aesthetically, his defenders dismissed aesthetic considerations as unimportant. "An author who believes that good is stronger than evil, and that a sinner may turn from his wickedness and live, and who embodies these convictions in his stories," wrote Julian Hawthorne, "deserves a success infinitely wider and more permanent than that of the skill-fullest literary mechanic: and it is to the credit of our nation that he has it." [11]

The best known defender of Roe was Lyman Abbott, prominent editor and early advocate of the social gospel. He, too, placed moral above aesthetic considerations in the evaluation of a writer. "I would rather minister to the higher life of ten thousand people," he said, "than win the plaudits of one self-appointed critic." Roe, of course, ministered to far more than ten thousand. His readers "in this country alone" were "numbered by the millions." Even more to the author's credit was the fact that, in Abbott's opinion, "no man, woman, or child ever read through one of Mr. Roe's books and arose without being bettered by the reading. . . ." [12] Abbott's admiration for Roe serves to underline the partial consensus among social gospelers, writers of succcess literature, and Christian novelists. All were middle class; all were shaken by the problems of industrialization; all sought to preserve cherished Christian values against the onslaught of urbanization and huge business combinations.

In the only children's book he wrote, Roe used a standard theme—the corrupting influence of the city as contrasted with the wholesome effects of rural living. Roe climbed on the bandwagon along with Charles Loring Brace and others who hoped to alleviate contemporary problems by getting people to leave the city for the country. He expressed the hope that the example of the Durham family in *Driven Back to Eden* would "lure other families from tenement flats into green pastures." [13]

The Durham family occupies an apartment in New York City. Mr. Durham is an office worker who just manages to support his family on his very moderate salary. The major difficulty confronting him is revealed in the opening pages of the book. His children, old enough to venture out alone, are being exposed to the immoral influences of city life. He finds his daughter looking at newspaper pictures whose "proper place" is "the gutter." He sees his son in a "very harmful kind of mischief . . . smoking cigarettes." When reprimanded, his son sullenly replies, "I'd like to know what there is for a boy to do in this street." Durham is taken aback and is unable to answer. Upon reflection, he admits the boy has a point. The city, he realizes, provides "very little range of action for a growing boy." [14] Yet smut and tobacco are dangers too serious to ignore. To protect and insure the moral well-being of his family, Durham decides to move to the country, where "there would be something for the children to do . . . pure air for them to breathe, and space for them to grow healthfully in body, mind, and soul." [15] After careful preparation he purchases a small farm. The family moves in winter so as to be settled in time for the spring planting. The difficulties of the first weeks of resettling are eased by the generous help of their rustic neighbors. The children join happily in the new family enterprise, and by the end of the first year Mr. Durham is able to express complete satisfaction. "There wasn't much chance for me to get ahead in the city, or earn a large salary," he tells his family. "Here, by pulling all together, there is almost a certainty of our earning more than a bare living, and of laying up something for a rainy day." The benefits of the move, however, are not primarily financial. The chief profit from the farm, Durham tells his children, "is not in my account book, but . . . in your sturdier forms." Most important of all is the fact that the family is "better and healthier at heart" than it was the year before.[16]

Roe's romantic rendition of farm life illustrates something of the anti-urban bias in his writing. Entering a demurrer against the movement from country to city, he even questioned the notion of the city as a place of opportunity. Clearly for a man like Durham—a man Roe obviously liked —the city did not offer much of a chance to "get ahead." Nor is getting ahead the chief end of life. Roe confined his hero's financial aspirations to "laying up something for a rainy day," a goal in marked contrast to the industrial fortunes of his time.

IV

The most direct attempts on the part of Christian novelists to confront the problems of industrialization were those of Charles M. Sheldon and other social gospel writers. Sheldon, like Roe, was a minister, and, like Roe, considered his novels an extension of his ministry. In 1888, he was called to the pulpit of the Central Congregational Church in Topeka, Kansas. When he had first come to Topeka, Sheldon had disguised himself as a laborer and had gone looking for a job. Distressed at the conditions he found and determined to do something about them, he used his pulpit to deliver sermons propagating the social gospel.

Frank Blackmar described this philosophy as a belief in "the regeneration of mankind through the personal application of the teachings of Jesus to the individual. . . ." [17] He summed up Sheldon's solution for a society racked by industrial conflict as follows:

> Each man must determine in his own mind what his own life will be, and while it is the duty of people to be helpful and thoughtful of one another, if each one will do what Jesus would do under similar circumstances, according to the best of his interpretation of the matter, there will be a grand harmony of life and service among all people. There will be no trouble about corruption in politics, the management of the state, the selfishness of trusts, the unequal distribution of profits, and the opposition of labor, or the excessive power of capital; all these will be settled in the simple formula of following the Master.[18]

The axiom that the total virtue of a society is equal to the sum of the virtues of all its parts is implicit in the writings of the Christian novelists. As individualistic as businessmen, they substituted virtue for profit as their goal. Just as men argued that pursuit of private profit contributed most to the general wealth of society, so early social gospelers argued that the pursuit of private virtue contributed most to the general moral health of society. They believed all social ills were founded in individual impiety, and focused their efforts at reform on individuals rather than institutions.

Sheldon's social gospel novels were an outgrowth of his Sunday evening sermons. His parishioners felt the morning service was enough, and enthusiasm for evening classes began to flag. To stimulate attendance, Sheldon delivered his evening sermons in the form of serialized stories. Each meeting ended at a suspenseful point in the narrative, "to be continued next week." The technique was as successful then as it was to be in movie theaters fifty years later. Sheldon's early novels were simply collections of these sermons.

In *His Brother's Keeper*,[19] Sheldon examines the problem of industrial conflict. Stuart Duncan, a wealthy mine owner, is confronted by a bitter strike led by his childhood friend, Eric Vassall. Willing to grant the workers' demands, Duncan refuses to admit the strike as a legitimate form of action or the union as a bona fide form of organization. The situation grows more tense when the state sends in troopers. Eric falls ill and loses leadership over his men. The presence of strikebreakers and state troopers, along with the lack of responsible leadership, makes for an explosive situation. Violence is averted only by the intervention of a Salvation Army group, led by Rhena Dwight, a renegade debutante from the East who has given up the frivolities of "society" to devote herself to God's work. The piety of her group restrains the workers from mob action. They finally accept non-recognition of their union, though their other demands are met. Stuart Duncan marries the New York socialite in the Salvation Army Hall. He devotes the rest of his life to administering his fortune for the benefit of mankind and becomes the perfect embodiment of the principle of the stewardship of wealth.

While the book is sympathetic to the plight of workers, it clearly opposes collective action. Reverend Burke, who speaks for the author, tells us there can be no solution to industrial strife unless "it is brought about by the appeal to and a belief in Christianity as the real source of final adjustment of men's relations with one another in the social compact." To live in harmony, men must "act like Christians" and follow the Golden Rule. When men learn to love one another, strife will disappear, for "love . . . is the great and final adjuster of all social problems and differences." [20] The inability of men to love one another has its roots in the inordinate desire for riches. The cause of the unrest of the age "lies in a disregard of humanity in a passion for getting wealth. . . ." The love of money "has wrecked empires" and unless checked "will smash our civilization." [21] The Christian novel has an undertone of foreboding which appears in non-fiction inspirationalists as well. While hopeful that harmony in society can be restored, they are fearful that, unchecked, the impulse toward accumulation will tear the social fabric apart. Many, indeed, who shared the basic values of Roe and Sheldon became prophets of doom, and saw the conflict of the period as a portent of the imminent collapse of American civilization. [22]

The classic social gospel novel is Sheldon's *In His Steps*, which first appeared in 1896 and sold over two million copies. [23] Reverend Henry Maxwell asks his congregation to ask themselves: "What would Jesus do?" before committing any action. The results are extraordinary. A railroad executive reports his company for accepting rebates; a singer gives up her concert career to devote herself to revivals; an ivory-tower professor decides to enter the next political campaign. "My plain duty," says the academic, "is to take a personal part in this coming election, to go to the primaries, throw the weight of my influence, whatever it is, toward the nomination and election of good men, and plunge into the very depths of the entire horrible whirlpool of deceit, bribery, political trickery and saloonism as it exists in Raymond today." [24] One of the town's wealthiest matrons comes to the realization that she is only God's steward. She denies that her generosity is "an occasion for vainglory or thanks from anyone." In dispensing her money wisely she is being honest in the "administration of the funds" God has asked her "to use for His glory." [25] With all its citizens guiding themselves according to what Jesus would do, the town is reformed in very short order. The implication is that such action everywhere would usher in the millennium.

Sheldon, in a typical success tract,[26] stressed the importance of honesty, thrift, and prudence as means to achievement. To be properly used, however, they had to be placed in the service of a noble end. True success required "some higher motive than . . . a big practice and a large income." The young lawyer, for example, should "enter personally into the battle for a clean, pure, honest city government," and while this might not bring wealth, it would develop "that fiber which has love of men at the heart of it and stalwart manhood at the back of it." [27] He warned the young man entering business against separating his personal morality from his business morality, and labeled such separation "monstrous." [28] He denied that love, gentleness, and tenderness could be confined to churches, families, and friendships. It was wrong to teach men that as soon as they emerged from these private spheres "they must begin a heartless war on their fellow men in order to succeed, in order to make business pay." Love must be the rule in "business as well as in churches and families." [29] Sheldon, subscribing to the success myth, refused to concede the validity of separating the drive for money from general moral considerations.

In advising artists and writers, Sheldon, like Roe and Abbott, emphasized their moral responsibility. The mission of the artist, he claimed, is "to teach men something they need to know." The first true principle of art is to lead men "to higher aims and purer acts." Were Christ to tour the great art galleries of the old world and the new, "he would sweep out of them a vast quantity of painting and sculpture" which was "ignoble, base, and impure." [30] The written word, too, was only worthwhile in so far as it helped to make the world better. Critics might sneer "at the novel with a purpose," but "no other kind" had "the right to exist." Writing, if "freed from the stain of mercenary motives . . ." would help move the world "along the track of millennial progress." [31]

Sheldon was most prescient in his advice to journalists. What more noble career "than to go into some town where sin ruled, and begin a paper that stood up for law, and temperance, and righteousness in business. . . ." Such a journalism was worth praying for. He predicted the new journalism would "dawn on the world at the beginning of the next century." It would be enlisted in the cause of righteousness and would "serve as the means by which Christian principle" would "be applied to every human condition. . . ." [32] We can easily imagine Sheldon's pleasure when muckraking journalism appeared, as he said it would.

V

Gene Stratton Porter and Harold Bell Wright were the most popular Christian novelists in the early part of the twentieth century. Gene Stratton Porter was born in Indiana in 1863, the twelfth child of a Methodist minister. During her girlhood she showed no particular literary bent, but early manifested the keen interest in nature which was to provide the impetus for her first writing effort. She married a businessman in Geneva, Indiana. He prospered, and they built a house just outside the town, on the edge of the Limberlost swamp which became the natural setting for most of her work. Her first book, *The Song of the Cardinal*, a nature study, appeared in 1903. Encouraged by its reception, she wrote her first novel, *Freckles*,[33] the following year.

We first meet Freckles seeking a job in a lumber camp. He is ragged, disheveled, and has no right hand. He was raised in an orphanage in Chicago, where his deformity prevented his adoption. He attributes his maiming to the cruel negligence of a mother he never knew. Assuming that only a wretched woman would allow such a thing to happen, he feels the shame of ignoble origins. Despite these inauspicious beginnings, however, Freckles manifests all the qualities of a noble character. He is honest, hard-working, and loyal. Sensing these qualities, Mr. McLean, the owner of the lumber camp, hires him. He is given the important and difficult job of guarding certain forest lands in the swamp. There, his constant contact with nature nourishes him and he grows stronger and healthier with each passing day. He works hard, does his job well, and saves most of his earnings. Whatever the obstacles, his determination always carries the day. "A man can do anything," says Freckles, "if he's the grit to work hard enough and stick at it. . . ."[34]

Mr. McLean, impressed by the boy's abilities, offers to pay for his education and finally adopts him. Freckles is overjoyed and deeply grateful. In the midst of all this good fortune, however, one difficulty arises to mar his happiness. Freckles meets a girl who accompanies a naturalist taking pictures of the swamp's natural wonders. He promptly falls in love, but is kept from his Angel by a feeling of unworthiness because of his low birth. Angel, however, refuses to believe that anyone as noble and fine as Freckles could have come from a mean background. "Thistles grow from thistles, and lilies from other lilies,"[35] she says, and proceeds to investigate the origins of her beloved. She goes to the orphanage where Freckles was raised, and manages to piece together the facts of his background from bits and snatches of evidence. The noble Freckles is noble indeed. The son of a lord, he is none other than Terence Maxwell O'More, of Dunderry House, County Clare, Ireland. As the mystery unfolds, we discover that his father had married against the wishes of his family. He had taken his bride to the New World, where they were stalked by poverty. Freckles' grandfather remained indifferent to their sufferings. Both perished in the attempt to save their son when their dwelling caught fire. It was at this time that the infant Freckles lost his hand. Convinced now of his proper origins and full of reverence for his unhappy parents, Freckles becomes engaged to his lovely Swamp Angel. All ends on a joyous note, with the assurance that the hero will spend the rest of his days in prosperity and happiness.

With the exception of its locale, the plot fits the classic Alger pattern. The hero is orphaned, but exemplifies the virtues of hard work, perseverance, and frugality. He finds a benefactor, meets a lovely girl, and lives happily every after. The idea of goodness being genetically transmitted crops up frequently, and seems difficult to reconcile with the idea of upward mobility associated with "rags-to-riches" themes. One implies continuity between generations, the other implies drastic change. The inconsistency can be explained simply by acknowledging the fact that Americans wanted both. A tension between emphasis on mobility and emphasis on stability is present in all literature stressing the middle-class virtues, and invests it with a chronic ambivalence. This is partially resolved by demonstrating mobility within a restricted framework. The heroes in this literature do not gain new positions in society so much as they regain old ones. "Rags to riches" might be better designated as "riches to rags to riches." Fictional examples of the dispossessed regaining their birthrights obviously struck a responsive chord. The appeal of this fantasy probably extended across class lines, but it seems to reflect most accurately the middle-class aspiration for a return to their former pre-eminence in the social order. Other characteristics of these novels point in the same direction. Their heroes are almost invariably of old American stock. The occasional foreigner, like Freckles, is generally of northern European origin. The benefactors they find are men of moderate means and modest taste, living simple lives in simple homes. The traditional middle-class ideal of moderation is everywhere. Poverty and profligacy, the extremes which typified the Gilded Age, are both abhorred. The Christian novel created a world in which neither is prevalent, a world which excluded both the immigrant and the millionnaire.

Porter's *Michael O'Halloran* is also reminiscent of the Alger stories. The hero is an orphaned city newspaper boy. His mother's legacy to him was a perfect formula by which to live.

> She had even written it down lest he forget. It was so simple that only a boy who did not mind his mother could have failed. The formula worked perfectly. "Morning: Get up early, wash your face, brush your clothes. Eat what was left from supper for breakfast. Put your bed to air and go out with your papers. Don't be afraid to offer them, or to do work of any sort you have strength for; but be deathly afraid to beg, to lie, or to steal, and if you starve, freeze, or die, never, never touch any kind of drink.[36]

Following his mother's advice, Mickey grows into such a fine lad that three people want to adopt him; his education is provided for, and he gets a good start in life working in the offices of the newspaper he once sold.

While Mickey's story provides the focus of the novel, subsidiary plots surround the success theme. The Minturn family, for example, illustrates the corrupting influence of great wealth. Mrs. Minturn is a prototype of the wealthy matron, neglectful of her family and taken up with "society." Her indifference to her children results in the death of the youngest. Spurred by this tragedy, Mr. Minturn leaves his wife, taking the other children with him. He moves to a simpler home, requires the boys to spend a lot of time in the country, and replaces their fancy clothes with simple ones. In short, he removes all the frills and luxuries which had surrounded them. The new regimen transforms his spoiled and unruly sons into model boys. Formerly contemptuous, they come to respect their father and realize the emptiness of their former lives. Mr. Minturn can scarcely restrain his joy when he hears one son tell the other: "Oh damn being rich! I like being *comfortable* a *lot* better. Malcolm, being rich has put us about ten miles behind where we ought to be. We're baby-girl softies!" [37] Ultimately even Mrs. Minturn sees the folly of her ways and is reunited with her family.

As Mrs. Minturn provides the example of what to avoid, so Leslie Winton is a paragon worthy of emulation. Miss Winton is a young woman of means engaged to a young lawyer. He has only recently come to the city, has small inherited means, and is busy conducting investigations into municipal corruption—a somewhat idealized embodiment of the Progressive profile.[38] Leslie, too, is interested in such reforms as "sweat shops, child labor, civic improvement, preservation of the wild and things like that!" [39] Her primary commitment, however, is to hearth and home. "If the nation prospers," she insists, "the birth rate of Americans has got to keep up, or soon the immigrants will be in control everywhere, as they are in places right now. Births imply homes. Homes suggest men to support them, women to control them." To those who are so "abominably obsessed with self, they refuse to become mothers," Leslie offers no quarter. "Such women should first have the ducking stool, and if that isn't effica-cious, extermination; they are a disgrace to our civilization and the weakest spot we have." [40] The whole of her senti-ment reflects rather accurately the feelings of large numbers of middle- and upper-middle-class people in the first decade of the twentieth century.[41] Indeed her remarks on women might have been made by Theodore Roosevelt.[42] The fic-tional romancers with their reformism, their distaste for the immigrant, and their idealization of the home and mother-hood, are of a piece with the Progressive mood.

The most popular of Porter's books, *The Harvester*, ap-peared in 1911.[43] The hero, David Langston, is strong, hard-working, and of perfect Christian character. These attributes stem from his upbringing in the woods, where nature nour-ishes these qualities. The plot centers around his finding a proper mate. He discovers her one day, fragile and fright-ened. She has just come from Chicago and shows all the de-bilitating effects of the city in her physical state. David woos her, restores her to health, and marries her.

His unique skill with medicinal herbs could bring him fame and fortune, but he refuses to use his talents toward these ends. "When a man accumulates more than he can earn with his two hands," he says, "he begins to enrich himself at the expense of the youth, the sweat, the blood, the joy of his fellow men." The lures of money and "society" are danger-ous, and David avoids both. He does not want "to know so-ciety and its ways," having seen "what it does to other men. . . ." He knows, too, of "the quick and easy ways to accumulating" money. Something inside him, however, holds him "to the slow, sure, clean work" of his "own hands," and this yields him "enough for one, for two even, in a reasonable degree. . . ." [44] A tale of contentment and moderation, *The Harvester* was not likely to inspire dreams of millions.

Porter was ridiculed for her "optimistic sentimentalism" and "her endless naive speeches" glorifying the "simple virtues." [45] Charged with creating unreal characters, she answered that all of them were drawn from people she had known "in the plain, old fashioned, country homes" [46] where she had lived. She claimed to know the seamier side of life, "its failures," even "its blackest depths of crime," but gladly left the analysis of these things to others. She was fortunate in that for every wicked person she had known, "she had met, lived with, and intimately known an overwhelming number of strictly clean, decent people." City critics might not know of their existence but they were real nonetheless. These critics might scoff "that there is not such a thing as a moral man, and that . . . her pictures of life are sentimental and idealised." "They are!" she declared. "And I glory in them! They are living pictures from the lives of men and women of morals, honour, and loving-kindness. They form idealised pictures of life because they are copied from life where it touches religion, chastity, love, home and hope of heaven ultimately. . . ." [47]

Her indignation at her critics stemmed from more than writer's vanity, however. Those who criticized her work cast shadows on an image of America she considered it vitally important to preserve. Persuaded that large numbers of young people drew their ideas on the proper conduct of life "from the books of half a dozen popular authors," she regarded her novels as weapons in a crusade for righteousness. The great virtue of idealized romance was that it made no one worse than he was. On the other hand, it might "fire thousands to higher inspiration." Conversely, unsavory literature could do great harm. With that combination of Christian social concern and Victorian prudery that made Anthony Comstock the self-appointed guardian of the nation's morals, Mrs. Porter called for the banning of improper writings. The interests of the nation's youth would be served "if the government actually censored books and forbade publication of those containing sensual and illegitimate situations which intimately describe how social and national laws are broken by people of wealth and unbridled passions." [48] The association of wealth with immorality was common in romantic literature with rags-to-riches themes. This, no doubt, reflects the perception which large numbers of Americans had of the society of their day. In consequence, one of the major aims of writers like Mrs. Porter was to show that despite social evidence to the contrary, success and virtue were not incompatible.

One admirer expressed appreciation of just this aspect of Mrs. Porter's novels.

> There is not only a high ideal held out to your readers which is beneficial to the reading public, but your books are especially different in presenting strong characters who succeed by right living and the right kind of effort. You make it appear always and strongly that to live right is not only good policy, but leads to the most successful life, and that good, honest effort in the true human spirit always brings satisfactory results. Such lessons cannot but be of great service to the public. . . .[49]

Those who wanted such lessons repeated found another ally in Harold Bell Wright.

VI

Wright was born in 1872 in Wrightstown, New York, into a family which traced its American ancestry back to 1640. The family was poor, however, its pedigree notwithstanding. Wright attended primary school and at fifteen went to work as a house painter and decorator. At the age of twenty, he decided to enter the ministry of the Christian Church, and studied briefly at Hiram College. He left there, presumably for reasons of health, and began a wandering life doing all manner of odd jobs including occasional preaching. From 1897 to 1908, he held various pastorates in Kansas, Missouri, and California, before leaving the pulpit to devote himself full time to writing. He regarded his books as an extension of his ministry, and remarked: "When I became convinced that, all things considered, writing was the work I could do best, I undertook that job in exactly the same spirit with which I had undertaken the work of preaching." [50]

Wright's early works followed the pattern of social gospel novels. His first, *That Printer of Udell's*,[51] appeared in 1903. The central character, Dick Falkner, as usual is an orphan. Making his way through life, he finds the most dangerous temptations are liquor and tobacco. At the same time hard work and frugality are extolled. Wealth without labor is ignoble. One sympathetic character remarks: "To be sure, I ain't rich yet. . . . But you bet I've worked for every cent I've got, and I didn't fool none of it away either. . . ." [52] Dick discovers that wealth often falls into the laps of the wicked and rails against the hypocrisy of rich men who, knowing nothing of Christianity, contribute to churches. One day, sitting in church, Dick is struck by the contrast between Christian principles and the rules of action men live by. If men could learn to live the Sermon on the Mount, instead of just talking about it, the world would be transformed. He forms a Young People's Church Society to begin the task of conversion. They are joined by other Christian groups, notably the Salvation Army, and start the job of reforming the town. Thus begins a movement which revolutionizes Boyd City and makes it a model "to all the world, for honest manhood, civic pride, and municipal virtue." [53]

Wright's attitudes toward wealth are further explored in his most popular novel, *The Winning of Barbara Worth*.[54] His two major characters serve as prototypes of the new and the old American. The new is represented by Willard Holmes, a representative of Eastern capitalism. His rise to a position of influence is due to his "connections" and "the strength of the proud social position to which he was born, rather than to hard work and experience." His approach to business is entirely amoral. Nothing concerns him "but the financial interests of the capital employing him." [55] He is simply a tool of the "interests"; and while he has all the refinements of genteel upbringing, he lacks the grit and guts that make the man.

The old type of American businessman is Jefferson Worth. Shrewd in business, he never allows money to obscure his social responsibilities. In this characterization, Wright provides the perfect synthesis of morality and success.

> Of old New England Puritan stock, Worth had come through the hard life of a poor farm boy with two dominant elements in his character; an almost super-human instinct for Good Business, inherited no doubt, and an instinct, also inherited, for religion. . . . It was his genius for business that led him, in young manhood, to leave the farm. . . . It was the other dominant element in his character that kept him scrupulously

honest, scrupulously moral. Besides this, honesty and morality were also "good business." [56]

Men like Jefferson Worth—neither "Jefferson" nor "Worth" is accidental—had penetrated the American wilderness and laid the basis for the nation's greatness. They were moved by something greater than mere profit. In their train, however, followed "saloons, gambling houses and dance halls," those inevitable "joys of civilization" [57] that undermine the classic virtues. Whatever decency remained in the country, however, was in the West, where men still lived close to nature. The East was urban, effete, and evil. Wright warned the "little Westerners . . . to watch out for" those "big eastern operators." Unless the West was careful, those Easterners would "take the whole blamed country. . . ." [58]

Wright's bitterest excoriation of "civilization" appears in *The Eyes of the World*,[59] the story of Aaron King, a young artist in genteel poverty, and his struggle to succeed without compromising himself. One of his first encounters is with a writer, Conrad La Grange, who has made a great "success" by selling his soul and indulging the public taste for "realism." A thoroughly bitter, jaded, and physically debilitated man, he describes himself as a "literary scavenger." He says:

I haunt the intellectual slaughter pens, and live by the putrid offal that self-respecting writers reject. I glean the stinking materials for my stories from the cesspools of life. For the dollars they pay, I furnish my readers with those thrills that public decency forbids them to experience at first hand. I am a procurer for purposes of mental prostitution. My books breed moral pestilence and spiritual disease. The unholy filth I write fouls the mind and pollutes the imagination of my readers. I am an instigator of degrading immorality and unmentionable crimes.[60]

This sums up the writer of realism as a panderer to public depravity. His moral sickness is reflected in his physical decrepitude.

La Grange describes the easy road to fame and fortune for Aaron King. All he must do is "paint pictures of fast women who have no morals at all—making them appear as innocent maidens. . . ." He must also paint portraits of those the world considers "distinguished citizens—making low-browed money-thugs look like noble patriots, and bloody butchers of humanity like benevolent saints." The patronage of these elements will bring success. A few artistic stunts, a few wires pulled in the right places, a few well-placed press releases, and all is done. Then, comments La Grange sardonically, "you will be what I am." [61] The depraved old writer tries to redeem himself by warning the innocent young artist of the perils that await him. King is perplexed. His mother had sacrificed everything for his education. He must succeed to be worthy of her effort. But could conventional success be destruction in disguise? His mother, herself, had advised him to be ambitious. It was important for a man to have high aspirations. "Without a strong desire to reach some height that in the distance lifts above the level of the present," she had written, "a man becomes a laggard on the highway of life—a mere loafer by the wayside—slothful, indolent—slipping easily, as the years go, into the most despicable of places —the place of a human parasite that, contributing nothing to the wealth of the race, feeds upon the strength of the multitude of toilers who pass him by." But, "like other gifts that lead men Godward," ambition could be used destructively. To be good, it must be noble and "nobly controlled." "A mere striving for place and power . . . is not a blessing but a curse. It is the curse from which our age is suffering sorely; and which if it be not lifted will continue to vitiate and poison the life of the race." [62] The novel has a jeremiad quality, carrying warnings to the wicked to repent.

As the plot unfolds, King is beset by every kind of temptation. Several times he comes close to irreparable compromise, but each time narrowly escapes perdition. Finally, he learns that success to be worth anything must be on terms consistent with integrity. Armed with the knowledge that nobility as a man is essential to his greatness as an artist, his future is assured. "Civilization" has lost a victim.

The book is merely a collection of caricatures, each epitomizing a single trait. Thus the millionaire in the story is called "Materialism"; the young girl whom King marries, "The Spirit of Nature"; the jaded society matron, "The Spirit of the Age"; the lustful young society buff, "Sensual," and so on. Wright is particularly obsessed with sensuality. Describing the sensualist, he writes: "He was not educated to the thought of *taking* life—he was trained to consider its *perversion*. The heroes in *his* fiction did not *kill* men—they *betrayed* women. The heroines in his stories did not desire the death of their betrayers—they loved them, and deserted their husbands for them." [63] Wright clearly was no stranger to some of the vagaries of the human animal, but clothed his discussion of them in an impenetrable moralism.[64] To do otherwise, to describe the human condition without the addition of a sermon, was a species of depravity in which only realistic writers indulged.

VII

The plots in Christian novels usually revolve around characters who are noble, who struggle with adversity and finally emerge on top. Behind this facile optimism, however, there runs an undercurrent of fear, a sense that the country is suffering from some terrible malaise. Its cause is never pinpointed, but has vaguely to do with the capitalist, the politico, the city, the lust for riches, and the loss of love between men. Nostalgic in tone, these novels are reminiscent of a time when the country was more rural and men stood closer to nature.

The writers of this genre were not alone in criticizing the new society that had emerged in America. The literary response to industrialism was broad and largely negative.[65] Realists like Phillips and Dreiser painted pictures of American life that were hardly flattering. Even the local colorists provided an implicit critique of American society. As one scholar has written:

> It does not seem accidental that the fashion of local color writing should have coincided with the hey-day of populism and the beginnings of muckraker journalism. All responded to the same kind of intuition about American society; and as the populists and muckrakers pointed an actively accusing, reformist finger at what industrial, metropolitan, corporate society was getting the country into, the local colorists, accusing passively through a submissive nostalgia, projected images of what the country was being led away from. . . ." [66]

The Christian novelists were active in their accusations but equally attached to their own image of an older America. This image, however untrue to the past, was a good index of their hopes and fears for the present and the future.

These writers saw their vision of America ridiculed in more realistic fiction, which, if able, they would have erased from the scene. Realism, to them, was the rotten apple in the literary barrel, and its practitioners the proverbial worms. This antagonism was part of the larger clash between tradition and modernism that gained such force in the industrial era. The tension between old and new showed in almost all areas of the national life: country versus city, religious orthodoxy versus science, immigrant versus native-born, industry versus agriculture, to name but a few. The Christian novelists' dislike for literary realism was another symptom of this tension. It was not the realists' subject matter or language that disturbed people like Porter and Wright. Certainly Wright could be as lurid as any writer of sex thrillers, and the treatment of the seamier side of life by authors like Dreiser and Herrick was still being conveyed in polite language. What was so irritating was the realists' insistence on a new perspective. Their writing reflected the modern temper, the romancers resisted it. That was the rub.

Nowhere is the conflict more evident than in the way adherents of these two schools handle success themes. The conception of success differs radically from one to the other. Yet scholars, for the most part, have ignored the distinction, lumping all rags-to-riches themes under the single category of the success myth. Kenneth Lynn's study of the myth's impact on the consciousness of five American novelists illustrates the point. Lynn writes that the myth, popularized by nineteenth-century success books, received "its classic expression in the work of Horatio Alger, Jr." [67] These stories, he tells us,

> reached the zenith of their fame and popularity in precisely those three decades—the seventies, eighties, and nineties— when the rate of industrialization and urbanization, the degree of social mobility, the absence of state control, the power of individuals reached levels never before attained in American society. The Alger hero fired the American imagination at the instant of his maximum credibility.[68]

This evaluation, though generally accepted, is incorrect. The popularity of the Alger stories reached its zenith in this century; we do not know that social mobility was dramatically rising when they were written; and the firing of the American imagination by the Alger hero had little to do with his credibility. The appeal of these stories lay as much in the realm of fantasy as that of a James Bond thriller. The fantasies they exploit are different, to be sure, but both types of hero appeal because they mirror desire, not reality.

This does not invalidate Lynn's study, which for the most part is excellent. It does, however, point up the prevailing habit of identifying the American worship of the dollar with the Alger stories, and by extension with the whole of the literature popularizing the success myth. Assuming this identification, Lynn writes: "Far from scorning the bitch-goddess, they [Dreiser, London, Norris, Herrick, and Phillips] grew up on the success myth [presumably represented by Alger] and in their maturity accepted it as the key to the meaning of American life." [69]

Lynn correctly perceived the fascination that wealth held for these writers and was perfectly justified in calling it their "dream of success." He was wrong, however, to equate this dream with the success myth as expressed in the Alger stories. The "dream" and the "myth" represent two separate and distinct threads in the fabric of American culture, and the use of them as synonyms assumes an identity where none exists. The "dream" grew out of the new possibilities for wealth and power that industrialization brought in its wake. It was fired by the advent of Napoleons of the market-place, men who commanded industrial armies, controlled vast resources, and lived in lordly opulence. The "myth," by contrast, reflected the values of a merchant-agrarian society, religious, moderate, and simple in tone.

The successes created by Lynn's novelists were fictional transmutations of the new millionaires, novelistic renditions of Rockefellers or Yerkes. As character types, they were as different from Ragged Dick and Tom the Bootblack as sharks from minnows. Surrogates of these Alger heroes appear in most Christian novels but never in realistic fiction.

Once we differentiate the "myth" from the "dream," the antagonism of Christian novelists to their less sanguine brethren becomes clear. The "myth" with all its moralistic trappings found continued expression in the work of Porter, Evans, and other fashioners of the storybook sermon. The "dream of success" which stamped realistic novels had no moralistic message, but represented money and power, pure and simple. It was the amorality of the realists that was so upsetting. Their refusal to moralize, their examples of vice rewarded and virtue trampled,[70] in short, their inversion of the classic Christian pattern, is what drew the anger of the sentimental romancers. The latter could not accept the idea that the universe was not moral, which was to say, in effect, that it was godless. Their insistence that art, to be valid, must be moral was part of their larger struggle to preserve the "myth of success" from the faithlessness of Lynn's dreamers.

NOTES

1. James D. Hart, *The Popular Book: A History of America's Literary Taste* (New York: Oxford University Press, 1950), p. 104.

2. William Perry Fidler, *Augusta Evans Wilson, 1835–1909* (University: University of Alabama Press, 1951), p. 151. Horatio Alger, Jr., in one of his few attempts at adult fiction, wrote a rags-to-riches story built around a heroine. This is his little-known *Helen Ford* (Boston: A. K. Loring, 1866).

3. Fidler, *op. cit.*, p. 223.

4. Augusta Jane Evans, *St. Elmo* (New York: Carleton Publishers, 1867). Frank Luther Mott estimates sales of *St. Elmo* at a million copies. He at-

tributes the popularity of Evans' books, in part, to their being "a success story, in each case, of an under-privileged girl . . . and a strong attack on the sins of the rich in comparison with the virtues of simple home life." Frank Luther Mott, *Golden Multitudes: the Story of Best Sellers in the United States* (New York: The Macmillan Co., 1947), p. 127. For a similar theme, see Augusta Jane Evans, *Beulah* (New York: Derby and Jackson, 1859).

Fidler notes another reason for her wide audience. He writes: "Perhaps the strongest appeal of Mrs. Wilson's books is that of 'remembrances,' as one critic wrote. Her novels are cherished reminders of social traditions and standards of conduct once honored but often forgotten in a latter day. Librarians and booksellers say that this appeal is chiefly responsible for her continued vogue." Fidler, *op. cit.*, p. 4. For an analysis of *St. Elmo* from a different perspective, see Beatrice Kevitt Hofstadter, "Popular Culture and the Romantic Heroine," *The American Scholar*, XXX (Winter 1960–1961), 104–106.

5. For a parody of *St. Elmo*, see Charles Henry Webb, *St. Twel'mo, or the Cuneiform Encyclopedist of Chattanooga* (New York: C. H. Webb, 1868).

6. E. P. Roe, *Barriers Burned Away* (New York: Dodd, Mead and Co., 1872).

7. *Ibid.*, p. 298.

8. Review in *The Christian Union* (February 19, 1873), p. 148.

9. Hart, *op. cit.*, p. 121. Mott estimates Roe's sales at somewhere between four and five million. Mott, *op. cit.*, p. 148. One contemporary noted that Roe's "income from books is much ampler . . . than the income of any other man of letters, obtained from the same source in America." George E. Montgomery, quoted in Mary A. Roe, *E. P. Roe: Reminiscences of his Life by His Sister* (New York: Dodd, Mead and Co., 1899), p. 203.

10. E. P. Roe, *Opening a Chestnut Burr* (New York: Dodd and Mead, 1874), p. 7.

11. Quoted in Mary A. Roe, *op. cit.*, p. 214.

12. Quoted in *ibid.*, p. 233.

13. E. P. Roe, *Driven Back to Eden* (New York: P. F. Collier and Son, 1885), Preface.

14. *Ibid.*, p. 15.

15. *Ibid.*, p. 22.

16. *Ibid.*, p. 220.

17. Frank W. Blackmar, "Charles M. Sheldon, A Man with a Mission," *Harper's Weekly*, XLIII (August 5, 1899), 769.

18. *Ibid.*, p. 772. This description applies to early social gospel ministers like Sheldon and Washington Gladden. It does not apply to the more radical Christian Socialists like Walter Rauschenbusch.

19. Charles M. Sheldon, *His Brother's Keeper: Or Christian Stewardship* (Chicago: Advance Publishing Co., 1898).

20. *Ibid.*, p. 179.

21. *Ibid.*, p. 178.

22. For this aspect of the response to industrialization, see Frederic C. Jaher, *Doubters and Dissenters: Cataclysmic Thought in America, 1880–1918* (New York: Free Press of Glencoe, 1964).

23. Charles M. Sheldon, *In His Steps* (New York: Hurst and Co., n.d.). The book first appeared in 1896. Estimate of sales is in Mott, *op. cit.*, p. 197.

24. Sheldon, *In His Steps*, p. 101.

25. *Ibid.*, pp. 124–125.

26. C. M. Sheldon, *New Opportunities in Old Professions* (Chicago: John A. Ulrich, 1899). This is a reprint of an address given at the Washburn College commencement, Topeka, Kansas, June 14, 1899. Sheldon also wrote a book called *How to Succeed.* I have not been able to locate this, but know of its existence through an advertisement on the fly-leaf at the end of C. M. Sheldon, *The Reformer* (Chicago: Advance Publishing Co., 1902).

27. Sheldon, *New Opportunities in Old Professions*, p. 7.

28. *Ibid.*, p. 9.

29. *Ibid.*, p. 10.

30. *Ibid.*, pp. 14–15.

31. *Ibid.*, pp. 23–24.

32. *Ibid.*, p. 26.

33. Gene Stratton Porter, *Freckles* (New York: Grosset and Dunlap, 1904).

34. *Ibid.*, p. 56.

35. *Ibid.*, p. 373.

36. Gene Stratton Porter, *Michael O'Halloran* (New York: Doubleday, Page and Co., 1915), p. 9.

37. *Ibid.*, p. 226.

38. For a description of the Progressive profile see George E. Mowry, *The Era of Theodore Roosevelt* (New York: Harper and Row, 1958), pp. 85 ff.

39. Porter, *Michael O'Halloran*, p. 43.

40. *Ibid.*, pp. 232–233.

41. Mowry, *op. cit.*, pp. 32 ff.

42. See Theodore Roosevelt, *An Autobiography* (New York: The Macmillan Co., 1913), pp. 176–184.

43. Mott estimates her sales by 1924 at between eight and nine million. Mott, *op. cit.*, p. 219.

44. Gene Stratton Porter, *The Harvester* (New York: Doubleday, Page and Co., 1911), pp. 273–274.

45. Robert Lynd, "Review of Michael O'Halloran," *Publisher's Weekly*, LXXXVIII (August 21, 1915), 563–564.

46. Quoted in Jeanette Porter Meehan, *The Lady of the Limberlost: the Life and Letters of Gene Stratton Porter* (Garden City, N.Y.: Doubleday, Doran and Co., 1928), p. 149.

47. *Ibid.*, pp. 155–157.

48. *Ibid.*, pp. 158–159.

49. Letter to Porter dated December 31, 1914, *ibid.*, p. 315.

50. Harold Bell Wright, *To My Sons* (New York: Harper and Bros., 1934), p. 219.

51. Harold Bell Wright, *That Printer of Udell's* (Chicago: The Book Supply Co., 1903).

52. *Ibid.*, p. 101.

53. *Ibid.*, p. 289. The social gospel theme is also used in Harold Bell Wright, *The Calling of Dan Matthews* (Chicago: The Book Supply Co., 1909).

54. Harold Bell Wright, *The Winning of Barbara Worth* (Chicago: The Book Supply Co., 1911). Wright's books were most popular before the First World War; afterwards, his sales dropped drastically. See Mott, *op. cit.*, p. 232. See too Bailey Millard, "The Personality of Harold Bell Wright," *The Bookman*, XLIV (January 1917), 463–469.

55. Wright, *The Winning of Barbara Worth*, p. 113.

56. *Ibid.*, pp. 156–157.

57. *Ibid.*

58. *Ibid.*, p. 309. For further expression of the east-west antagonism in Wright's work, see Harold Bell Wright, *When a Man's a Man* (Chicago: The Book Supply Co., 1916).

59. Harold Bell Wright, *The Eyes of the World* (A. L. Burt, 1914).

60. *Ibid.*, p. 42.

61. *Ibid.*, pp. 44–45.

62. *Ibid.*, p. 460. Wright wrote in his autobiography: "Through some devil's process our boasted 'progress' seems to have brought us to this—that the one great end and aim of life is to achieve the privilege of living upon the work of others, and of doing nothing for ourselves or in return for what we receive." *To My Sons*, p. 177.

63. *The Eyes of the World*, p. 424.

64. Revealingly, Wright wrote: "After all, one writes the sort of thing one writes because one's mind is mostly occupied with that sort of thing." *To My Sons*, p. 39.

65. See Walter Fuller Taylor, *The Economic Novel in America* (Chapel Hill: University of North Carolina Press, 1942).

66. Warner Berthoff, "The Art of Jewett's Pointed Firs," *New England Quarterly*, XXXII (March 1959), 51.

67. Kenneth S. Lynn, *The Dream of Success* (Boston: Little, Brown and Co., 1955), p. 4.

68. *Ibid.*, p. 9.

69. *Ibid.*, p. 251.

70. Any one of the following of David Graham Phillips' novels may be used as examples: *The Great God Success* (1901); *The Plum Tree* (1905); *The Fashionable Adventures of Joshua Craig* (1909); *The Conflict* (1911).

Chapter 4

How to Succeed:
Conduct-of-Life Literature
in the Industrial Era

I

Books on "how to succeed" swelled from a trickle to a flood after the Civil War. At first glance, this inspirational outpouring, wearing the word "success" as its insignia, appears to be a testament to America's worship of the bitch-goddess. That this worship was widespread and growing is attested to by success books themselves. Inspirationalists referred constantly to America's worship of Mammon. On the whole, however, they criticized this aspect of the American character. Success literature contained much advice on the general conduct of life, very little on the art of accumulating fortunes.

In part, the impression that this literature was devoted to inspiring dreams of riches derives from a semantic confusion. In current parlance "wealth" and "success" are used as synonyms; this was not so through much of the nineteenth century. The first American dictionary in which I found success defined as "the gaining of money" was William Dwight Whitney's, *The Century Dictionary*, published in 1891. As late as 1893, Webster's *International Dictionary of the English Language*, did not contain this definition.[1] The *Oxford English Dictionary* dates the use of success to mean money to 1885, and cites the following passage from Holmes' *Ralph Waldo Emerson* as illustration:

> Reading about "Success" [this was the title of one of Emerson's essays] is after all very much like reading in old books of alchemy. "How not to do it," is the lesson of all the books and treatises. Geber and Albertus Magnus, Roger Bacon and Raymond Lully, and the whole crew of "pauperes alcumistae," all give the most elaborate directions showing their student how to fail in transmuting Saturn into Lune and Sol, and making a billionaire of himself. "Success," in its vulgar sense,—the gaining of money and position,—is not to be reached by following the rules of an instructor. Our "self-made men," who govern the country by their wealth and influence, have found their place by adapting themselves to the particular circumstances in which they were placed, and not by studying the broad maxims of "Poor Richard," or any other moralist or economist. For such as these is meant the cheap cynical saying quoted by Emerson, "Rien ne réussit mieux que le succès."
> But this is not the aim of Emerson's teaching:—
> "I fear the popular notion of success stands in direct opposition in all points to the real and wholesome success. One adores public opinion, the other private opinion; one fame, the other desert; one feats, the other humility; one lucre, the other love; one monopoly, and the other hospitality of mind."
> And so, though there is no alchemy in this lecture, it is profitable reading, assigning its true value to the sterling gold of character, the gaining of which is true success, as against the brazen idol of the market-place.[2]

Thus, while money and success were becoming equated in popular parlance, the word was still ambiguous enough to permit more varied usage. Young people, particularly those most in need of the counseling of moralists, were less likely to dip into a tome called "Christian Living" than one entitled "Success"; and inspirationalists, in exploiting the word's ambiguity, probably touched a wider audience than they would have reached otherwise.

Whatever the allurements of their titles, the contents of success books quickly dispel any illusion of their yielding the secrets of making millions. Success itself was variously defined: as "the highest order of usefulness, in whatever condition it may have pleased Providence to place us";[3] as living "the Christian life and profession, accepting the Bible as . . . guide and teacher";[4] or as living "an earnest, honest and pure life." [5] Francis Clark hit the point directly when he wrote: "Every rich man is not, by any means, truly successful; every poor man is not, by any means, unsuccessful." [6]

II

The fortunes made after the Civil War altered the meaning of success even monetarily defined. For a generation that remembered a time when "a man that had a farm worth $1,500 or $2,000 was considered 'A No. 1,' " and when the "richest man in town was worth some $4,000 or $5,000" and "a village where, if a man had $50,000, he was supposed to be a magnate," [7] the change was hard to assimilate. The number of millionaires grew from a handful in 1865 to over 4,000 by 1892.[8] Popular estimates of the period placed the figure several times higher.[9] There is little question that "the million-aire class" impinged forcefully on the popular imagination. The names of Rockefeller, Carnegie, Fisk, Gould, and Harriman were much more generally known than those of leaders in the industrial and financial hierarchy are today. Despite their notoriety, however, the business magnates of the Gilded Age were not the heroes of the popularizers of the mobility ideology. These idealized the man "who is content with comfort rather than luxury, who prefers great principles to a great bank account, who considers 'enough better than a feast,' who prefers a competence to a colossal fortune. . . ." Such men were "not only among the happiest people, but among those who, like Lincoln and Garfield and Lucy Stone and Miss Willard, have been the real benefactors of mankind." [10] Post-bellum success literature rarely emphasized the new possibilities for accumulating money. It encouraged more modest aspirations, usually advising the young to "master some occupation or calling that will afford . . . a livelihood, and in time, a competence." [11] Not everyone could be a magnate, and only "a few" were "competent to start a large factory. . . ." For the majority of men it was best to enter a business which could "be set up in a small way, such as blacksmithing and carpentry. . . ." Such a trade enabled a man to "accumulate enough to educate his children and make himself comfortable in his declining years." With this most men should be content, for "all cannot be captains . . . and all cannot be at the head of rich establishments. . . ." [12] This kind of advice urged satisfaction with small blessings. It did not, however, promote the belief that unlimited possibilities awaited everyone. The estimate of mobility potential conveyed in success literature was a rather sober one. In so far as the success myth contributed to social cohesion, then, it did so by stressing the acceptability of modest social advance rather than fostering grand illusions.

As disorienting as the new quantitative dimension of wealth, was the rapidity of its accumulation. The fortunes of the period were amassed with tremendous speed. This was symptomatic of the general quickening of tempo in all areas of life and clashed with the conservative outlook of self-help advocates. They saw the age as one of "fast men," "of steam and electricity," of travel by "lightening lines." "The cry on all sides is for 'shortcuts' to the professions, and science-made-easy methods of intellectual culture," complained one author.[13] "Nothing is to be more deplored than this feverish haste, this passion for 'shortcuts' in everything, which seems so universally to prevail," joined another. "The young man who means to reach the heights . . . should understand that broad and easy roads, and shortcuts, so popular in these modern days, do not lead to them."[14] The virtues of patience, hard work, and prudence were being undermined by the spectacle of men who seemed to blossom into millionaires overnight.

Similarly, inspirationalists attacked the growing distaste for manual labor. William Mathews, whose *Getting on in the World* was one of the most widely circulated self-help books, criticized "the growing disposition of . . . young men to get their living by their wits, and to leave manual labor, agricultural or mechanical, to be monopolized by foreigners." "Bodily toil," he noted, "except of the lightest kind, is becoming to young America more and more distasteful."[15] For success ideologists, this was another symptom of the rejection of traditional values ushered in by industrialization. The conservatism of the rags-to-riches myth placed its adherents in a position critical of the new social and economic order. To work with one's hands had been the mark of an honest man; it was quick becoming the mark of the loser. Success writers deplored the change. "Happy will be that country where [labor] is crowned with dignity, and woe will it be to the land where it is held in contempt." [16] These recurrent caveats recall the jeremiads of the Puritan divines. This strain of complaint in American Protestantism was pervasive in books on how to succeed. The ascetic virtues of the Protestant ethic clashed with the weakening of restraints that accompanied economic expansion. Success literature manifested a chronic ambivalence to the rapidity of American development.

III

For the most part inspirationalists aimed their warnings at the sins of character—greed, gluttony, intemperance, and the like. The one impersonal force which drew their fire was the city. Movement from rural to urban areas rose sharply after 1860. It has been estimated that for every city laborer who moved to a farm between 1860 and 1900, twenty farmers flocked to the cities in search of better lives.[17] Ironically, the apostles of opportunity uniformly dreaded its greatest symbol. They warned that the city's temptations were almost insurmountable, sapping both the moral and physical stamina of youth. As proof of this, they contended that "boys from the country coming into the cities" were "taking the prizes of wealth and power and position away from the fellows that were reared in the city. . . ." The explanation offered for the rustics' superiority was that they had "had their will disciplined by regular and steady work and [had] not had their sensibilities deluged and overstimulated by a superabundance of amusement." [18] The young man reared close to nature, nurtured by sun, earth, and fresh air, was bound to be a finer specimen than his urban brother. Whatever wealth the city might boast of, it could never duplicate the healthfulness of rural conditions. Orison Swett Marden, editor of *Success* magazine, wrote:

> Nature gives a life-draught that artificiality knows not how to brew. Our nation has become great through its newness, its nearness to primitive conditions, through the opportunities that come from tapping the storehouses of nature at first hand; and through such manly qualities as vigor, energy, and enthusiasm, which have been developed in overcoming natural conditions and living face to face with the real world. Our great cities would decay from their own unnatural conditions were it not for the constant stream of fresh, honest, vigorous manhood and womanhood constantly flowing in from the suburbs and the country at large. The artificial crop will no more supply the demand than the hothouses will supply the food of the world. The sun-kissed fields and wind-purified hills must always be relied on for men and bread. [19]

Just as the country was the backbone of the nation, so the farmer was God's nobleman. The growing contempt for the hayseed disturbed success writers. "It will be a sad day for the true prosperity of our country," John Dale wrote, "when the best brain and intelligence of the land hold in contempt the cultivation and ownership of the soil; for it is to the country that the nation must look for those conservative and renovating forces, which are necessary to perpetuate our government." [20] That "sad day," however, was approaching swiftly. Farmers, carpenters, and mechanics were leaving the country in droves for what they believed was "the nobler work of weighing sugar, selling tape, hawking books, soliciting insurance, or posting ledgers." [21] Once in the city, they were dazzled by "the glittering, dashing, captivating forms of moneyed success. . . ." They saw the "splendid houses and equipages" of the rich; they read of the "luxurious entertainments" which the rich attended; they witnessed "the fawning obsequiousness of sycophants" which the rich commanded. On all sides they heard "the rich quoted as the successful, until wealth and success" became "synonymous terms." Subject to these surroundings, it was but natural that young men came "to believe that the chief end of man is to glorify gold and enjoy it forever." [22] The desire for riches was compared to the moth's fatal attraction to flame. Men were consumed by the passion for wealth. Success writers sought to dampen rather than fire this passion. They cautioned against overweening ambition. Ambition became vice, and vice bred failure. Other evils of the time were "boundless credits, overtrading, speculation and luxurious living." [23] These, however, were only secondary manifestations. The real trouble, "lying deeper in the popular character," was the love of money. Mathews summed it up as follows:

> Mammon-worship—devotion to "the almighty dollar"—the intense, all-devouring ambition to be the Napoleon of the mart, the man who owns a greater amount of real estate, bank, and railroad stocks, and solid cash or mortgages, than any other man on "change," the impatience to attain to wealth by a few brilliant and daring strokes, instead of by a slow and tedious uphill journey; the subordination of health and happiness, the highest interests of body and soul to money, *money*, MONEY, which is made the end instead of the means of existence,—*this* is the root from which spring not merely the marvellous activity, but the giant vices, of the American mercantile character. The race after riches in this country is not a

healthy, bracing race, but a steeplechase, a headlong, maddening rush.[24]

In the scramble after money, morality went the way of all flesh. Criticisms of a growing ruthlessness in the national character were often shrill.

> Away with the cold dictates of virtue and prudence and honor! Fling honesty to the winds. Extend no helping hand to your comrades sinking by your side. Think only of your own safety, and less of that than of the glorious end you have in view. Press on with all your energies, though the balls rain thick and fast about your ears. Stop not to stanch your wounds. Make a bridge, if necessary, of your dead and dying companions, and when you have carried the stronghold of Mammon, plant your flag on its topmost battlement, look around with a smile of triumphant satisfaction, and say "I'm a rich man." [25]

Such was the passion which put many a man into "an insane asylum or into the grave," [26] and success literature in attacking it took on the tone of a holy crusade.

The race for riches was matched by the impulse to spend. Urbanization intensified the tendency toward invidious display. Moralists worried over the mansions built more for show than comfort. They criticized the social competition that absorbed the energy of the distaff side of the upper class. "To outshine all rivals in the giddy circles of Newport, Niagara, and Saratoga," one complained, "is the height of many a woman's ambition, whose husband, instead of discouraging, exults in her extravagance. . . ." Furthermore, they noted with distress that the antics of the upper classes were imitated at the lower levels. "The hoop-skirts now in vogue typify the swelling conceit, the empty pride and vanity, which beginning with the upper circles, is mimicked and caricatured by all the orders of society, from the millionaire down to that of the humble grocer and fruit dealer. . . ." The merchant, it was said, "who half a century ago would have lived upon five hundred dollars a year, now spends four thousand." [27]

Success writers called on "all good people to unite in an effort to stay the tide of wild excess." "All noble and true women" were asked to voice "their disgust at the extravagant and indecent display of the followers of fashion." Nothing short of concerted action by "good people" could save "the nation from the mill-stone that has dragged other republics to destruction." Sane values had to be restored so that young men might "find a larger and nobler devotion than that of money, and modesty and dignity [might] not wholly desert American womanhood." [28]

The entertainments of high society were criticized as slavish imitations of European custom. "Is there anything more un-American than what we call 'society,' whose aristocratic code was imported from Paris and London into New York, and thence spread to other large cities of our land?" asked one author.[29] As a corrective, he prescribed a return to true American tradition. Rather than late and lavish dinners, good Americans should

> meet in the early evening, at a simple supper . . . and discuss cheerfully great questions of politics and education and welfare and religion, with music and speaking furnished by themselves, and just as little of formality as possible, and with no shibboleth of wealth as a test of position but only so much education and refinement of manners and dress as would be necessary to form a homogeneous and congenial group.[30]

When the taste for extravagance showed itself in the political arena, the normally non-partisan editors of *Success* broke policy and upbraided the errant politicos. The following article appeared in the April 8, 1899, issue of the magazine.

> *Success* has no political views. We stand for justice, truth, and right, for everything that tends to elevate and improve humanity. . . . At the same time, *Success* takes note of passing events in politics, as well as other fields, and the controversy between William Jennings Bryan and Perry Belmont appears to be an incident well worthy of attention. . . .
>
> Mr. Belmont, in behalf of the Democratic Club of New York City, invited Mr. Bryan to a banquet of the club,—the cost to be ten dollars a plate,—in honor of Thomas Jefferson. Mr. Bryan declined to accept the invitation on two grounds: first, because a ten-dollar-a-plate banquet could not be called democratic; and secondly, for the alleged reason that Mr. Belmont and his associates are not really Democrats, because they opposed the Chicago platform in 1896. . . . Mr. Bryan in the meantime, has accepted an invitation to a Jefferson "banquet" at the popular figure of one dollar a plate.
>
> Whether the Chicago platform is right or wrong, logic and policy seem to be on the side of Mr. Bryan. Ten-dollar banquets are class affairs, within reach only of the moneyed few. . . . It is the duty of every public man . . . to see that banquets are not brought into striking contrast with dinner pails.[31]

In general, it can be said that the values of rural, Protestant America, which Bryan exemplified, were more in accord with those of success writers than the value system industrial and finance capitalism was creating.

IV

Yet condemn excesses as they would, inspirationalists rarely advocated forced restraints upon the individual. Likewise, though they were aware that great fortunes encouraged immoderation, they could not bring themselves to condemn wealth in and of itself. "Trade and money-making," one wrote, were "the necessary elements of a healthy society; without them the blessings of the earth could not be developed, and man would relapse into barbarism." Just as "money-making is not forbidden," he went on, "so no limit to money-making can be set with mere respect to amounts. . . ." [32] Esteeming individual freedom and wealth, and loathing the excesses of both, inspirationalists were caught on the horns of a dilemma. They retained the Puritan ideal of moderation while rejecting Puritan conceptions of social regulation in favor of nineteenth-century political liberalism. Thus they were left with an ethic but without the means of enforcing it. The problem of seeking ends without means, so to speak, accounts for the steady stream of guidebooks that poured from the pens of success writers in the Gilded Age. Reluctant to use government to compel proper behavior, they resorted to personal persuasion on a grand scale.

The concern of success writers over the excesses symbolized by mansions of marble and ten-dollar-a-plate dinners was matched by their distress at the squalor and wretchedness of the poor. Urban growth had caused an increase in slums and all the evils attendant upon overcrowding. The poor were more visible. Vices which in rural surroundings were spread thin and inconspicuous became glaring sores in urban concentrations. Chief among these was the increased consumption of alcohol.[33] Saloons proliferated as cities grew and they provided a constant target for the moralizing of inspirationalists. All success books could qualify as temperance tracts. Smoking was also criticized, and tobacco joined alcohol as one of the chief causes of failure. "One form of improvidence, which commands world-wide attention," noted one success writer, "is the enormous waste of substance for liquors and tobacco." According to the census of 1890, it was observed, "eight hundred millions of dollars are spent annually for liquors, and six hundred millions more for tobacco, and that together they exceed the cost of all the bread, meat, woolen and cotton goods, and boots and shoes, used by the whole country." [34] The same writer predicted that if the money spent on these forms of self-indulgence were spent properly, "in a few years every family might dwell under its own roof; there would be no ragged children growing up in vice and ignorance, no despairing mothers, or squalid houses." The fault lay with "the men who squander their hard earnings, and thus invite the poverty of which they complain." [35]

Unwilling or unable to attribute the indigence of large numbers of people to other than individual causes, success writers found in the vices of drinking and smoking a convenient explanation for large-scale poverty. At the same time, though, they equally criticized those who profited from and encouraged the vices of the poor. Furthermore, liquor was only the most glaring of the evils "Mammonism" fostered. For example, success writers warned against the "pernicious literature with which American greed for gain [was] flooding our land. . . ." [36] They attributed the growth of amusements which subverted the Sabbath to the unrestrained pursuit of profit. Gambling, too, flourished "in spite of the law, and actually under its license, *because there* [was] *money in it*." [37] Liquor, Mammon, and the city were the great trinity of evil.

V

To discourage people from flocking to the urban fleshpots, writers warned that opportunities for success in the cities were less than believed. William Mathews wrote:

> . . . if any fact has been demonstrated beyond the shadow of a doubt, it is the deceitfulness of the apparent facilities for getting rich in the cities. The fact that while in other careers the mass of men are successful, ninety-five at least out of every hundred who embark in commerce either make shipwreck or retire sooner or later in disgust, without having secured a competence, has not only been verified again and again by statistics, but is a stereotyped observation which drops from the lips of businessmen daily.[38]

Others frankly expressed the hope of turning "the thoughts of young men to the desirability of reversing the order of things," and urged them "instead of seeking the city with its congestion to seek the country with its freedom. . . ." [39] The removal of people to rural areas was often offered as a panacea for all social ills. Francis E. Clark, author of success books, and founder of the Christian Endeavor Union, urged the "Gospel of Out of Doors" as "the most efficacious antidote for the peculiar evils of our own day and generation." He went on to say:

These are the evils of the city, not of the country. The reeking misery of the slums, not the stolid animalism of the fields, is our danger in America today. Anarchy is hatched in the city. The brothel is a product of the city. Bribery and political corruption, "graft" of every sort, find their hotbed in the city. If by some master stroke the slums could be transported to the Vermont hills or the Adirondack woods or the South Dakota prairies . . . half the problems of our every-day civilization would be solved.

The other half would disappear if the "members of the Four Hundred at the other end of the social scale . . . were planted in another garden and made to dress it and keep it. . . . For then justice will spring out of the ground and righteousness will look down from Heaven." [40] Clark's proposal underscores the alienation of the middling elements in the new America. Penetrating far beyond the agricultural community, the myth of the yeoman became part of varied expressions of protest. It appeared in contexts as diverse as agrarian radicalism, religious fundamentalism, or mild reformism. Different though they were, all these movements shared a common antagonism to the forces of modernization at work in America. As one of the most important of these forces was the new economic organization of the nation's resources, success writers were perforce ambivalent toward it. Changes in the Gilded Age, however, involved more than a revolution in economic relations. The period also saw important shifts in thought patterns. Here it is important to emphasize that the success myth was more than an expression of attitudes toward getting ahead in the world; the idea of rags-to-riches generally appeared in the context of a definable set of ideas and values concerning man, society, and the cosmos. In short, the success myth encompassed a world-view. Hence, success literature was a manifestation of the protest, not only against material changes in the nation, but of ideational changes as well.

VI

The ideological concerns of success writers are seen in their fear of changing attitudes toward the relation of conduct to achievement. They complained of a growing tendency in the popular mind to dissociate commercial success from virtue, or even to regard them as mutually exclusive. The association of personal virtue and material prosperity, which had deep roots in American tradition, was breaking down in the postbellum period. In 1883, Wilbur Crafts wrote "that an importation of principles into trade is greatly needed," as was "significantly shown by the fact that the Congregational Club of New York recently and seriously discussed the question, 'Can Business Be Conducted Successfully on Strict Christian Principles?' " [41] The fact that the question could be seriously raised before such a group was symptomatic of how bad things were. The corruption of the post–Civil War period in all areas of the national life was making a mockery of moral standards. Young men came to regard the linkage of virtue and success as absurd. Too many Tweeds, Fisks, and Goulds afforded striking evidence to the contrary. Referring to corruption in the political arena, *Success* magazine editorialized:

> Honesty in the performance of public duties is fully as important to the well-being of society as rectitude in private transactions. Corruption in high places is a demoralizing example

for the youth of our land, who ought to be able to regard official station as one form of honorable success, and as the just reward of firm integrity and conspicuous ability. Unhappily, there is evidence too strong to be disregarded, that dishonesty is the rule, and not the exception, in the legislatures of some of our states, and that Congress itself is not free from the power of those who are willing to corrupt the very source of government.[42]

This association of venality with worldly rewards, both pecuniary and political, threatened to turn the idea of a Christian universe upside down. Much more was at stake than clean government. Supernaturalism itself would be undermined if men ceased to believe in a world governed by moral principles. Christian believers could never accept the idea of a naturalistic universe. To deny morality as a crucial factor in the destiny of men was to court rejection of the most basic tenets of religious faith. It is for this reason that so many ministers entered the ranks of the inspirationalists.[43] At a time when riches were so highly valued, it was especially important to retain the ancient connection between virtue and material well-being. Hence success books were full of warnings against the belief

> that there is any necessary antagonism between success and downright integrity of character—uprightness of heart and life. The long array of Christian jurists and statesmen and merchant-princes which might be cited would seem to give to an error like this a sufficient refutation. Amid the prevailing irreverence and scepticisms and frivolities of the day seek ever to cherish and cultivate a reverent spirit.[44]

Further insight into the motives of success writers is gained by examining the personal struggles recorded by one of the most prominent advisers to young men, Josiah Strong. He received a "Puritan training" which gave him "individualistic and rather severe ideas of life and religion." In his young adulthood he "felt the shock of great changes, theological and social. . . ." "Broken from their ancient moorings," he said, "men seemed to me to be drifting." The "new views fostered by science were believed to be hostile to religion, paralyzing to faith, and demoralizing to conduct." The rejection of old views was not nobly motivated either. "Impatience of restraint rather than love of truth seemed to inspire the attacks on many beliefs which the fathers held sacred." Science was used as an excuse for moral nihilism. "When would these changes cease?" he asked. "How much of the old structure of society and of belief would they leave standing? Such were the questions which troubled a serious mind that could not be blind to what was actually taking place." [45] Not all were as articulate as Strong, but the popularity of a literature dedicated to strengthening traditional beliefs and values indicates how widely these problems were felt. The proliferation of success books was symptomatic of the need of large numbers of people to assure themselves that "the old structure of society and of belief" would remain intact.

VII

Virtually every development of the Gilded Age was criticized by popularizers of the success myth. They deplored the movement from farm to city; they felt the growth of extremes of rich and poor to be destructive of social well-being; they condemned the corruption in business and politics and feared the cynicism it promoted; they sensed the threat to religion that science posed and tried to check it by an almost compulsive reassertion of faith.

In their eagerness to preserve belief, however, they resorted to appeals more worldly than religious. By repeating that all success was dependent upon "principles derived directly from the Bible," [46] and opting for the "acceptance of the Christian life and identification with some church because they pay," [47] success writers contributed to the reduction of religion to a narrow functionalism. In this way success literature resembled religious evangelicalism. In the postbellum period, whatever remained of orthodox Calvinism began to crumble before the onslaught of Darwin and the higher criticism. Unable to muster a coherent intellectual defense against these trends, Protestant theology became increasingly vapid. More and more, techniques of conversion replaced doctrine as the chief concern of clergymen. Henry Ward Beecher indicated this when he said: "I gradually formed a theology by practice—by trying it on, and the things that really did God's work in the hearts of men I set down as good theology, and the things that did not, whether they were true or not, they were not true to me." [48] In some of his preaching he "made it appear . . . that for salvation good intentions were the chief necessity." [49] This emphasis on the easy means to salvation was strongest in the revivalism of the period, where millions were assured that heaven was open to them if they would only believe.[50] Success writers played a similar game, but dangled a different reward before the would-be victor. As revivalists brought men to God by promising salvation, inspirationalists brought men to goodness by promising success.

To judge from its tone and content, success literature was

directed toward elements of the middle class, to Protestants of "native" stock. These "essays on the good" were not aimed at the immigrant who made up such a large proportion of the American industrial proletariat.[51] The nativist bias of this literature clearly marks it as one intended for a home-grown audience. Furthermore, the success myth promoted the occupational ideal of the independent farmer, merchant, or artisan. These aspirations were not geared to producing an obedient working class congenial to the rulers of a factory economy. They were more likely to encourage dissatisfaction with the lack of independence, the forfeiture of self-direction, and the loss of individuality that attached to the industrial worker. It is dubious, then, that success books had any significant latent function as a means of social control. Their importance is as a symptom of the widespread unrest brought on by rapid and dramatic social change.

One of the most striking features of this literature is its anachronistic quality. The values it fostered were not so much supportive of industrial capitalism as irrelevant to it. Several philosophical alternatives presented themselves to the post–Civil War generation as possible ways of interpreting the disruptive phenomena of industralization. Both Marxism and Social Darwinism offered guidelines for explaining what was happening in America. Either of these philosophies, both of which placed conflict at the center of man's existence, provided a coherent interpretation of contemporary realities. Social Darwinism had the further virtue of giving a much desired rationalization for the inhumane consequences of rapid industrial development. It also provided a cogent moral justification for the activities of the leaders of the industrial hierarchy. Yet success writers continued to cling to a *weltan-schauung* that denied the necessity of conflict as a factor in social development. Their social theory, if it can be called that, was post-Newtonian. Its emphasis was on the balanced, ordered, harmonious nature of the social organism. They could not offer an explanation for industrial conflict. They merely insisted that it was unnatural and unnecessary—an aberration resulting from the failure of individuals, at both ends of the social spectrum, to behave like Christians. Success writers would not admit any necessary antagonism between the boss and his workers. All were engaged in a common enterprise with *mutual* obligations. The employee owed his boss loyalty, hard work, and intelligence. The employer owed his worker a fair living wage, decent working conditions, and courteous consideration. Hard feelings and conflict were due to personal misunderstanding and suspicion. The solution to the problems between labor and capital was to make both aware of their real identity of interest and their Christian duty to one another. One success writer had the following bit of advice for employers: "The most efficient, loyal, and contented workers are always developed under employers who make the Golden Rule their motto. In factories, stores, and offices where this rule is adopted, we don't hear of strikes or lockouts, or conflicts between employers and employees." [52] In relations between capital and labor, as in everything else, Christian principles would resolve conflict. Spencerian social theory did not have much of an impact on success literature. The idea of progress by means of the strong eliminating the weak was alien to the genre. It might be a while before labor and capital "discovered that their interests are really one, that they must cooperate like the two wings of a bird; but that discovery will come in time, and then they will combine." [53]

VIII

Such a body of beliefs was severely strained by the realities of American life. Toward the end of the century, success writers were forced to qualify the old teachings more and more. They had to take into account a new economic man—the corporation employee. "Doubtless," they were forced to admit, "a greatly increased proportion of young men must expect to work on salaries in large corporations." [54] The new American soil was not fertile ground for the yeoman individualism of an earlier day. For salaried men in corporations, however, success literature in the classic vein had little meaning. Its world of farmers, carpenters, and blacksmiths was not relevant to generations urban born. The myth of success and the literature it produced in the nineteenth century was an expression of the pre-industrial mind in America. Its decline was prefigured by the disappearance of its social frame of reference. This is not to say that the inspirational tradition died; it did not. It continues to run strongly even in the present. It did, however, find a new mold, a new set of images and associations. What these were are the subject of the following chapters. Suffice it to say, here, that as the nation entered the new century, the classic rags-to-riches ideology was on the wane.

In the first decade of the twentieth century, many who shared the values of success writers rejected their facile optimism and entered the ranks of reform. Like Louis Post, they attacked success writers for deceptively inculcating the "idea that social conditions permit the rewards of industry to find their natural objects." [55] Preaching was a far cry from what was really necessary for "the highest ideals of morality" [56] to triumph. Men of good will must "attach themselves to the causes that harmonize with the great order of things." [57] Interestingly, however, the good society reformers envisaged was much like the one success writers described. If reformers resented the illusional quality of success literature, it was only because they sought to make the illusion a reality. There was not a total identity of ideas between Progressives and success ideologists, but their areas of common belief were substantial. Both groups shared the same moralism; both believed that in a just society reward must be commensurate with labor; both disliked conspicuous display and idealized the virtues of simplicity; both resented the immigrant; both feared monopoly and political graft; and, finally, both found the centers of infection for the nation's ills in its cities. It is revealing of the relationship between the success ethic and reform that Orison Swett Marden's *Success* magazine advocated municipal ownership of public franchises as early as 1889.

> The American people have too long submitted not merely to be robbed, but to be decimated also by corporate greed. The time will doubtless come when posterity will think it almost incredible that the lives of hundreds of innocents should have been sacrificed in one city to the lawless covetousness of corporations whose very privileges, in the first place, were purloined from the people.[58]

The advocacy of public ownership may appear to contradict the individualistic bias of the success ideology. It is important to remember, then, that in this period, the corporation, not the state, appeared the great subverter of individualism. The sympathy for reform in success literature was often matched by a sympathy in reform literature for success. An examination of *La Follette's Weekly Magazine*, for example, reveals that it advertised numerous self-help tracts.[59] This further supports the view that reformers did not find the values embodied in the rags-to-riches tradition antagonistic to their purposes.

The discontent success writers expressed about almost everything that typified the Gilded Age indicates that their position vis-à-vis the new industrial order was not a happy one. They did, of course, encourage the belief that anyone could succeed, and in this way, perhaps, served to inhibit social resentments. This belief, however, was attached to a complex of values that could only provoke antagonism to existing conditions. Enormous accumulations of private wealth gave rise to a new leisure class with all the conspicuous trappings, if not the titles, of nobility. The ascetic principles of the Protestant ethic, enjoined in all success literature, were as hostile to the lord of the exchange as they had been to the lord of the manor. Furthermore, the belief in opportunity had a prescriptive aspect. It may have been false, but it promoted an ideal and defined a level of expectation. If Americans had not been taught that opportunity was part of their birthright, they might never have resented the lack of it. Expectations that are unfulfilled easily become sources of resistance to the social forces that frustrate them. In this way the belief in opportunity was instrumental in bringing about protest. There was, of course, a reactionary potential in the success myth. This came into full glare in the 1920s with the revolt against modernism. The rural, religious, individualistic emphasis of the success ideology was present in the Ku Klux Klan, in the movement for prohibition, in the anti-evolution crusade. This cast of mind, however, could cut different ways. Its meaning for a society in transition was different from that for a society already transformed. This is exemplified in the career of William Jennings Bryan who, running for the presidency in 1896, could be viewed as a harbinger of radical social upheaval, and who, a quarter of a century later, died a symbol of reaction. Bryan's ideology remained constant, only its significance had changed.[60] The thrust of identical ideas, then, may vary in different historical periods. In the Gilded Age, the innovative forces in American society were, in political terms, conservative. On the other hand, the forces of tradition, in good part because of their resistance to change, were somewhat to the left in the political spectrum. In the context of a society being revolutionized from above, the traditionalism of the success myth had a progressive cast. In an age of corporate exploitation, the rags-to-riches ideology pointed in the direction of reform.

NOTES

1. See William Dwight Whitney, *The Century Dictionary* (New York: The Century Co., 1891), p. 6037, and Webster's *International Dictionary of the English Language* (Springfield, Mass.: G. & C. Merriam Co., 1893).

2. Oliver Wendell Holmes, *Ralph Waldo Emerson* (Boston: Houghton, Mifflin and Co., 1885), pp. 260–261. Not the whole passage, of course, is quoted by the *Oxford English Dictionary*, which uses only the following sentence: " 'Success,' in its vulgar sense,—the gaining of money and position,—is not to be reached by following the rules of an instructor." See too Ralph Waldo Emerson, *The Conduct of Life* (Garden City: The Masterworks Program, n.d. [1860]), *passim*.

3. Joseph Henry Dubbs, *Conditions of Success in Life* (Philadelphia: Reformed Church Publication Board, 1870), p. 3.

4. John T. Dale, *The Secret of Success: or Finger Posts on the Highway of Life* (Chicago: Fleming H. Revell, 1889), p. 160. See too William M. Thayer, *Ethics of Success* (Boston: Silver, Burdett and Co., 1894), p. 6.

5. F. E. Clark, *Our Business Boys* (Boston: D. Lathrop and Co., 1884), p. 48.

6. *Ibid.*, p. 14. J. S. Chamberlain, another success writer, wrote: "Wealth is not always a synonym of success. Many men whom the world delights to honor grasped the full glory of glittering success, although they never acquired anything of wealth. The truly successful are those who have achieved the greatest good in their respective callings whether that success has brought them riches or not." J. S. Chamberlain, *Makers of Millions: or the Marvelous Success of America's Self-Made Men* (Chicago: George M. Hill Co., 1899), p. 11.

See too Charles H. Kent, *How to Achieve Success: A Manual for Young People* (New York: The Christian Herald, 1897), p. 17, and H. A. Lewis, *Hidden Treasures: or Why Some Succeed While Others Fail* (New York: A. W. Richardson, 1887), p. 512.

7. Quoted in Edward Chase Kirkland, *Dream and Thought in the Business Community, 1860–1900* (Chicago: Quadrangle Books, 1964), p. 6, from testimony given before the Senate Committee on Education and Labor in 1885.

8. *New Light on the History of Great American Fortunes*, ed. Sidney Ratner (New York: Augustus M. Kelley, 1953), p. 92.

9. *Ibid.*

10. *Success*, II (March 11, 1899), 264.

11. Dale, *op. cit.*, p. 156.

12. Nelson Sizer, *The Royal Road to Wealth: How to Find and Follow It* (San Francisco: J. Dewing and Co., 1883), p. 41.

13. William Mathews, *Getting on in the World: or, Hints on Success in Life* (Chicago: S. C. Griggs and Co., 1883), pp. 242–243. Mathews' book, which first appeared in 1873 and sold 70,000 copies, first saw light as a series of articles in the *Chicago Tribune* in 1871.

For the expression of similar sentiments, see Alexander Lewis, *Manhood-Making: Studies in the Elemental Principles of Success* (Boston: The Pilgrim Press, 1902), p. 47; H. A. Lewis, *op. cit.*, p. 499; "A Dangerous Time," *The Outlook*, LXVIII (May 11, 1901), 105–106; James D. Mills, *The Art of Making Money or the Road to Fortune: A Universal Guide for Honest Success* (New York: International Publishing, 1872), p. 172; Clark, *op. cit.*, pp. 47–48.

14. William J. Tilley, *Masters of the Situation: or Some Secrets of Success and Power* (New York: N. D. Thompson Publishing Co., 1890), pp. 315–317.

15. Mathews, *op. cit.*, p. 304.

16. John T. Dale, *The Way to Win: Showing How to Succeed in Life* (Chicago: Hammond Publishing Co., 1891), p. 447. See too Jonathan B. Harrison, *Certain Dangerous Tendencies in American Life, and Other Papers* (Boston: Houghton, Osgood and Co., 1880), p. 6.

17. Fred A. Shannon, *The Farmer's Last Frontier* (New York: Farrar & Rinehart, 1945), p. 357.

18. Washington Gladden, *Straight Shots at Young Men* (New York: Thos. Y. Crowell and Co., 1900), p. 27. See too Tilley, *op. cit.*, pp. 550 ff.

19. Orison Swett Marden, *The Young Man Entering Business* (New York: Thos. Y. Crowell and Co., 1903), p. 2.

20. Dale, *The Way to Win*, p. 521. Russell Conwell, author of *Acres of Diamonds*, wrote of farming: "He who would fill his life with the greatest number of happy days may get it in other professions perhaps, but the widest experience shows that the country farmer is the most sure of securing it." R. H. Conwell, *The New Day, or Fresh Opportunities* (Philadelphia: The Griffith and Roland Press, 1904), p. 39.

21. Mathews, *op. cit.*, p. 304.

22. Howard Crosby, *A Sermon to Young Men* (New York: B. Stradley, 1876), p. 4.

23. Mathews, *op. cit.*, p. 327.

24. *Ibid.*, pp. 328–329.

25. *Ibid.*

26. *Ibid.*, p. 330. Mathews' feelings were typical of the genre. For examples, see the following: Clark, *op. cit.*, p. 41; John T. Davidson, *Sure to Succeed* (New York: A. C. Armstrong and Son, 1889), p. 4; H. A. Lewis, *op. cit.*, p. 499; Tilley, *op. cit.*, pp. 315–317; *Success*, II (August 5, 1889), 604.

27. Mathews, *op. cit.*, p. 315.

28. Dale, *The Way to Win*, p. 550. Along with the concern over extravagant living, anxiety was often expressed at the increasing informality of women's manners. Washington Gladden, prominent social gospeler and author of success tracts, wrote: "This habit of running loose, of constantly seeking the street for amusement, and even of making chance acquaintances there, is practiced by some of the girls of our good families; and it is not at all pleasant to see them on the public thoroughfares, and to witness their hoydenish ways. I know that they mean no harm by it, but it often results in harm; the delicate bloom of maiden modesty is soiled by too much familiarity with the public streets of a city, and a kind of boldness is acquired which is not becoming in a woman." Washington Gladden, "Girls and Their Mothers," *Modern Home Life*, Vol. V of *Modern Achievement*, ed. Edward Everett Hale (New York: The University Society, 1902), 135.

The concern for female modesty was an aspect of the idealization of the mother in success literature. William Thayer, for example, wrote: "If a boy must forget his father or mother, let him forget his father. We never knew a son, who forgot or spoke ill of his mother, to make much of a man." William M. Thayer, *Nelson: or How a Country Boy Made His Way in the City* (New York: T. Y. Crowell, 1878), p. 71. William D. Owen, another success writer, said: "Henry Clay had a mother. A mother is everything to a child. . . ." William D. Owen, *Success in Life and How to Secure It* (Chicago: Howe, Watts and Co., 1882), p. 179. John Dale wrote: "It it a beautiful tribute to the influence of motherhood to observe how the greatest and purest minds recur with ever increasing satisfaction to the maternal influence and training in their early life, and to attribute all their successes to her gentle teachings." Dale, *The Way to Win*, p. 191.

29. Wilbur F. Crafts, *Familiar Talks on that Boy and Girl of Yours: Sociology from the Viewpoint of the Family* (New York: The Baker and Taylor Co., 1922), p. 350. This book appeared in the last year of Crafts' life but represents the sentiments of success writers of an earlier period, of whom Crafts was one. See, for example, his earlier work, *Successful Men of To-day* (New York: Funk and Wagnalls, 1883).

30. Crafts, *Familiar Talks*, p. 350. On the theme of simplicity versus extravagance, Oliver H. G. Leigh wrote: "This much is certain, the men and women truly great, or worthy of veneration, have preferred simplicity of life to ostentatious display. Simplicity in attire, in speech, in manner, in habits, accords naturally with strength of character and it enhances dignity.

"A practical moral comes out of this, namely, that simple, gracious manliness is actually the most inexpensive first-rate outfit a young beginner can procure as an unfailing help and solace in the struggle for a career of success." Leigh, Introduction to *Business and Professional Life*, Vol. II of *Modern Achievement*, x–xi.

31. *Success*, II (April 8, 1899), 330.

32. Crosby, *op. cit.*, p. 5.

33. For the increased consumption of alcohol and increase of the saloon in the period between 1870 and 1900, see Arthur M. Schlesinger, *The Rise of the City, 1878–1898* (New York: The Macmillan Co., 1935), pp. 355 ff.

34. Dale, *The Way to Win*, p. 433.

35. *Ibid.*, p. 434. See too H. A. Lewis, *op. cit.*, p. 488; Tilley, *op. cit.*, pp. 467 ff., Sizer, *op. cit.*, p. 108; and Kent. *op. cit.*, pp. 159–209.

36. John V. Farwell, Introduction to Dale, *Secret of Success*, p. vii.

37. Josiah Strong, *Our Country: Its Possible Future and Its Present Crisis* (New York: The Baker and Taylor Co., 1891), p. 168.

38. Mathews, *op. cit.*, p. 304. See too Henry Hardwicke, *The Art of Getting Rich* (New York: The Useful Knowledge Publishing Co., 1897), p. 131. The statistic was used by success writers at the turn of the century as an argument to urge young men to work for others rather than try to open businesses of their own. See Marden, *op. cit.*, p. 110. Interestingly, Andrew Carnegie had similar advice for the young. Carnegie wrote: "Out of every hundred that attempt business upon their own account statistics are said to show that ninety-five, sooner or later, fail. I know that from my own experience." Andrew Carnegie, "The Man of Business," in *Science of Business*, Vol. I of *Modern Achievement*, 84.

39. Erastus Wiman, *Chances of Success* (New York: American News Co., 1893), pp. 31–32.

40. Francis E. Clark, *The Gospel of Out of Doors* (New York: Association Press, 1920), pp. 1–2. Though this book appeared in 1920, its sentiments are typical of the success writers of the post–Civil War period. By the 1920s, the idealization of the farmer was rarely, if ever, found among success writers. Clark by 1920 was an old man, and his sentiments represent an earlier period.

See also Wilbur F. Crafts, *Practical Christian Sociology* (New York: Funk and Wagnalls, 1895), pp. 139–141. In a later work, Crafts lists thirteen increasing evils in America since the Civil War. They are: (1) consumption of liquors; (2) murders; (3) divorces; (4) lynchings; (5) labor riots; (6) municipal corruption; (7) Sabbath desecration; (8) impure shows; (9) yellow journalism; (10) brutal sports; (11) judicial maladministration; (12) graft; (13) general lawlessness. W. E. Crafts, *National Perils and Hopes* (Cleveland: F. B. Barton Co., 1910), p. 1. Almost all these evils were ones associated with the city and industrialization, the two dominant changes in American life since the Civil War. In this connection, one should see C. Wright Mills' analysis of sociology textbooks on social problems, entitled "The Professional Ideology of Social Pathologists," *Power, Politics and People*, ed. I. Horowitz (New York: Oxford University Press, 1963), pp. 525–552. The "social orientation" which Mills describes as common to these American texts on social pathology seems firmly rooted in the value system embodied in the success mythology.

41. Crafts, *Successful Men of Today*, p. 116.

42. *Success*, II (March 18, 1899), 282. The magazine printed articles expressing similar sentiments toward corruption in business. In one, Andrew H. Green is quoted as saying: "The people are running after strange gods, after money Kings. . . . The man is most admired who makes the most millions in the fewest years. It is unfortunate that such a perverted taste exists, for it exalts the conscienceless capitalist and casts down the champion of the people's rights. The popular method of getting rich is not to earn money legitimately . . . but to secure franchises for far less than their value." *Success*, II (August 5, 1889), 604.

43. I take issue here with Irvin Wyllie's contention that clergymen merely endorsed the values of the business community. Wyllie writes: "By teaching that Godliness was in league with riches such spokesmen [clergymen] put the sanction of the church on the get-ahead values of the business community. And by so teaching they encouraged each rising generation to believe that it was possible to serve both God and Mammon." Irvin G. Wyllie, *The SelfMade Man in America: the Myth of Rags to Riches* (New Brunswick, N.J.: Rutgers University Press, 1954), p. 56. Clergymen who wrote success tracts considered God and Mammon absolutely incompatible and repeatedly said so. Mammonism and success

were very different things in the minds of nineteenth-century Christian moralists.

44. Tilley, *op. cit.*, p. 766. See also Lyman Abbott, *How to Succeed* (New York: G. P. Putnam's Sons, 1882), pp. ix, 121–131.

45. Josiah Strong, *The Times and Young Men* (New York: The Baker and Taylor Co., 1901), pp. 13–14.

46. William M. Thayer, *Onward to Fame and Fortune* (New York: The Christian Herald, 1897), p. 5.

47. Alexander Lewis, *op. cit.*, p. 195.

48. Henry Ward Beecher (1882), quoted in Henry F. May, *Protestant Churches and Industrial America* (New York: Harper and Bros., 1949), p. 86.

49. *Ibid.*

50. For a discussion of evangelical pragmatism, see Richard Hofstadter, *Anti-Intellectualism in American Life* (New York: Alfred A. Knopf, 1963), pp. 84–87. See too Sidney E. Mead, *The Lively Experiment, The Shaping of Christianity in America* (New York: Harper and Row, 1963), pp. 32–33, 121–124.

51. For a discussion of the proportion of the industrial labor force which was immigrant see Edward C. Kirkland, *A History of American Economic Life* (New York: F. S. Crofts & Co., 1939), pp. 511 ff.

52. Marden, *op. cit.*, p. 248.

53. Strong, *The Times and Young Men*, p. 52. On labor conflict Wilbur Crafts wrote: "There should be no conflict between labor and capital. They are as necessary to each other as to the bow the cord is, useless without the other. . . . Let us all, rich and poor, join the Society of the Royal Law and love our neighbors as ourselves." Crafts, *Successful Men of Today*, p. 193.

54. Albert Shaw, *The Outlook for the Average Man* (New York: The Macmillan Co., 1902), p. 38. Andrew Carnegie wrote: "In the olden days . . . everything was done upon a small scale. There was no room for great ideas to operate upon a large scale, and thus to produce great wealth to the inventor, discoverer, originator, or executive. New inventions gave this opportunity, and many large fortunes were made by individuals. But in our day we are rapidly passing, if we have not already passed, this stage of development, and few large fortunes can now be made. . . ." Carnegie, "The Man of Business," *Science of Business*, Vol. I of *Modern Achievement*, 84.

55. Louis F. Post, *Success in Life* (New York: The Civic Publishing Co., 1902), p. 14. For other critiques of success literature, see W. J. Ghent, *Socialism and Success* (New York: John Lane Co., 1910); Ham Jones, *About Money: A Lively Tract for the Present Time* (Boston: New England News Co., 1872); and Joseph Dana Miller, "Apostles of Autolatry," *Arena*, XXIV (December 1900), 608–617.

For a recent spoof on success literature, see Carl Winston, *How to Run a Million into a Shoestring* (New York: G. P. Putnam's Sons, 1960).

56. Louis F. Post, *Ethics of Democracy* (Indianapolis: The Bobbs-Merrill Co., 1903), p. 360.

57. *Ibid.*

58. *Success,* II (April 1, 1889), 310. The situations being criticized were the deaths resulting from the failure to take proper safety precautions with streetcars in New York City.

59. See, for example, the inside cover of *La Follette's Weekly Magazine,* IV (January 6, 1912). On this theme as it appeared in socialist literature, see Daniel Bell, "Marxian Socialism in the United States," *Socialism and American Life,* ed. Donald Drew Egbert and Stow Persons (Princeton, N.J.: Princeton University Press, 1952), I, 298–299.

60. For a perceptive treatment of Bryan, in this connection, see Lawrence W. Levine, *Defender of the Faith, William Jennings Bryan: The Last Decade 1915–1925* (New York: Oxford University Press, 1965), pp. 358–365.

Chapter 5

The Revival of the Transcendentalist Dogma

PART I

The Defense of Idealism

I

By the turn of the century, the truths taught by the old tradition of uplift had acquired a hollow sound. Though, as far as we know, possibilities for advancement were not contracting at this time, patterns of mobility were changing. There was, as C. Wright Mills noted, a shift from entrepreneurial to white-collar patterns of success.[1] This may account for the feeling that the ordinary man had fewer chances than at an earlier time.[2] Randolph Bourne noted that his contemporaries had "a very real feeling of coming straight up against a wall of diminishing opportunity. . . ." This made them suspicious of "ideals, which, however powerful their appeal once was, seem singularly impotent now."[3] The worst fears of the older generation of success writers were being realized;

the belief that Christian virtue led to worldly well-being was dying. The hero of a Utopian novel at the end of the century voiced a common experience when he described his own disillusionment with the "faith of the fathers." As a boy on the farm he had believed in the blessings of Christianity and the rewards of righteous living. When he grew older, however, belief turned to disenchantment. Unemployed, he found his virtue of little avail in finding work. "Christianity," he concluded, "may be a fine thing for those whose wants are supplied, but I, for one, cannot see that Christ's teachings have had sufficient influence to make it easier for a man to earn an honest living." [4]

The moral uncertainty revealed by this reaction ran deep. The bed-rock assumptions by which men understood their lives were in process of erosion. The classic self-help tradition no longer provided a coherent set of concepts for explaining everyday occurrences. As in all periods of rapid change, traditional modes of thought in the industrial era ceased to comport with daily experience. The broadening gap between traditional beliefs and modern realities called forth the torrent of conventional guides to living in the postbellum era. They were, in effect, a compulsive reassertion that all was the same despite changing externals. The beliefs they propagated, however, were rooted in a religious and agrarian society. These ideas and values could not, without substantial revision, withstand the skepticism engendered by science and the growing urbanization of American culture. Industrialism fostered a naturalistic world-view which contradicted theological notions of a purposive and moral universe. The machine threatened to dwarf the individual, while science appeared to deny the centrality of man within the cosmic scheme of things. These changes, mundane and intellectual, shattered the psychic prism through which men perceived and structured reality. As one contemporary noted, the nineteenth century "began with man inventing the machine and discovering the methods of the laboratory, it ends with man the helpless slave of what his own mind and hands have builded." [5] This was temporarily obscured by the orgy of activity and exploitation that marked the closing decades of the century. When the smoke had cleared, however, the legacy of the industrial age was painfully apparent. Along with its mammoth corporations, it bequeathed "a materialistic philosophy, a mechanistic science and a commercialized view of life that . . . sapped the vitality of all our idealisms." [6] Age-old conceptions of God, immortality, and morality were no longer tenable.[7] Bereft of earlier faiths, what were men to believe? Uncertainty abounded. "A chief characteristic of the situation," wrote Santayana, "is that moral confusion is not limited to the world at large . . . but that it has penetrated to the mind and heart of the average individual." [8]

In consequence a demand arose for a new "philosophy of life," one that would "more adequately interpret the facts of experience and at the same time satisfy the deep yearning of the human spirit." [9] A "new thought" was needed to meet the inspirational requirements of a new age. This appeared at the turn of the century, and took the form of a spontaneous religious movement. It came from no particular denomination, and drew its major exponents from outside the ministry. It had no official source of doctrine, and lacked, for example, any authoritative statement of creed such as Mary Baker Eddy had given to Christian Science in *Science and Health*. It lacked any central organization, but found expression in a great variety of groups which went under such names as New Thought, Mind, Mental Science, Harmony, Metaphysical Healing, and Mind Cure. The promoters of the new philosophy claimed that it transcended denominational differences, hence rejection of regular church affiliations was not considered necessary to an acceptance of the new teachings. Lacking any precise institutional definition, New Thought, nonetheless, is an identifiable set of beliefs which together comprise a world-view.[10] An integral part of this doctrine was a new gospel of success which came to supplant the earlier rags-to-riches myth. The new success ideology gave belief in the individual's power for self-direction a new lease on life by providing it with a rationale viable in the context of an industrialized society.

II

Like nineteenth-century success books, New Thought inspirational writing was directed toward Americans of native stock. It differed from the earlier literature, however, in that its orientation was entirely urban.[11] It carried no praise for the farm boy or the rural way of life, so prominent in earlier success guides. Similarly, the classic virtues of prudence and frugality found no endorsement in its pages. On the contrary, proponents of the new doctrine were severely critical of the older inspirational literature. The most caustic of the critiques was Bolton Hall's *Thrift*. Hall searched libraries for " 'success' books for the blind mind" as he called them. "Anyone who can succeed in reading them," he remarked acidly, "could succeed in anything." The world portrayed in these books, however, bore no relation to the America Hall knew. "These 'honesty-and-industry-lead-to-affluence' boys did not have to explain away the dear good franchise grabbers, not to show how a traction magnate graduated from state prison, not how a great monopolist 'made good' by blowing up his early competitor's oil works. . . ." [12] Clearly, Hall shared the concerns of Progressives of his day. A minister's son and a practicing lawyer, he combined his writing with an active involvement in the reform movement.[13] He rejected traditional success writers because "the ideal principles inculcated by these thrift-tooters" were "directly opposed to the objects of nearly all business. . . ." [14] Yet he continued to affirm that success remained a possibility for everyone. New Thought did not deny the illusion of the earlier success cult; it merely provided it with a more relevant and defensible contextual framework.

Not content just to topple old idols, Hall offered new ones in their stead. He advised people against becoming "so possessed with the idea that present conditions are against them and against all others in their position that they believe they cannot succeed. . . ." They need only look at the successful people around them. A glance would show these were ordinary folk without unusual endowments of any kind. "Only hopelessness or thick-headedness," he admonished, "will enable you to deceive yourself into a belief that you cannot succeed just as easily and just as well as they." The immigrant furnished the most conspicuous evidence of continuing possibilities. Foreigners came here to make money—and did, despite their poverty and ignorance of the language.

We flatter ourselves that it is because they live so cheaply— "below the American standard." When American families wallow in luxury on an average income of less than nine dollars per week for each worker, the amount that the Dagos and Huns and Kikes save by living still cheaper would not make them very rich. The Chinese live the cheapest of any. Do you happen to know any Chinese millionaires who save a million out of the laundry charges? Of course, as long as people are miserably poor they spend very little, but that is not the reason they thrive.

The true cause lay in their mental set. "The reason they succeed is mainly that they expect to succeed and accordingly do succeed. . . ." [15] This, then, was the core of the new success cult—states of mind rather than traits of character were the keys to success or failure.

III

Like the Protestant ethic, the belief in mind-power was only part of a more comprehensive cosmology. This emerged, as I have noted, around the turn of the century. Explaining the rise of their doctrine, New Thoughters stressed that "the time was ripe for a marked spiritual reaction." Materialism "had subtly permeated science, philosophy, ethics, sociology, and therapeutics. . . ." Even the churches felt its influence. A whole list of "isms"—realism, pessimism, agnosticism, and atheism—troubled people's minds.[16] This evoked a counter movement "toward a spiritual interpretation of life and toward a practical use of the occult powers of the soul." [17] The upsurge of religious energy was so intense that William James found it "analogous in some respects to the spread of early Christianity, Buddhism, and Mohammedanism. . . ." To the academically nurtured, the utterances of New Thought writers were "tasteless and often grotesque" but the importance of their movement as a social phenomenon was not to be denied.[18]

James, with his characteristic tolerance, was sympathetic,

but even critics conceded the movement's popularity and influence. One such observed unhappily that its literature sold "almost as well as fiction." Commenting on its quality, he wrote:

> Most of it is of a character to repel persons of critical taste. Its language is crude. It makes assertions in regard to scientific matters that cannot be proved—or, at least, have not been proved. It is mixed up with spiritism, astrology, mind-reading, vegetarianism, reincarnation, and all sorts of other "crank" doctrines and fads—and with a few actual "fakes." The very names of its publications are enough to make sophisticated persons smile. . . .
>
> And yet, *it goes*—and not merely with the ignorant and credulous. In fact, the intelligent common-school-educated middle class furnishes most of its patrons.[19]

The impact of New Thought was further enhanced because certain of its key ideas were disseminated by other groups, among them Christian Scientists, Spiritualists, Theosophists, and psychical researchers.[20] Their common ground was an antipathy to "mere" materialism and a commitment to some kind of philosophical idealism. All affirmed the primacy of spirit over matter which was fundamental to the new gospel of success.

This renascent idealism provides one of the most striking continuities in popular currents of thought between the nineteenth and twentieth centuries. Just as the Puritanism of Boston gave birth to the old success myth, so the transcendentalism of Concord gave birth to the new. In *The Transcendentalist*, Emerson stated that "What is popularly called Transcendentalism among us, is Idealism; Idealism as it appears in 1842." [21] What was popularly called New Thought was idealism; idealism as it appeared in 1900.[22] The new movement acknowledged Emerson as its "great prophet." [23] Borrowing from the Concord sage, New Thoughters declared the "necessity in spirit to manifest itself in material forms" and insisted "that day and night, river and stream, beast and bird, acid and alkali, pre-exist in necessary ideas in the mind of God." [24] All that men knew as reality was merely the objective manifestation of a pre-existing idea. The new inspirationalists found this notion pregnant with meaning and used it to infuse the individual with a new sense of possibilities.

Contrasting the materialist and the idealist, Emerson had written: "The materialist insists on facts, on history, on the force of circumstances and the animal wants of men; the idealist on the power of Thought and of Will, on inspiration, on miracle, on individual culture." [25] The latter aptly described the disciple of New Thought who, along with Emerson, replied to the materialist's assertion that men were made by circumstances by answering: "I make my circumstances."

> Let any thought or motive of mine be different from that they are, and the difference will transform my condition and economy. I—this thought which is called I—is the mould into which the world is poured like melted wax. . . . You call it the power of circumstances, but it is the power of me.[26]

For New Thoughters, the promotion of this idea took on the urgency of a cause. They saw themselves as active combatants in the struggle for human dignity, fighting to preserve the individual ego from the crushing effects of scientific determinism. In promoting idealism, they were asserting that men were "not mere machines and automata" but "rational, self-conscious, free, and self-determining beings." [27] If facts indicated otherwise, inspirationalists again followed Emer-

son's example and simply ignored experience when it conflicted with their optimism.[28]

IV

Idealism, however, was insufficient unless accompanied by
the means of translating itself into objective realities. New
Thoughters were sensitive to the disaffection afflicting established creeds. They exploited the growing feeling that religion had lost all relevance to the day-to-day problems people
encountered.

> If religion simply means attending church services, listening
> to the choir and the preacher, or taking part in some of the
> various activities of church life; if religion brings to daily ex-
> perience only the instruction as to life's programme but not
> the divine strength to carry out that programme, only the
> description of life's ideals but not the dynamic power by
> which these ideals may be realized in character, then we are
> justified in asking whether we are getting out of our religion,
> whether our beliefs in God are yielding us, all we have the
> right to expect.[29]

To avoid this pitfall, New Thought called its idealism
"practical," and subjected all beliefs to the measure of usefulness. "The final test of a creed," declared one popularizer,
"is not whether it has remained unchanged for hundreds of
years, but whether it is giving men and women strength to
resist the temptations of life and build unassailable moral
characters. This is a utilitarian age in more senses than one.
The religions of today must bow to this requirement." [30]

New Thought did so, and thus brought the functional defense of faith to its logical conclusion. The utilitarian argument, once merely a means for bolstering religious belief, now became its exclusive *raison d'être*. Ralph Waldo Trine, the most widely read disciple of New Thought, insisted that "adequacy for everyday life here and now, must be the test of all true religion." Any creed that did not bear this test, he peremptorily dismissed as "simply not religion." [31] The new inspirationalists were not content to preach idealism; they sought to apply it. This led them to focus on success and the problems of health and disease. William James remarked that the spread of New Thought was "due to its practical fruits." "The extremely practical turn of character of the American people," he went on, "has never been better shown than by the fact that this, their only decidedly original contribution to the systematic philosophy of life, should be so intimately knit up with concrete therapeutics." [32]

The new transcendentalists' emphasis on utility served as a bridge between idealism and the emerging philosophy of pragmatism. These two modes of thought, customarily regarded as polarities in American philosophy, were melded in New Thought. The union was not altogether unnatural, as James's affinity for Emerson reveals. Frederic Carpenter's examination of the underlinings and marginal notes in James's copy of Emerson's works provides us with some notion of those aspects of Emerson's thought that appealed most to the psychologist-philosopher. Among the passages cited are those dealing with "the creative I," "psychic energy," and expansiveness or power in general. Also noted is Emerson's sentence in *Nature*, "Build therefore your own world." [33] Both men placed strong emphasis on the power of the mind to ameliorate the material and physical difficulties of life. "Emersonian transcendentalism," then, "clearly belongs to the intellectual heritage of William James and of the pragmatic movement of which he was a leader." [34]

Sharing a common ancestor, pragmatism and New Thought shared certain similar concerns. The common ground between what is probably America's most distinctive contribution to Western thought and what is generally regarded as one of the crudest expressions of popular philosophy, highlights the interrelatedness between apparently disparate elements of culture. James, himself, was aware of the relevance of popular thinking to the problems which were then being discussed in the most arcane reaches of the academe. Of the great philosophical trio at Harvard at the turn of the century—James, Royce, and Santayana—James was most in tune with the popular mind. All of these men were troubled by the uncertainties brought about by the immense changes in American society since the Civil War. But it was James who "became the friend and helper of those groping, nervous, half-educated, spiritually disinherited, passionately hungry individuals of which America is full." [35] As their spokesman in the world of learning, and as the most lucid interpreter of what that world had to offer the relatively untutored, James enables us to better perceive the concerns that motivated thinking, at both levels, at the turn of the century.

The English philosopher, F. C. S. Schiller, had suggested to James that he call his philosophy humanism. The use of this word would have given emphasis to James's "proposal to deal with philosophies by referring them, in the last analysis, not to nature but to *human* nature." [36] Science had downgraded the importance of man in the cosmic scheme of things. Both James and New Thought again placed man in the center of the universe. Ready to "defend the sciences against obscurantism," James "was equally ready to rebuke the 'scientific point of view' if it denied men's right to believe in God, free will and immortality." [37] The reigning skepticism of the period challenged belief in all three. One New Thought spokesman complained that the scientific age was "also an unbelieving and faithless era." If science destroyed faith, its wonders could never compensate man for the loss. "Accomplish what we may in the luxuries of a material civilization, man will yet be restless and unhappy. He may penetrate the earth, travel under the water, navigate the air, and pile up invention without limit, but with all he will be miserable so long as he lacks a simple faith." [38]

James, though not an idealist, joined arms with them in their crusade against positivism and its denial of the supernatural. He derided the positivists for their sacrifice of all other gods to the new divinity of Science. The naïve belief that these men had conquered their subjective propensities by rejecting theism, he labeled a delusion. "They have simply chosen from among the entire set of propensities at their command those that were certain to construct, out of the materials given, the leanest, lowest, aridest result—namely, the bare molecular world,—and they have sacrificed the rest." [39]

In an even more important area, James lent support to an idea which was central to the new success cult. This was his defense of the notion that belief could, and often did, condition reality. In one instance he used the example of a mountain climber confronting a chasm he had to leap across in order to survive. If the man believed it was possible, this would aid immeasurably in its accomplishment.

Have faith that you can successfully make it, and your feet are nerved to its accomplishment. But mistrust yourself, and think of all the sweet things you have heard the scientists say of *maybes*, and you will hesitate so long that, at last, all un-strung and trembling, and launching yourself in a moment of despair, you roll in the abyss. In such a case (and it belongs to an enormous class), the part of wisdom as well as of courage is to *believe what is in the line of your needs*, for only by such belief is the need fulfilled.[40]

His most popular address on this subject was "The Will to Believe," delivered before the philosophical clubs of Yale and Brown in 1896. There, again, he emphasized the functional power of belief. Lashing out at the positivists, he declared that *"where faith in a fact can help create the fact*, that would be an insane logic which should say that faith running ahead of scientific evidence is the 'lowest kind of immorality' into which a thinking being can fall! Yet such is the logic by which our scientific absolutists pretend to regulate our lives!"[41]

James was stating what is commonly spoken of as the self-fulfilling prophecy. This term is usually reserved for un-pleasant or negative results, such as, for example, the neurotic's creation of the situation he most fears. James argued that this mechanism could function positively. In New Thought this notion was greatly exaggerated in the assertion that belief not merely could, but did, create fact. Both the common-sense notion and its exaggeration, however, were aimed at giving the individual a renewed sense of power to regulate his own life. Thus James and the neo-transcendentalists were engaged in a common effort to preserve belief in the power of self-direction—a belief implicit in the earlier rags-to-riches tradition—which science had undermined.

Similarly, when science challenged the belief in immortality, James joined the fray in defense of the spirit. He wrote:

One hears not only physiologists, but numbers of laymen who read the popular science books and magazines, saying all about us, How can we believe in life hereafter when Science has once for all attained to proving, beyond possibility of escape, that our inner life is a function of that famous material, the so-called "gray matter" of our cerebral convolutions? How can the function possibly persist after its organ has undergone decay? Thus physiological psychology is what is supposed to bar the way to the old faith.[42]

As a physiological psychologist he denied the inevitability of such conclusions, and affirmed the possibility that life might continue even "when the brain is dead."[43] For New Thoughters, the belief in immortality was "morally proved valid because it [was] best for man." Those who sought to undermine it destroyed the "natural faith and hope of the young" and were, to that extent, "anti-social enemies of man."[44]

Even if the positivists' dictum that proof must precede belief were accepted, the affirmation of immortality was as valid as its denial. Since scientists could not conclusively prove that man's existence terminated at death, their position rested on no firmer ground than the idealists'. Thus advocates of negative certainty were declared victims of their own argument. New Thoughters finally argued that to all intents and purposes immortality was a fact because men had always believed it to be so. Here they cited James's assertion that a fact of consciousness was as real as any other. Only death could bring absolute verification of the existence of the hereafter. "But for all practical purposes," as one spokesman declared, "the verification of what I find in my consciousness is found in the fact that a similar consciousness exists in most other individuals of all ages and in every clime."[45] Unsatisfactory as this intellectual sleight of hand might be, it was eagerly seized upon by those clinging to this most cherished fragment of the crumbling edifice of Christian belief.

Nowhere was this need more clearly demonstrated than in

the movement for psychical research, formed principally to provide proofs of an after-life. The movement attracted men of considerable prestige in both England and America and received enthusiastic support from New Thought adherents. The urgency of the quest for evidence of life's continuance after mortal death may be largely attributed to man's disinclination to accept the finiteness of human existence. There were, however, less egocentric motives involved. Many feared that the denial of immortality, and the consequent rejection of belief in future rewards and punishments, threatened the entire moral fabric of Western civilization. James Hyslop, occupant of a chair in logic and ethics at Columbia University and the leading psychical researcher in the United States, warned that the situation was fraught with danger. The belief in immortality was "so closely related to Ethics that its decay threatened the destruction of all ethical and spiritual endeavor." [46] New Thought writers went even further. Ignoring the fact that belief in immortality had for centuries failed to reform mankind, they saw in it a new means to social regeneration. "Suppose," one wrote,

> it were proved that our social or unsocial conduct here actually limited and injured our soul's life after death . . . and that by the law of reaction or retributive justice, all the social wrongs we commit here, consciously or unconsciously—our exploitation of others, our indifferent selfishness, our scorns and contempt—would in some form be visited upon ourselves in that "other life." If these facts could be proven true and men generally accepted them as such, we should not only have a clew to the solution of the industrial problem, but of all our social and international problems of today. For the reverence of all other individuals, equally with ourselves, would mean the beginning of the reign of justice here on earth. . . .
>
> At any rate, if it can be proved that the materialistic theory

of consciousness is false, and that man has a more important
end than the satisfaction of his bodily wants and his merely
earthly happiness, we shall then have established a new fulcrum for the moralist.[47]

V

New Thought writers, then, were engaged in a defense of
beliefs which had previously been bolstered by traditional religion. Their works preserved the comforts of the faith for a
de-Christianized generation. While New Thought produced
no full-fledged theology, it did venture answers to such questions as the nature of God, the quality of his relationship to
man, the sources of good and evil, and the means for achieving salvation here and beyond.

As a religious movement, it belongs in the tradition of liberal theology. Its disciples were not troubled by the fact that
God was not getting his due in this world, and made no attempt to put the "fear of God" into the hearts of men. Harangues about sin and damnation repelled them. Hell-fire and
brimstone have no place in their teachings. Morality, rather
than piety, was their objective.

In the minds of its advocates, New Thought was a kind of
reformation dedicated to purifying the church and restoring
to Christianity "that primitive vitality which so early slipped
from its grasp when it became allied with the state and enslaved by dogma." [48] They condemned all barriers among
denominations. Stripped to their essence, all religions were
the same. Therefore, a Jew, a Catholic, or a Buddhist might
worship equally well in the other's temple. "Or all can wor-

ship equally well about their own hearthstones, or out on the hillside, or while pursuing the avocations of every-day life. For true worship, only God and the human soul are necessary." [49]

Similarly, New Thoughters dismissed the priesthood as superfluous. Adopting an extreme antinomian position, they held to a direct relationship between God and man and denied the need for institutional or personal intermediaries. They declared the age of authority in religion gone forever. "The only authority is the authority of truth as known and felt and experienced in the individual consciousness." [50] Thus, in matters of faith, they employed a rhetoric of radical individualism.

The reformist nature of New Thought extended beyond matters of organization to questions of doctrine as well. The new dispensation denied the doctrine of original sin. The well-known couplet from the New England primer—"In Adam's fall, we sinned all"—had "no truth in it at all." [51] The biblical Adam was a man like all others and his failure in no way devolved upon his progeny. Conceptions of innate depravity were pernicious superstitions to be discarded along with "all other forms of orthodoxy implying emphasis on man's sinfulness, an atoning sacrifice, and a future punishment." [52] The Calvinist's ideal of asceticism met a similar fate. Work was good, but its motive should be the desire to realize one's potentialities. Men must be re-educated to understand their labor as a means of self-expression and enjoyment. As one author put it: "The ascetics and the Puritans made this great mistake. They thought that duty was doing what is hard and what you *hate*. The truth is that duty is doing what is hard and what you *love*." [53] In this sense New Thought has a strikingly contemporary sound. The words fulfillment and self-realization—so worn out in contemporary usage—first appear in its literature.[54] "Work is a necessity to life," instructed one popularizer, "and if we are not working—if we are not expressing, then we are not fulfilling life." [55]

The good life, always the object of guides to success, now became synonymous with the full life. "Cultivate your talents" was the new watchword. Inspirationalists advised their readers not to concentrate their efforts exclusively on business, and to leave plenty of leisure time for the cultivation of hobbies, family life, and enjoyment of nature. Balance in the new success literature took the place which moderation had occupied in the old.

VI

Given their attitude toward work, it is not surprising to find New Thought writers discouraging parents from forcing careers on children against their inclinations.[56] More generally, their attitude toward child-rearing shows a marked departure from the past, and illustrates the progressive mood which permeated their thinking. They taught that children were not young adults, but a species apart.

> For the child is not the man in miniature—he is, in some respects, another order of being. We would not put him at once upon the food which he must have in later life, because we plainly perceive the lack of teeth. . . . The little baby does not need to be "early inured to self-restraint" or anything of that sort. . . . Like the plant, the baby wants proper environment, and food, plenty of the sunshine of love, and room to grow in.[57]

New Thoughters also recognized the importance of the first few years of life in forming the character and personality of the individual. "There is no room in the house more important than the nursery," one counselor wrote. "It is the child's first home, the spot which represents the world that he has so recently entered, and much depends upon his earliest impressions. For that reason great care should be taken in making his surroundings not only comfortable, but bright and happy." [58] Happiness was added to the list of obligations parents had to their children. Along with honesty and industry, adults were enjoined to cultivate "mental sunshine" in the young. Lack of it took on the dimensions of a serious flaw. "No person, young or old, is well developed or perfectly equipped until habitual cheerfulness is as much a part of him as are his limbs or his eyes." [59]

The New Thought method for teaching ethics also represented a departure from traditional norms. It deplored the emphasis on the struggle with evil, and criticized the "thou shalt nots" of the decalogue which continually brought pictures of wickedness before the child's mind. Repeated negative injunctions also suppressed the natural spontaneity of childhood. "Joy will go out of the heart of a child . . . if he is constantly suppressed," warned one popularizer. "Mothers who are constantly cautioning their little ones not to do this or not to do that, telling them not to laugh or make a noise, until they lose their naturalness and become little old men and women, do not realize the harm they are doing." [60] Instead, New Thoughters advised a more positive approach, the stressing of "do's" rather than "don'ts." "Do not denounce vices, but preach the virtues," was the New Thought injunction. [61] It was even suggested that a child brought up naturally, as if right conduct were as normal as good eyesight, would form stable habits of character without any formal ethical training. "There is no question that it is such habits of right conduct, and not the knowledge of moral obligations, which hold a man in time of stress." [62] Character conceived as the sum of good habits accurately mirrored the psychological thinking of the day, and references to academic works, particularly to James's *Psychology*, were frequent in inspirational literature.

New Thought attitudes toward education generally, had a progressive cast. Writers criticized coercive techniques of teaching. While they admitted that inducements might be necessary in getting a child to learn, these "should be inducements which lead him to do the work, not to do it against his inclination." Teaching did not consist in making "the child go against his desire, but to desire to do the right thing, and to desire it so strongly as to do it." [63] These ideas were similar to those of John Dewey and the progressive school of educators.[64] New Thought inspirational literature was instrumental in disseminating new notions of child-rearing and in creating a climate congenial to the acceptance of the "new education."

VII

The New Thought attitude toward children was derived from its conception of the fundamental nature of man. Whereas the Puritan viewed the child from a conviction of man's sinfulness and depravity, the New Thoughter viewed the child from a conviction of man's goodness and divinity. The new inspirationalists never tired of drawing the contrast.

The "old" thought emphasized the sovereignty of God, and looked upon man as a miserably unfortunate creature; the

147

"new" dwells rather on the splendid powers and noble possibilities of men. The old conception of man was that of a relatively depraved being, suffering for the sins of his first parents, and needing salvation for his own sins; the new emphasized the native goodness of man, and has little to say about sin. . . . It was customary in terms of the outworn view to paint the miseries of this our natural existence, the horrors of hell, and the darker aspects of life in general; but the new picture is essentially cheerful, affirmative, ideal. The new has little or nothing to say about suffering, pain, or sorrow; little about sacrifice, the atonement, or salvation through acceptance of the cross; and little about heredity, environment, or other supposed "limitations." The tendency is to break down all doctrinal barriers, adverse beliefs, and all exclusive distinctions; and hence to open up wide vistas into realms of hope and ambition.[65]

Followers of the "new" called on individuals to awaken to an awareness of their divinity. Men were but individualized parts of the Infinite Spirit and so in essence the life of God and of man were one.[66] Consciousness of this union was "the secret of all peace, power and prosperity." [67] It was in this realization that the genius of Jesus lay.

Not since the sublime declaration of Jesus that "I and the Father are one"; that is the I AM, the soul which was in Jesus and is in all men and the Father . . . are one, has a greater or more universal truth been spoken to man. . . . The greatness of man was the supreme thought and theme of Jesus. Emerson said of him: "Alone in all history he estimated the greatness of man. . . ." [68]

Thus Christ was not intrinsically different from other men. This was not to deny his divinity, but to extend it to everyone. The Saviour, in New Thought, became the epitomization of human potentialities.[69] He was not regarded any less as the son of God, merely "vastly more the Son of Man." For the prophets of the new individualism, his life was "the norm, the type, the example, the real inspiration for the life of every individual." [70]

The problem of relating finite man to an infinite God is as old as Christianity itself. Traditional doctrine taught that the miracle of the incarnation was singular. God became man in the person of Christ, thus providing a pathway to salvation, a bridge between the mundane and the sacred. New Thought conceived the miracle of the incarnation as continuing, repeated with the creation of every man or woman. Vested with divinity, each person became his own instrument of grace, both redeemer and redeemed, the complete master of his destiny, if he would but believe it. In this cosmology, material success has a supernatural connotation. Prosperity is evidence of the individual's realization of oneness with the Infinite and the power this bestows. The parallel between this and the Puritan's view of worldly well-being as an outward sign of grace is clear. For Americans, whether disciples of the "old" thought or the "new," success and the supernatural are inextricably bound together. On the level of symbol, the pursuit of the material and the pursuit of the ideal have a symbiotic relationship in the American mind that is one of the most distinctive and enduring marks of our culture.

NOTES

1. C. Wright Mills, *White Collar, The American Middle Classes* (New York: Oxford University Press, 1956), p. 272.
2. See "About Opportunities," *The World's Work*, XI (January 1906), 7034–7035.

3. Randolph Bourne, "The Two Generations," *The Atlantic*, CVII (May 1911), 594–596.

4. Albert Chavannes, *In Brighter Climes, or Life in Socioland* (Knoxville: Chavannes and Co., 1897), p. 16.

5. John Herman Randall, *The New Light on Immortality, or The Significance of Psychic Research* (New York: The Macmillan Co., 1921), p. 123.

6. *Ibid.*

7. For a discussion of the breakdown of former certainties around the turn of the century, see Thomas C. Cochran, "The Social Scientists," *American Perspectives: The National Self-Image in the Twentieth Century*, ed. Robert E. Spiller *et al.* (Cambridge, Mass.: Harvard University Press, 1961), pp. 94 ff. See too Henry F. May, *The End of American Innocence* (New York: Alfred A. Knopf, 1959), p. 121.

8. George Santayana, *Winds of Doctrine: Studies in Contemporary Civilization* (New York: Charles Scribner's Sons, 1913), p. 3.

9. John Herman Randall, *The Philosophy of Power, or What to Live For* (New York: Dodge Publishing Co., 1917), pp. 11–12. See too Henry Frank, *The Mastery of Mind in the Making of a Man* (New York: R. F. Fenno and Co., 1908), p. 231.

10. I use New Thought as a generic label for the body of ideas I am examining.

11. A. Whitney Griswold, "New Thought: A Cult of Success," *The American Journal of Sociology*, XL (November 1934), 311.

12. Bolton Hall, *Thrift* (New York: B. W. Huebsch, 1916), pp. 2–4.

13. The relation of New Thought to the Progressive reform movement is discussed in greater detail in Chapter 6.

14. Hall, *op. cit.*, p. 5.

15. *Ibid.*, pp. 6–7.

16. Henry Wood, *The New Thought Simplified: How to Gain Harmony and Health* (Boston: Lee and Shepard, 1904), pp. 146–147. See also Horatio W. Dresser, "What is New Thought," *Arena*, XXI (January 1899), 30, and Alfred W. Martin, *Psychic Tendencies of Today* (New York: D. Appleton and Co., 1918), pp. 1–33.

17. John B. Anderson, *New Thought, Its Lights and Shadows: An Appreciation and a Criticism* (Boston: Sherman, French and Co., 1911), p. 1.

18. William James, "The Powers of Men," *The American Magazine*, LXV (November 1907), 64.

19. Frances M. Björkman, "The Literature of 'New Thoughters,'" *The World's Work*, XIX (January 1910), 12471. Also see John Herman Randall, Foreword to *A New Philosophy of Life* (New York: Dodge Publishing Co., 1911), pp. 8–10, and Paul Tyner, "The Metaphysical

Movement," *American Monthly Review of Reviews,* XXV (March 1902), 316.

20. Henry C. Sheldon, *Theosophy and New Thought* (New York: The Abingdon Press, 1916), *passim.*

21. Ralph Waldo Emerson, "The Transcendentalist," *The Selected Writings of Ralph Waldo Emerson,* ed. Brooks Atkinson (New York: Random House, 1950), p. 87.

22. See Stanton D. Kirkham, *The Philosophy of Self-Help* (New York: G. P. Putnam's Sons, 1909), pp. 8–9.

23. Dresser, *op. cit.,* p. 31.

24. Emerson, quoted in A. L. Allen, *The Message of New Thought* (New York: Thos. Y. Crowell Co., 1914), p. 67. The quote is from Emerson's *Nature.*

25. Emerson, "The Transcendentalist," *Selected Writings,* p. 87.

26. *Ibid.,* p. 90.

27. Frank, *op. cit.,* p. 233.

28. F. O. Matthiessen, *American Renaissance: Art and Expression in the Age of Emerson and Whitman* (New York: Oxford University Press, 1941), p. 52.

29. Randall, "The Universal Mind," *A New Philosophy of Life,* pp. 4–5.

30. Allen, *op. cit.,* p. 199.

31. Ralph Waldo Trine, *In Tune With the Infinite* (New York: Dodd, Mead, and Co., 1921), p. 210. This book first appeared in 1897 and became one of the non-fiction bestsellers of the twentieth century. On its continuing popularity, see the following: Alice Payne Hackett, *60 Years of Best Sellers, 1895–1955* (New York: R. R. Bowker Co., 1956), p. 18; "The Lounger," *The Critic,* XXXIX (July 1901), 6–7; Paul Tyner, *op. cit.,* pp. 312–320; *Publisher's Weekly,* CXIX (March 14, 1931), 1387–1388; *Publisher's Weekly,* CLI (February 22, 1947), 1251–1252; and "In Tune With Trine," *Newsweek,* XXIX (May 26, 1947), 84.

32. William James, *The Varieties of Religious Experience* (New York: Random House, 1929), p. 94. The essays composing this book were first delivered as the Gifford Lectures on Natural Religion in Edinburgh, 1901–1902.

33. Frederic I. Carpenter, "William James and Emerson," *American Literature,* II (March 1939), 42–43.

34. *Ibid.,* p. 57. See too Harvey Gates Townsend, *Philosophical Ideas in the United States* (New York: American Book Co., 1934), p. 134. For the influence of Emerson on John Dewey, the second leading figure in the development of pragmatism, see Matthiessen, *op. cit.,* p. 4.

It should be noted, too, that James's father was a Swedenborgian. This may also have contributed to James's sympathy for New Thought, which claimed Swedenborg as one of the fathers of this philosophy. For the influence of Swedenborg on New Thought, see Grace M. Brown, *Mental Harmony, Its Influence on Life* (New York: Edward J. Clode, 1916), pp. 27, 40–41.

35. Santanyana, *op. cit.*, p. 205.

36. William James, Introduction to *Essays in Pragmatism*, ed. Alburey Castell (New York: Hafner Publishing Co., 1948), p. x.

37. *Ibid.*, p. viii.

38. Wood, *op. cit.*, pp. 66, 71.

39. William James, "Reflex Action and Theism," *The Will to Believe and Other Essays in Popular Philosophy* (New York: Longmans, Green and Co., 1909), p. 131. This article appeared first in the *Unitarian Review* for October 1881.

40. William James, "Is Life Worth Living," *The Will to Believe and Other Essays*, p. 59.

41. William James, "The Will to Believe," *The Will to Believe and Other Essays* (New York: Longmans, Green and Co., 1909), p. 25. Commenting on its reception, Alburey Castell has written: "It came at a time when the religious consciousness was hard pressed by the more aggressive representatives of the nineteenth century's conception of the 'scientific point of view'; and seems to have been welcomed as though by defenders of a besieged city." Castell, "Introduction," James, *Essays in Pragmatism*, p. xii.

42. William James, *Human Immortality: Two Supposed Objections to the Doctrine* (Boston: Houghton Mifflin and Co., 1898), p. 7.

43. *Ibid.*, p. 12.

44. James A. Edgerton, *Invading the Invisible* (New York: The New Age Press, 1931), pp. 193–194.

45. Randall, *The Philosophy of Power*, pp. 317–318. See too Martin, *op. cit.*, pp. 141, 148.

46. James H. Hyslop, quoted in Randall, *The New Light on Immortality*, p. 82. Hyslop became Secretary of the American branch of the Society for Psychical Research in 1906 and held that position until his death in 1920.

47. *Ibid.*, pp. 136–137. For William James's attitude toward psychical research, see his "Frederic Myers' Services to Psychology," *Memories and Studies* (New York: Longmans, Green and Co., 1912), pp. 145–170. See too James, "What Psychical Research Has Accomplished," *The Will to Believe and Other Essays*, pp. 299–327. On the felt connection between ethics and immortality, see James, "The Sentiment of Rationality," *ibid.*, pp. 99–108.

48. Wood, *op. cit.*, p. 135.

49. Trine, *op. cit.*, pp. 205–206.

50. Randall, *The Philosophy of Power*, p. 30.

51. Ralph Waldo Trine, *Character-Building Thought Power* (New York: Thos. Y. Crowell and Co., 1899), pp. 47–48.

52. Horatio W. Dresser, *Handbook of the New Thought* (New York: G. P. Putnam's Sons, 1917), p. 11.

53. E. L. Cabot's *Everyday Ethics*, quoted in Horatio W. Dresser, *Human Efficiency: A Psychological Study of Modern Problems* (New York: G. P. Putnam's Sons, 1912), p. 365. See too Charles B. Patterson, *Dominion and Power: or The Science of Life and Living* (New York: Funk and Wagnalls, 1910), p. 163.

54. For examples, see Randall, *The Culture of Personality* (New York: H. M. Caldwell and Co., 1912), p. 247.

55. Patterson, *op. cit.*, p. 166.

56. Orison Swett Marden, "What Shall I Do?" *The Consolidated Library*, ed. Orison Swett Marden (New York: Bureau of National Literature and Art, 1907), XIII, 270. See too Dorothy Grenside, *Little Builders: New Thought Talks to Children* (New York: Dodge Publishing Co., 1916), *passim*.

57. "The Order of Development," *The Consolidated Library*, II, 63.

58. "The Nursery," *ibid.*, I, 21.

59. "Cheerfulness, The Great Life Tonic," *ibid.*, XIV, 65.

60. O. S. Marden, quoted in Margaret Connolly, *The Life Story of Orison Swett Marden: A Man Who Benefited Men* (New York: Thomas Y. Crowell Co., 1925), pp. 26–27.

61. John Herman Randall, "The Rediscovery of Jesus," *A New Philosophy of Life*, p. 59. See too Allen, *op. cit.*, p. 176.

62. Kate E. Blake, "Fitting for Life," *The Consolidated Library*, II, 247.

63. "Faults of Weakness and Suggestive Remedies," *ibid.*

64. For example, see John Dewey, *Democracy and Education* (New York: The Macmillan Co., 1916), pp. 402–418.

65. Dresser, *Handbook of the New Thought*, pp. 16–17.

66. Trine, *In Tune With the Infinite*, pp. 12–13. See too Charles G. Davis, *The Philosophy of Life* (Chicago: D. D. Publishing Co., 1910), p. 123.

67. Orison Swett Marden, *Peace, Power and Plenty* (New York: Thos. Y. Crowell and Co., 1909), p. ix.

68. Allen, *op. cit.*, pp. 95–97. It is interesting to note that one New Thought cult which grew up in the 1930s called itself I AM.

69. Kirkham, *op. cit.*, p. 51.

70. Randall, "The Rediscovery of Jesus," *A New Philosophy of Life*, p. 76.

Chapter 6

The Revival of the Transcendentalist Dogma

PART II

The Religion of Optimism

I

The rapid transformation of society in the post-Civil War decades and its consequent dislocations caused the rise of a strongly pessimistic cast of mind in America. Prophets of doom multiplied and dire prognostications of the nation's future became commonplace. Henry Adams announced the universe was running itself down, dragging us all to oblivion. Others saw the threat to our survival in an upheaval of the working classes or in the influx of barbarian hordes to our shores. Still others quaked before the Asiatic menace, which, through sheer force of numbers, might overrun Anglo-Saxon civilization.[1] The nation had reached its natural boundaries, and its days of buoyant expansiveness appeared over.

New Thought advocates condemned this inclination to morbidity and gave continued assurances of progress. This did not, however, preclude an awareness of social problems. Despite their easy optimism, many New Thoughters were deeply involved in the Progressive movement. Prominent among these was Benjamin O. Flower, who combined "a lively sympathy for the poor and oppressed" with "an enthusiastic belief in a coming reign of human brotherhood with all its attendant blessings."[2] The son of a minister, Flower planned to enter the ministry of the Disciples of Christ until "a change in his theological views, which ultimately resulted in his becoming a Unitarian, led him to turn to journalism."[3] He founded *Arena*, a New Thought magazine, in 1889 and edited it until 1896. In 1904, he rejoined the magazine as editor-in-chief, by which time it had come to occupy an important position in the journalistic arsenal of the reform movement. In 1909, he launched his last important magazine venture, when he founded the *Twentieth Century Magazine*, another reform journal which at various times editorialized for direct legislation through initiative, referendum, and recall, government ownership of public utilities, and compulsory arbitration.

Flower attributed what he believed to be the American loss of confidence to the grip which materialism had on the thought of his contemporaries. This orientation, he contended, was "always found side by side with aggressive selfish egoism, a profound unrest and a tendency to pessimism on the part of multitudes of people." Pessimism advanced as idealism declined. The consequence for society was the displacement of good-fellowship and harmony by the "fierce spirit of competition." At such times, it was "above all else important that a strong optimistic spirit be infused into society; that the devils of pessimism and doubt be routed by the angels of courage, faith and love; and that man's belief in himself as a son of the Infinite Father be reawakened."[4]

New Thought writers, like Christian novelists, felt that

the preservation of an optimistic world-view was a social necessity. From the viewpoint of social reform, this had a relevant kernel of truth. New Thoughters correctly perceived that efforts at social improvement rested on hopefulness, and they were extremely sensitive to the threatened paralysis of despair. As with so many of their preachments, it was not the idea so much as its overstatement that brought them to the edge of absurdity. It is important, then, to realize that their roseate view of the world stimulated, rather than inhibited, their sympathies for efforts at ameliorating actual social ills. One reviewer caught their spirit when he praised Orison Swett Marden's *Secret of Achievement* as "an excellent antidote to that morbid class of literature sometimes called 'realistic'—whose squalid and dreary pessimism" [5] was poisoning the atmosphere. Here again, New Thoughters shared a common perspective with the Christian novelists. Both feared literary naturalism because they believed it bred hopelessness. Their optimism was, to be sure, based on a kind of sentimental Christian meliorism, but this was a significant aspect of the Progressive mentality, and while it helped define the limitations of that reform movement, it also provided it with much of its force.

II

Whatever their reform proclivities, the prime concern of inspirationalists was the individual and most of their writings were addressed to his needs. In the case of Orison Swett Marden, inspirationalist par excellence, the desire to give reassurance stemmed from a sympathy developed through the difficulties of his own life. Born in New Hampshire in 1850, he was orphaned at the age of seven. His guardian "bound him out" to five different families, all of whom treated him poorly. His experience in the home of a Baptist minister soured him forever on religious orthodoxy. In later years, he recalled: "When out there with nature, I loved God. When in there, listening to Elder Strong, I feared and shrank from Him." [6] This youthful experience probably enhanced the appeal which the liberal theology of New Thought had for him. The harshness of his youth left him with a chronic sense of inadequacy that caused him to marvel at his later accomplishments. His biographer quotes him as saying:

> To hear that I would never amount to anything was no new thing for me. . . . The unfortunate suggestion seemed to be ingrained in the very marrow of my being, for all through the different stages of my career I used to be amazed at my successive promotions. Could it be that the "good-for-nothing" boy who had been told so often that there was no chance for anyone like him, away back in the woods, without friends or money, ever to do anything but work on a farm, or in a saw-mill in the forest—could it be that he was, in a measure, after all, succeeding in doing something he had longed to do? . . . [7]

It could be and it was. Marden, supporting himself, received a degree from Boston University in 1877 and four years later graduated from Harvard Medical School. In 1882 he received a law degree from Boston University, and spent the next decade in various business enterprises. In 1894 his first book, *Pushing to the Front*, appeared, and by 1925 had gone through 250 editions. Marden, forsaking medicine, law, and business, became one of the leading inspirational writers of his day.[8]

As an antidote to despair, he assured his readers that "the sons and daughters of God were planned for glorious, sublime lives, and the time will come when all men will be kings and all women queens." Poverty and vice were destined for extinction. "The plan of creation," he declared, "will have failed if every human being does not finally come into his own and return to his God as a king." [9] This was not a deferral into the bliss of the herafter. New Thoughters were certain that "death will give place to life incorruptible, right here on this earth." [10] Hardship was an unnatural condition, though no time was set for the fulfillment of the divine injunction of a good life for all. Earthly perfection was assured, but men might hasten it by assuming a cheerful expectancy. The new faith enjoined optimism as a duty and stigmatized pessimism as both un-Christian and irreligious.

> Melancholy, solemnity, used to be regarded as a sign of spirituality, but it is now looked upon as the imprint of a morbid mind. There is no religion in it. True religion is full of hope, sunshine, optimism, and cheerfulness. It is joyous and glad and beautiful. There is no Christianity in the ugly, the discordant, the sad. . . . "Laugh until I come back" was a noted clergyman's "good-by" salutation. It is a good one for us all.[11]

III

The optimism of earlier popularizers of America's sunlit future was nurtured, in part, by the belief that the American environment was uniquely suited to the development of superior individuals. Jefferson, for example, found comfort in the conviction that generations of his countrymen would grow up in contact with nature. In the Jackson period, men argued that American superiority rested on her "natural" men, who were greater in wisdom and prowess than the effete products of overcivilized surroundings.[12] By the end of the century, however, confidence in the special healthfulness of the American milieu was lost. Conditions which enveloped the individual were seen as destructive rather than sustaining, something to be surmounted if men were to survive whole. Thus New Thought found it important to say that "man need not be the victim of his environment, but can be the master of it." [13]

As if to compensate for the loss of the supports of nature, inspirationalists trumpeted man's "god-like attributes," and his potential of almost limitless power.[14] In focusing on latent sources of energy in the individual, New Thought was in company with the advocates of "muscular Christianity." [15] Along with the promoters of the strenuous life, New Thoughters called on men to summon their unused capacities. Here again William James lent support. In an article citing Theodore Roosevelt as the exception to the rule, the famed psychologist stated that "the human individual . . . lives usually far within his limits; he possesses powers of various sorts which he habitually fails to use. He energizes below his *maximum*, and he behaves below his optimum." [16] At the same time he observed that the nation was then witnessing "a very copious unlocking of energies by ideas, in the persons of those converts to 'New Thought,' 'Christian Science,' 'Metaphysical Healing,' or other forms of spiritual philosophy, who are so numerous among us today. . . ." All of these systems, he noted, operated "by the suggestion of power." [17] Popularizers of these mind-power creeds placed the ability for achievement in the realm of belief. In effect, they taught that as a person thinks, so he is.

The New Thought conception of God dovetailed neatly with its stress on human potentialities. It discarded anthropomorphic descriptions of the deity as man writ large or as some "Magnified Being apart from the universe, sitting on a great white throne. . . ." [18] Instead, God was described as power or force, the primal energy of life, and was variously called the Over Soul, the Spirit of Infinite Life and Power, or the Universal Intelligence.[19] According to this pantheistic notion, divinity permeated the whole of the universe, "manifesting itself in all forms of creation." [20] It was a mistake to regard God "after the manner of an absentee landlord." To the degree that men recognized "Him as immanent as well as transcendent," they were "able to partake of His life and power." [21] New Thoughters explained that individuals were "expressions of Being projected into existence." By opening themselves to the influx of the divine essence, they could acquire its attributes. Thus men would be "gradually changed from the natural to the Spiritual, from earth-men to God-men. . . ." [22] Considered in this way, man was a storehouse of unfulfilled potentialities, able to draw at will on an infinite energy or intelligence. "Realizing this, no one is limited in any absolute sense, and the possibility of 'tapping new levels of power,' is always ours, for the supply is inexhaustible." [23] This gave mystical expression to the traditional American sense of abundance. As if to compensate for the loss of the frontier, New Thoughters offered a new realm for future exploitation, a realm without limit and without end.

IV

Given their orientation, it is not surprising that New Thought writers used Bergson and Hegel to bolster their arguments. Both philosophers were enjoying some vogue in the United States at the turn of the century, and were easily fitted to the needs of the new inspirationalists. Bergson's *élan vital* could be roughly equated with the "universal intelligence" of New Thought.[24] Similarly congenial was Hegel's conception of history as successive materializations of the Idea.[25] Eclectic in its borrowings from all types of speculation, New Thought ignored the concept of the dialectic but seized upon the evolutionary principle in Hegel. This offered something akin to Darwinism within an idealistic context, which might serve to harmonize that most disturbing of scientific theories with philosophical idealism. The prestige of science was so great that a concordance was necessary if idealism, in any form, were to survive. New Thoughters took heart in the movement of science away from a materialistic bias in the early years of the new century. They were pleased to find "the advocates of the materialistic conception, with their strange ideas of creation's origins, in the minority, and that minority constantly diminishing in the light of scientific investigation." At the same time, they noted that the majority of scientists and philosophers, "men whose useful discoveries are attracting the attention of the world, are outspoken in their declarations that back of all nature and all its manifested forms is an unseen intelligence, the divine cause of all existing things." [26] Science, they perceived, was "becoming more and more mystical" or, at least, "less and less hostile towards things of the spirit. . . ." [27] Given their belief in the ultimate unity of all things, they felt this reconciliation was natural and declared there was no essential conflict between "true religion" and "real science." [28]

They used the theory of evolution, rejecting only those interpretations that conflicted with their humanism. Consequently, they dismissed Spencerian Darwinism because it conveyed "the same sort of enervating and hopeless meaning to the individual that the Calvinistic creed once carried in theological terms." [29] Both bodies of thought presumed a group of elect human beings, relegating the rest to damnation. Battling the Spencerians, various spiritualistic groups joined the reform Darwinists in arguing that men could consciously direct events and mold their own destinies. "Thus," one observer remarked,

> all these movements that are grouped within or near the general field of the "New Thought" possess in common a vitalized kernel of truth . . . the truth that the individual is not meant to be the frightened and helpless sport of "malicious chance" (itself an unthinkable absurdity); the truth that every man is, in his own inalienable right, an agent for the expression and manifestation of power; a being possessed of the right to affirm not only "I am," but "I can," and "I will." [30]

New Thoughters rebelled at the separation of individualism from the egalitarian ideal. Their argument with social Darwinists was not that the latter denied individualism, but simply that they restricted it to the "fittest."

On other counts, New Thoughters and Spencerians could agree. Both shared a faith in progress and the ultimate perfectability of the race. One prominent New Thoughter noted that, as knowledge progressed, man's discoveries revealed the laws and forces of the universe as "finer and finer in their nature." This he attributed to "the process of evolution, so developing, so unfolding us, that we are getting nearer and nearer to the essence, the inner nature—the soul of things." [31] Construed in this way, evolution re-enforced millennialist dreams. As William James perceived, Darwin's discoveries had laid the ground for a new religion of nature.

> The idea of evolution lends itself to a doctrine of general meliorism and progress which fits the religious needs of the healthy-minded so well that it seems almost as if it might have been created for their use. Accordingly we find "evolutionism" interpreted thus optimistically and embraced as a substitute for the religion they were born in, by a multitude of our contemporaries who have either been trained scientifically, or been fond of reading popular science, and who had already begun to be invariably dissatisfied with what seemed to them the harshness and irrationality of the orthodox Christian scheme.[32]

Exploiting the prestige of science, New Thoughters called aspects of their teachings the science of the mind, which they defined as the "laws of thought as they pertain to man's relationship to the universal creative Mind and to health, happiness, and success." [33] The premise that fixed laws govern the universe, a premise basic to all scientific inquiry, was taken over by New Thought and applied to the realm of the spirit. Evolution dictated ultimate perfection in matters spiritual as well as physical. "In a universe of law," one writer explained, "the final mastery of evil by man is assured." [34] Obstacles marred the way, but all would ultimately topple before the "cosmic urge, forever pushing and projecting man forward into higher physical, mental, and spiritual development." [35] For all its touting of the freedom of the individual, New Thought, ironically, had its own brand of determinism. It sustained an illusion of freedom, at the same time, using the laws of evolution as an iron-clad guarantee of salvation. The old inspirationalists had assumed the universe was governed by moral law. The new had to defend this notion, and evolution provided a convenient fulcrum for their argument. It had the further virtue of bringing time-worn belief in line with modern scientific discovery. Thus, on the level of ideology, an accommodation between traditionalism and modernism was achieved.

V

A corollary to New Thought concepts of natural law was their belief in an orderly and harmonious universe. Inspirationalists held that the seemingly divided and distracted life of men was an illusion, and studded their writings with such words as "unity," "oneness," "wholeness," and "harmony." One popularizer advised her readers to "get in swing with the universe," and not to be notes of "discord in the universal harmony." [36] Accordingly, all that was jarring and inharmonious was considered unnatural. Wickedness had no permanent place in the New Thought cosmology. Demonstrating their only point of agreement with the early fathers of the Christian church, the New Thoughters recognized evil "only as the absence of good and as possessing only negative qualities. . . ." [37] Furthermore, they argued, "all voices, powers, and energies in the universe are created for good purposes and are good in themselves," and only become evil "as they are improperly applied and misdirected" by man.[38] The similarity to classical dogma, however, ends there. Traditionally, Adam's attempt to liken himself unto God by tasting the fruit of the tree of knowledge was taken as the source of man's troubles. The original sin was the sin of pride. New

Thought rejected this belief and ascribed human shortcomings to what might be termed the sin of humility. Men suffered from aspiring to too little rather than too much. Humility, and self-depreciation, characteristics which had so long distinguished the saint, were declared by New Thought to be the stigmata of the sinner. Bred by centuries of "wrong thinking," these notions poisoned the thoughts of men. Redemption now required a reconstruction of man's self-image in line with the rediscovery of his divinity. As one writer explained: "There is no evil in the universe but has its root and origin in the mind, and sin, sickness, sorrow, and affliction do not, in reality, belong to the universal order, are not inherent in the nature of things, but are the direct outcome of our ignorance." [39] Ignorance was defined as bad thinking, rather than lack of knowledge; and its most serious consequence was the sin of fear. This was "parent to all such mentally debilitating moods as apprehension, timidity, cowardice, depression, superstition, self-depreciation, doubting and worry." The last, this writer contended, was "the most prevalent form of the Fear thought," and the "worry habit" had become the great national vice. It lay behind what was "called the great disease of modern times—nervousness or nervous prostration. . . ." [40] Before this could be ameliorated, men would have to recognize the inherent evil of fear and worry. They would have "to look them straight in the face, and give them their real name—sin, just as truly sin as getting drunk or robbing a bank." [41] The faults of character were thus extended to include unpleasant states of mind. Conversely, happiness held first place on the New Thought list of virtues.

Thoughts of courage and hope were anodynes for apprehension and despair. Cultivating the habit of optimism and cheerfulness was the first step in curing the worry habit. Though men could not immediately dissolve their anxieties, they might begin by confining their manifestations, which, in the long run, would ameliorate the anxieties themselves. This New Thought doctrine was a somewhat exaggerated restatement of the James-Lange theory of emotions. According to this theory, the bodily response associated with an emotion is what gave it its force rather than the emotion itself. Remove its physical counterpart and the emotion was less acutely felt. James wrote:

> An emotion of fear, for example, or surprise, is not a direct effect of the object's presence on the mind, but an effect of that still earlier effect, the bodily commotion which the object suddenly excites; so that, were this bodily commotion suppressed, we should not so much *feel* fear as call the situation fearful; we should not feel surprise, but coldly recognize that the object was indeed astonishing. One enthusiast has even gone so far as to say that when we feel sorry it is because we weep, and not conversely. . . . Now, whatever exaggeration may possibly lurk in this account of our emotions (and I doubt myself whether the exaggeration be very great), it is certain that the main core of it is true, and that the mere giving way to tears, for example, or to the outward expression of an anger-fit, will result for the moment in making the inner grief or anger more acutely felt. . . .
>
> Thus the sovereign voluntary path to cheerfulness, if our spontaneous cheerfulness be lost, is to sit up cheerfully, to look round cheerfully, and to act and speak as if cheerfulness were already there. . . . So to feel brave, act as if we *were* brave, use all our will to that end, and a courage-fit will very likely replace the fit of fear.[42] *

New Thought went a step further, advising cheerful thoughts as well as cheerful actions. In the manner of "folk

* William James, *Essays on Faith and Morals*, Ralph Barton Perry, ed. (New York: Longmans Green and Co., 1949). Reprinted by permission of David McKay Co., Inc.

remedies," the notion that despondency was remediable through "thought power" probably was functional in aiding some people to cope with their anxieties. At any rate, the New Thought idea of mind over mood had its parallel in a theory of emotions widely accepted in academic circles.

VI

By the turn of the century, tension, nervousness, and anxiety were already recognized as distinguishing American traits. James reported that his contemporaries attributed American tension to the "extreme dryness of our climate," coupled "with the extraordinary progressiveness of our life, the railroad speed, the rapid success" which characterized the national scene. James, however, dismissed these as "utterly insufficient to explain the facts," [43] and offered instead an explanation congenial to the New Thought point of view; one which focused on subjective factors as the primary cause. He doubted that objective conditions were responsible for the "American over-tension and jerkiness," or for the frequency of nervous breakdowns in our society. These were the consequence of "*bad habits* . . . bred of custom and example and the cultivation of false ideals. . . ." Neither natural conditions nor work were accountable for the trouble. Its source was in "those absurd feelings of hurry and having no time, in that breathlessness and tension . . . that lack of inner harmony and ease," that characterized the American's approach to life.[44] The remedy, of course, lay with the cause. Taste and habit had to be altered. "We must change ourselves from a race that admires jerk and snap for their own sakes, and looks down upon low voices and quiet ways as dull, to one that, on the contrary, has calm for its ideal, and for their own sakes loves harmony, dignity, and ease." [45]

As these habits were learned by example, the cure could best be effected by each individual's providing a fresh example for others to emulate. James, therefore, endorsed the "gospel of relaxation," as popularized by Annie Payson Call, a New Thought writer from Boston.[46] He hoped that by getting "not only our preachers, but our friends the theosophists and mind-curers of various religious sects, and such writers as Mr. Dresser, Prentice Mulford, Mr. Horace Fletcher, and Mr. Trine to help, and the whole band of school teachers and magazine readers" to join the effort, "it really looks as if a good start might be made in the direction of changing our American mental habit. . . ." [47]

New Thought further encouraged a "take-it-easy" approach to life with its principle of non-resistance. Phrases like "struggling upward" or "climbing life's ladder" saturated the nineteenth-century literature of uplift; in the newer guides these were replaced by "opening the shutters to let the sunshine in" or "letting down the barriers." Encouragements to overcoming objective obstacles gave way to advice on ridding the mind of subjective inhibitions. By way of comparison, the non-resistant attitude resembled the patient forbearance of the Lutheran rather than the rational self-discipline of the Calvinist, and fostered a calm and passive, as opposed to a tense and voluntaristic, cast of mind.

Preparation for the cosmic inflow was the aim of the new mystics. Accordingly, they assured their readers: "As we give the laws of life, both mental and physical, free course through us they yield a rich blessing in strength and harmony. Through a non-resistant attitude toward all things we lubricate life, dismiss friction, and thereby make existence a privilege and delight." [48] In a similar vein, another New

Thoughter wrote: "No great success ever came through forced effort. It creeps in easily, gently, happily. Let your life go on smoothly, feeling and knowing that you will reach your aim, careless as to how." [49] Don't "try to live up to anything," advised another, but "let go and let the impulse from within move [you] to every action." [50]

New Thought did not discourage work, in itself, however, but taught that labor approached with a proper attitude was never an undue strain. Unhealthful enervation stemmed from the negative associations which men brought to their tasks rather than from the tasks themselves. That certain kinds of labor were intrinsically destructive of health and well-being was ignored for the most part by a literature clearly directed more to clerks than to coal miners.

A corollary to the principle of non-resistance was the law of attraction.[51] Men violated it by seeking to achieve their objectives through the law of force—that is, through struggle. Inspirationalists argued that to think struggle was to invite it. In this way men generated the obstacles they feared by thinking about them. As Ralph Waldo Trine explained: "The great law of the drawing power of the mind, which says that like creates like, and that like attracts like, is continually working in every human life, for it is one of the great immutable laws of the universe." [52] Therefore, those "desiring better conditions must keep in mind a greater vision of a greater life even while apparently accepting lesser conditions." [53] This positive expectancy would gradually realize itself. The internal impediments to success were much greater than the external. As Marden wrote:

> Morbid thoughts are infinitely greater hindrances to success than opposition from outside. No health, no beauty, no harmony, no real success can exist in the atmosphere of abnor-

mal melancholy, or morbid ideas. If we are inclined to be pessimistic, to look on the dark side of things, to predict failure in everything we undertake, to anticipate trouble, we shall, most assuredly attract those things to us. . . . On the other hand, a harmonious, healthy, vigorous brain is a friend, a producer of success. Bright, cheerful, hopeful thoughts, and belief in one's ability to accomplish the thing undertaken, are friends that will insure success to their possessor.[54]

VII

This exaggerated belief in the power of thought buoyed up the traditional conviction of individual power. Ultimately, it rested on "the profound truth, which has been the teaching of idealism in every day and generation, that in the inner consciousness, in the will, in the actual thought of the individual, lie the real sources of power, of health, of true progress." [55] Accordingly, men might create their circumstances by controlling their states of mind, and therefore any achievement was in the reach of all. In the past, failure had been attributed to the violation of moral precepts. In the new dispensation, it was considered the consequence of a violation of the laws of mind and nature. This is what Elbert Hubbard meant when he assured his readers, "Success is the most natural thing in the world. The man who does not succeed has placed himself in opposition to the laws of the universe." [56] New Thoughters denied the teachings of nineteenth-century political economists that scarcity of resources dictated a society inevitably composed of haves and have-nots. Such notions, they contended, were anti-democratic, undermined harmony, and fomented social conflict. With some insight,

Marden explained that the competitive ideal had "its origin in the pessimistic assumption that it is impossible for everybody to be wealthy and successful; in the thought of limitation of all things which men most desire; and that, there not being enough for all, a few must fight desperately, selfishly for what there is, and the shrewdest, the longest-headed, those with the most staying power, the strongest workers, will get the most of it. This theory," he concluded, "is fatal to all individual and race betterment." [57] Condemning notions of scarcity and struggle as sacrilegious, New Thought affirmed that supply was limitless. "There is nothing in this world which men desire and struggle for," wrote Marden, "of which there is not enough for everybody." [58] Men seeking success must regard their task as one of realizing an abundance which, though latent, was infinite. Creation of fresh resources, rather than competition for those at hand, was the key to achievement. In this vein, one New Thoughter declared:

> In order to master your environment and your destiny it is not at all necessary that you should rule over your fellow men; and indeed, when you fall into the world's struggle for the high places, you begin to be conquered by fate and environment, and your getting rich becomes a matter of chance and speculation. Beware the competitive mind! No better statement of the principle of creative action can be formulated than the favorite declaration of the late "Golden Rule" Jones of Toledo: "What I want for myself, I want for everybody." [59]

This sense of abundance has been crucial to the configuration of American reform movements. It is certainly one of the strongest reasons for the absence of an enduring radicalism in this country. Reformers felt no hypocrisy in tendering the notion that material well-being for all required no basic re-orientation of society. Radical social change was rendered superfluous by the very richness of the nation. In some degree, this myth of infinite supply has been realized. The improvements in living standards we have seen in the twentieth century have resulted from an absolute increase in wealth produced, rather than from a redistribution of existing riches. The new success cult's emphasis on tapping "new sources of supply" found enough resonance in reality to remain plausible.

VIII

New Thought literature continued the tradition of earlier inspirational writing in equating the good with the practical. "To do to others as we would have them do to us is the practical, and the only practical road to such financial success as brings with it the happiness for which we are all seeking." [60] Only virtue brought success worth having. Similarly, in teaching the means to success, New Thought retained a broad construction of the word. "The useful life, the constructive life, the life that lights the pathways of others to higher ideals, and awakens their consciousness to the divine powers within themselves and brings peace and contentment to him who lives it, is the successful life." [61] Like earlier moralizers, the new inspirationalists railed against the passion for riches. One author complained:

> While there is no record of an age which was not in some sense commercial, no other has been as completely and abnor-

mally so as the present. Literature, music, art, religion, politics —all that should be free from the commercial spirit—are tainted; every stream is polluted. Our creed is to get rich; we are money mad. We own everything but ourselves; control everything but our minds; buy everything but health and happiness. The root of the evil is not money, but love of money to the exclusion of all else; not riches, but indifference to capacity which is the real wealth; not assets, but the failure to develop inner resources. We are the victims of a false and vulgar ideal, and this is the substance of the whole matter.[62]

New Thoughters called for the abandonment of a value system that "frankly construes success in terms of the dollar sign and estimates the value of human lives literally by the abundance of things they possess." Here the success ideology stands opposed to the unrestrained impulse for acquisition. The two, generally regarded as one and the same, were quite distinct aspects of American culture. While defending the belief that opportunity was open for all, success cultists decried the general passion for possessions. "Never was there a time when the need to 'see life steadily and see it whole' was greater than today, for our eyes are blinded by the glare of things, our minds are absorbed with the demand of things, our hearts are choked with the love of things, and our souls are stifled with the dead weight of things."[63] The fabled "materialism" of Americans, then, was not encouraged by popularizers of the success myth. Mind-power inspirationalists, like Alger before them, disseminated a brand of secular idealism, and were more concerned with the proper conduct of life than the accumulation of fortunes. Similarly, they retained the belief that moderation in all things must serve as the basis of the good life. Writing of money, Trine advised: "It is the medium ground that brings the true solution here, the same as it is in all phases of life."[64] The moderate bourgeois was just as much a hero of the new success writers as of the old.

Describing the titans of wealth, a New Thought writer with a Hegelian streak wrote:

> Rockefeller, Carnegie, Morgan, et al., have been the unconscious agents of the Supreme in the necessary work of systematizing and organizing productive industry; and in the end, their work will contribute immensely toward increased life for all. Their day is nearly over; they have organized production, and *will soon be succeeded by the agents of the multitude, who will organize the machinery of distribution.*
>
> The multimillionaires are like the monster reptiles of the pre-historic eras; they play a necessary part in the evolutionary process, but the same Power which produced them will dispose of them.[65]

As if extinction were not sufficient revenge, people were assured that plutocrats had "never been really rich; a record of the private lives of most of this class will show that they have really been the most abject of the poor." [66] This was the result of the inexorable law of compensation, which guaranteed that ill-gotten gains would be balanced by a future retribution in the form of "poverty, sickness, or misery of some kind." [67] One who had studied "strong men of shady financial reputations" until he knew their inner selves, came up with the soothing observation that "not one of them enjoyed his life." And for those who were not satisfied by this, he added that "ninety per cent of them die in poverty." [68] Pity, it would seem, is the last resort of the envious. Portrayed as wretched, millionaires appeared to be a breed of unfortunates.

New Thought further addressed itself to those who had known disappointment by reviving the Emersonian notion that even calamity had its compensations.[69] A typical illustration of this is the following story of a businessman who had spent much time and energy effecting a certain business combination. "When the crucial time came," the story goes, "the thing failed in a perfectly inexplicable way; it was as if some unseen influence had been working secretly against him." Being a disciple of mental science, however, he was not disappointed, "thanked God that his desire had been over-ruled, and went steadily on with a grateful mind." Some time passed, and "an opportunity so much better came his way that he would not have made the first deal on any account; and he saw that a mind which knew more than he knew had prevented him from losing the greater good by entangling himself with the lesser." [70] The story also illuminates how frequently New Thought writers turned common sense insight into extravagant exaggeration. This was particularly true of the notion that states of mind can affect objective reality. Clearly, the results of most objective conditions are to some degree determined by our subjective response to them. But inspirationalists encouraged the belief that thought did not only condition circumstances, but controlled them entirely. That some took the power of thought "overseriously was seen, for example, when members of a New Thought club met to 'hold the thought' for the benefit of the sufferers at the time of the San Francisco earthquake." "It was seen again," continued the same author, "when a New Thought leader expressed surprise at the outbreak of the Spanish-American war; for, said he, 'I supposed the New Thought had gained a greater hold in this country than that.' " [71]

"Holding the thought" was similarly applied to less earth-shaking events. The following story is typical of those illustrating its supposed efficacy in times of personal need. It is the story of a businessman who needs a thousand dollars desperately. Tapping every source available to him, he is unable to raise the money. In spite of this he continues to "think" that the money will be there when required. On the day payment has to be made, he goes to his office, undaunted, expecting the money will be there. Opening his mail, he finds that a friend, who knew of his plight, has sent it. " 'Pure luck and just a matter of chance,' the unthinking would say, but it was nothing of the kind." Rather, the author assures us, it was the natural outcome of the operation of "Universal Law." [72] Many New Thought writers also advertised "mind-power" as a get-rich-quick formula, by which one could accumulate a fortune just by thinking about it. Even disciples of the movement perceived these excesses. One admitted "the idea of 'success vibration' has been overworked in the name of New Thought," and warned that "no one can sit down and think money into his pocket. . . ." [73] Horatio Dresser, disciple and historian of the movement, also cautioned his readers that there was "no formula for success" [74] and was critical of inspirationalists who promised more than they could provide.[75] At the same time, however, he was able to associate himself with an inspirational column in *Good Housekeeping* magazine called "Happiness and Health Insurance Co., Mutual," [76] which also offered readers rather exaggerated assurances. Many inspirationalists, then, were guilty of the very excesses they deplored in others.

IX

Probably any inspirational literature is prone to excessive claims. Its function is dependent on a measure of exaggeration, and much of this may be attributed to "inspirational license." More remarkable than the overstatement in this kind of writing is its reformist tone. Given the movement's subjective emphasis and its conviction that the cause and cure for all problems rested within the individual, it is surprising to find among its adherents so many advocates of social reform. Despite the inwardness of New Thought mysticism, the movement was sympathetic to Progressivism, and many leading inspirationalists engaged in reform work.

Arena, which advertised itself "as an influential, thought-building force in the reform Movement," [77] was a New Thought magazine, and claimed as one of its editors Charles Brodie Patterson, a prominent reformer and author of inspirational tracts. One commentator remarked that Patterson's association with "the radical review . . . [was] significant evidence of the lively interest in the social movement that the new metaphysics is sure, sooner or later, to awaken in its students." [78] Marden's *Success* magazine, as we have noted earlier, was full of endorsements of reform, condemnation for franchise grabbers, and encomiums to men like "Golden Rule" Jones. James Arthur Edgerton, sometime poet of the New Thought movement and president of the National New Thought Alliance from 1909 to 1914 and of the International New Thought Alliance from 1914 to 1924, was secretary of the Populist National Committee from 1896 to 1904, and a member of the national executive committee until 1908. Mr. Edgerton's last stint in American politics was as the Prohibition party's vice-presidential nominee in 1928. Bolton Hall, prominent New Thought spokesman, was a single taxer and a devotee of Tolstoy, who wrote many books in which he suggested ways to reform America, bitterly attacked monopolies, and expressed admiration for such reformers as Jane Addams. [79] Elizabeth Towne, publisher of the popular inspirational magazine *Nautilus*, in 1910 expressed an eagerness to see "Edward Bellamy's dream come true." [80] In the same year, Ralph Waldo Trine, the most popular inspirationalist of his day, published *The Land of Living Men*,[81] a book which marks him as being as much a prototype of the American Progressive as of the American New Thoughter.

The reform impulse in the self-help ideology derives, in part, from the messianic tradition in America, which also had its origins in the New England experiment. The early Puritans conceived of their settlement as a city upon a hill which would radiate a beacon of light to reform the world. The notion persistently recurs throughout our history.[82]

Nurtured on the idea that one people by its example might reform the whole family of nations, it is not altogether surprising that Americans confronted with the task of reforming themselves should emphasize the power of each individual to improve the whole of society. The reform urge itself is, in part, attributable to an individualistic bias which carried with it a respect for the worth and dignity of all men. Moreover, the inspirationalists' commitment to personal power was joined to the conviction that every individual bore responsibility for the general welfare.[83] One brand of individualism minimized personal responsibility by depending on natural law to convert individual selfishness to moral purposes. Such was the rationalization of the nineteenth-century liberal who, in a manner of speaking, foisted on the universe the responsibility he refused to accept himself. The heirs of the American self-help tradition had no such easy out. While they drew confidence from the belief that natural law was on their side, this did not relieve them of responsibility for a just society any more than predestination absolved the early Calvinist from responsibility for the kind of life he led.

By the dictates of New Thought morality, men were in

fact their brothers' keepers. Accordingly, one inspirationalist warned: "Individual success must never be considered apart from its effect upon society." [84] Echoing this sentiment, another declared: "The welfare of others is essential to the success of every man. . . . While thousands of people are in dire need no millionaire may rightly be called successful." Nor was charity a sufficient discharge of duty. "He [the millionaire] may give thousands to found charitable institutions or endow universities, but he cannot hide the fact that the social organism of which he is a member has still a demand upon him." [85]

The rich, in general, fared poorly at the hands of New Thought writers. Their extravagance, their competitiveness, and their social irresponsibility played havoc with the sensibilities of the inspirationalists. This antagonism caused one author to observe: "In its sociological aspect, we are presented to-day with a curious spectacle, the world always afflicted with a criminal poor—for whom there is much excuse—is now afflicted with the criminal rich—for whom there is no excuse at all." [86]

The poor fared better, and received sympathetic treatment. The earlier literature of uplift had viewed poverty as having positive effects on moral growth, as a crucible for forging character. New Thought saw poverty as an unmitigated evil, entirely destructive of moral growth.[87] Unlike its predecessor, the new inspiration insisted that prosperity was "necessary to a useful and well-rounded life." [88] Because of the importance they attached to states of mind, New Thought writers saw in poverty an encouragement to the sin of negative thinking, or "poverty thought." Poor surroundings deluged the mind with unhealthy images that were dangerous to psychical well-being. And while they might be overcome, it was best to avoid them in the first place.[89]

Discussing poverty, Trine observed in 1910 that there were ten million Americans without adequate food, clothing, and shelter. What appalled him even more were the large numbers who "each year . . . through no fault of their own [were] dropping into the same condition." [90] Some poverty, he explained, was due to "intemperance, shiftlessness, laziness [and] depravity," and was perhaps inevitable. He contended, however, that most indigence, in this country and elsewhere, was caused by conditions beyond the control of the individual. Most poverty, he argued, grew out of "certain social and industrial evils and wrongs that a truly great or even self-respecting nation [could not] continue to permit," and he called upon the people to "put an end to the causes that deliberately make paupers out of the citizens of a great and free nation, and then turn around and take care of them out of the public funds." [91] This view echoed that of more secular writers of the same period. Discussing changing conceptions of poverty, Robert Bremner has written:

> By 1900 there was a widespread conviction that the causes of failure were to be found, in most cases, in circumstances outside and beyond the control of individual personality. Robert Hunter voiced the opinion of nearly all the reformers of the Progressive generation when he declared that twentieth-century poverty was due "to certain social evils which must be remedied and certain social wrongs which must be put right." [92]

New Thoughters shared this belief, though it was contrary to their avowed individualism. In so doing, however, they merely reflected the ambivalence of the reform movement as a whole. Society had grown large and complex, and some awareness of a distinct social reality could not be avoided. On the other hand, the commitment to individual

power was too great to be surrendered to a social determinism. The problem of drawing the line between individual and
social causation was certainly not exclusively American, but
our particular history did give it a unique emphasis. No other
nation had experienced such an unsupervised development;
no other country was so lacking in communal controls; no
other people had known such freedom from institutional
restraint. In other societies, existing institutional restrictions might be adapted to changing social needs; in America
they had to be created from scratch. Historically, Americans had been compelled to discover individual solutions
where social ones were lacking. Self-sufficiency, developed
in response to need, in time became a cherished value and,
even when inadequate, was too deeply ingrained to be
scrapped overnight. Thus the pattern of American reform
was spotty, a story of abrupt starts and sudden stops, a series
of halfway measures which attempted to cope with social
forces without relinquishing notions of individual responsibility.

New Thought, sharing the ambivalence of the reform position, continued to place primary responsibility on the individual even while admitting certain evils to be beyond his
direct control. To do otherwise, they claimed, was tantamount to running away. "Radical socialism," scoffed one
writer, was only, "a device for cowards who lack the manliness to be souls in the presence of heartless corporations." [93]
The apparent inconsistency of the New Thought position
also arose from the conflict of roles between the inspirationalist as personal therapist and as social analyst. Whatever insight the New Thoughter had into the causes of large-scale
poverty, it was foolish, from an inspirational point of view,
to tell the poor that as individuals they were impotent to
change their condition. Men dedicated to the principle of self-

improvement had to assume such improvement was possible, whatever the circumstances, or throw in the sponge altogether.

Institutions, however troublesome, were only the embodiment of men's thoughts and were therefore no greater than the minds that created them. Change the minds, the argument went, and the institutions would be transformed. Realizing this, the greatest teacher of all time had preached to "individuals, and not to churches or institutions." [94] Using Christ's example, New Thoughters contended that *the way to reform a nation . . . was for each man to formulate and think reformation for himself.* [95] Moreover, through thought transference, one person might influence the minds of many. Here again, as with success, notions of thought power could be taken to ludicrous extremes. For example, one inspirationalist assured his readers "that public feeling and sentiment, social, political, and religious, [was] due, primarily to the fact that a number of individuals . . . [were] holding certain thoughts . . . and their thoughts . . . [went] forth in great thought vibrations, to influence and even to radically change the thinking of multitudes of other minds." [96] This was not to deny that such impersonal forces as the machine and industrialism created perplexing problems. The New Thought solution rang clear. "Spiritualize mankind and all these questions will take care of themselves." [97] After all, had not Jesus "directed all his efforts toward the evolution of spiritual character in the individual, well knowing that social, political, and ethical standards would respond"? [98]

New Thought reformers, however, had no monopoly on illusion, nor did it always blind them to a more accurate assessment of contemporary social evils. Trine, for example, while advocating the "spiritual solution," bitterly attacked the railroads and other industries for "criminal negligence" with regard to the safety of employees, and, in the best Progressive tradition, produced a host of statistics to support his charges. Sufficient public indignation, he argued, would force change.[99] In a similar vein, he attacked child labor and the corrosive effects of urban living. While earlier apostles of uplift had blamed much of poverty on intemperance, Trine took the opposite view and argued that as far as drinking went, "poverty precedes more often than it follows." [100] In other ways, however, he continued in the older tradition. For example, he was as fearful as earlier moralists had been of the polarization of society into extremes of rich and poor. Whatever aspects of the older moralism New Thought rejected, it retained the conviction that a rough equality of condition and the continuance of opportunities for improvement were essential to social well-being. "As soon as extremes of wealth and poverty begin to manifest themselves," warned Trine, "and privilege grows, resulting in still greater inequality in the distribution of wealth and power, that moment the destructive force begins its work—a force that grows by what it feeds upon, an evil that will never correct itself, and that, unless it be checked by the great common people, will carry the nation to destruction." [101] The poor and the rich alike must be brought to an awareness of their identity of interest. In the short run, each group might grab something by the selfish pursuit of its own interests, but ultimately the loss would far exceed the gain.

To support this notion, New Thoughters seized upon the gospel of efficiency which had wide currency during the Progressive period. The efficiency movement and the new transcendentalism had much in common, not the least of which was their shared belief in the naturalness of social harmony. Their respective views on employer-employee conflict may serve to illustrate the point. New Thoughters took the position that when the worker shirked in his work, or cheated his employer, he was hurting himself. Only by learning that "every malicious thought he sends forth will return to torment himself" would the worker be able to "get rid of the distrust and hatred that now control his life." Likewise, the employer must learn that his workers' interests and his own are one. "When he fully realizes that whenever he oppresses and enslaves the employee, he oppresses and enslaves himself . . . he will deal fairly, justly, and kindly with him." [102] The position taken by Frederick W. Taylor, whose *Principles of Scientific Management* was the bible of the efficiency cult, is strikingly similar. Taylor argued that the identity of interest between worker and boss was self-evident. Despite this, throughout the industrial world, workers and employers saw themselves at war.

> The majority of these men believe that the fundamental interests of employés and employers are necessarily antagonistic. Scientific management, on the contrary, has for its very foundation the firm conviction that the true interests of the two are one and the same; that prosperity for the employer cannot exist through a long term of years unless it is accompanied by prosperity for the employé, and *vice versa;* and that it is possible to give the workman what he most wants—high wages— and the employer what he wants—a lower labor cost—for his manufactures.[103]

Taylor's remarks echo the sentiments of the new mystics. The same bond united them that was common to so much of the thinking of the period—the belief in a fundamental harmony of interests in society which men, in their ignorance, violated to their own destruction.

Efficiency became a rallying ground, too, because it appealed to people as diverse as the laborer and the capitalist, the middle-class reformer and the socialist, and the religious and secular idealist. Here the neutrality of its supposed scientific detachment came into play: "A man can be persuaded to be more efficient who cannot be persuaded of anything else." [104] Inspirationalists labeled the efficiency cult "a new form of idealism" [105] and adopted it as their own. There was in fact a literature of personal efficiency which falls into the conduct-of-life genre.[106] The professional self-helpers made efficiency moral with as much ease as they had made idealism practical. "The well organized, proficient life, whatever the calling, whatever the type of person, is the basis of the moral life at its best," pronounced one inspirationalist. "To be wholly moral one must be efficient, and no one can become really efficient without being moral." [107] Indeed, such phrases as "pragmatic idealism" and "efficient moralism," which summarize the contents of early twentieth-century success tracts, aptly describe the Progressive impulse as a whole, and underscore the relationship between the tradition of self-help and social reform.

The New Thought emphasis on harmony had another dimension, which made it adaptive to the demands of industrial America. The restructuring of society in the industrial era brought increased bureaucratization. The Progressive preoccupation with administration was symptomatic of the rise of the bureaucratic cast of mind.[108] We were, to borrow William Whyte's phrase, becoming a nation of "organization men." For this new man, that which produced harmony was good, that which produced conflict, tension, and frustration, was bad.[109] The new success ideology's stress on balance and equilibrium suited this ethos perfectly. As the yeoman and the independent entrepreneur had been the object of the older literature of success, so the organization man was the object of the new.

Whatever efficiency and scientific management might accomplish in the field of industrial relations, mind-power advocates, in typical Progressive fashion, urged the need for political reform as well. Justice could not return to the American scene unless the governmental branches of our democracy were cleansed. The responsibility for rampant political corruption rested with the people themselves. It was the "people"—that elusive entity in the Progressive mind that everyone referred to and no one defined—who permitted their representatives to turn over the public wealth to private groups. This only fed the arrogance of the rich. "Little wonder then," complained one inspirationalist, "that certain business and propertied classes have grabbed and are still grabbing everything in sight, as well as appropriating to themselves the machinery of government." [110]

The situation required that ordinary men assert their rights and assume their obligations. At heart, the problem was one of too little individualism rather than too much. A few self-reliant individuals were able to run the show because the average man was content to depend upon others, and through "such dependence" was "dominated and controlled. . . ." [111] With the aid of such reforms as the initiative, referendum, and direct primaries—the panaceas of the Progressive imagination—popular rule and hence clean government would be restored.[112] Moreover, the New Thoughter joined the Progressive in seeking "cooperation and brotherhood," "true service and social justice," and like him believed that "the love which Christ taught . . . would overcome the class hatreds which have organized themselves to bar the way." [113]

X

Such was the context in which the belief that all could succeed was carried into the twentieth century. Though different from the old, the new success ideology retained many of its values. New Thought, though far removed from the Protestant ethic, was actually its heir. The theological basis of this ethic had been progressively eroded in the nineteenth century; and New Thought, by explicitly rejecting Calvinism, merely brought to their logical conclusion those liberalizing tendencies which had produced the humanistic theology of the earlier transcendentalists.[114]

Fresh problems confronting inspirationalists also contributed to the changed content of the new success ideology. Nineteenth-century writers might complain of a decline in morals, but faith had remained intact. By the turn of the century, belief itself had to be defended. Age-old notions of social harmony and a moral order withered in the face of social conflict. At the same time, science and scholarship threatened to drown religion in a sea of skepticism. Some met this confusion with a protective cynicism, but for many the retention of some kind of faith was important; and if the traditional supporting structure was inadequate, a new one had to be built. So, to those confused and in quest of a world-view that allowed for optimism and for hope, New Thought offered a welcome list of certainties. To men who felt crushed by imponderable forces, it offered the assurance of unlimited personal power; to those for whom justice seemed dead, it provided a new basis for a belief in a moral order; for others, rushed and harried to distraction, it offered the balm of "the gospel of relaxation"; to those bereft of traditional religion, it offered a new faith and a new conviction of immortality; for men haunted by the specter of failure, it offered a fresh sense of opportunity and a new gospel of success.

NOTES

1. See Frederic C. Jaher, *Doubters and Dissenters: Cataclysmic Thought in America, 1880–1918* (New York: Free Press Glencoe, 1964), *passim.*

2. Harris E. Starr, "Benjamin O. Flower," *Dictionary of American Biography,* ed. Dumas Malone, VI (1943), 477.

3. *Ibid.*

4. B. O. Flower, " 'Peace, Power and Plenty': A Book Study," *Arena,* XLI (August 1909), 595. This was a review of Orison Swett Marden's *Peace, Power and Plenty.*

5. Review of Marden's *Secret of Achievement* in *The Occult Review,* XX (December 1914), 306.

6. Quoted in Margaret Connolly, *The Life Story of Orison Swett Marden: A Man Who Benefited Men.* (New York: Thomas Y. Crowell Co., 1925), p. 62.

7. *Ibid.,* pp. 114–115.

8. In 1925, Connolly estimated his total sales at nearly three million. *Ibid.,* p. 286.

9. Orison Swett Marden, *Peace, Power and Plenty* (New York: Thos. Y. Crowell and Co., 1909), p. 49. Numerous letters thanking Marden for the "inspiration" he provided can be found in Connolly, *op. cit.,* pp. 283 ff. Among them is one from the famous juvenile judge Ben Lindsey, who wrote: "I owe you a debt I can never repay, for all unconsciously you have been in large measure responsible for the success of our little work out here. I have been inspired, cheered, encouraged, helped, and uplifted, as, I am sure, thousands of others have been by your gospel and your message. . . . I always keep your books on my desk in the court room." Quoted in *ibid.,* p. 283.

10. Elizabeth Towne, *15 Lessons in New Thought, or Lessons in Living* (Holyoke: The Elizabeth Towne Co., 1921), p. 55. This was originally published in 1910.

11. Marden, *Peace, Power and Plenty,* pp. 299–300. See too Horatio

Dresser, *A Book of Secrets* (New York: G. P. Putnam's Sons, 1907), p. 48, and Henry Sherin, *Individual Mastery* (New York: The Trow Press, 1915), p. 75.

12. See John W. Ward, *Andrew Jackson, Symbol for an Age* (New York: Oxford University Press, 1962), pp. 13–97.

13. Marden, *Peace, Power and Plenty*, p. ix.

14. John Carleton Sherman, *The Stunted Saplings* (Boston: Shuman, French and Co., 1911), p. 24. See too John Herman Randall, *The Culture of Personality* (New York: H. M. Caldwell Co., 1912), p. 244, and Grace M. Brown, *Mental Harmony, Its Influence on Life* (New York: Edward J. Clode, 1916), p. 140.

15. It is interesting to note in this connection that Elbert Hubbard, author of the famed *Message to Garcia*, wrote a representative New Thought tract in 1913 called *The Book of Business* (New York: The Roycrofters, 1913).

16. William James, "The Powers of Men," *The American Magazine*, LXV (November 1907), 59.

17. *Ibid.*, p. 64.

18. John Herman Randall, "The Universal Mind or, the Immanent God," *A New Philosophy of Life* (New York: Dodge Publishing Co., 1911), p. 9.

19. See Ralph Waldo Trine, *In Tune With the Infinite* (New York: Dodd, Mead, and Co., 1921), p. 12.

20. A. L. Allen, *The Message of New Thought* (New York: Thos. Y. Crowell Co., 1914), p. 43.

21. Trine, *op. cit.*, p. 38.

22. Trine, *The Land of Living Men* (New York: Thos. Y. Crowell and Co., 1910), pp. 271–272.

23. Randall, "Awakening Latent Mental Powers," *A New Philosophy of Life*, p. 14.

24. Allen, *op. cit.*, p. 141. William James was also an enthusiastic admirer of Bergson. See the *Letters of William James*, ed. Henry James (Boston: Little, Brown and Co., 1926), II, 178–180.

25. It is interesting to note that Horatio Dresser, prominent exponent of the New Thought, studied philosophy under Royce and James at Harvard and later taught there. His doctoral dissertation was on Hegel. See Horatio Dresser, *The Philosophy of the Spirit* (New York: G. P. Putnam's Sons, 1908), pp. 387 ff. On the influence of Hegel, see also William James, "Philosophy," *The Varieties of Religious Experience* (New York: Random House, 1929), p. 439, and Wallace D. Wattles, *Financial Success Through Creative Thought* (Holyoke: The Elizabeth Towne Co., 1927), pp. 6–7.

26. Allen, *op. cit.*, pp. 23–24.

27. Randall, *The Culture of Personality*, pp. vii–viii.

28. Allen, *op. cit.*, p. 107; Henry Wood, *The New Thought Simplified: How to Gain Harmony and Health* (Boston: Lee and Shepard, 1904), p. 103.

29. Sherman, *op. cit.*, p. 3.

30. *Ibid.*, p. 19.

31. Trine, *The Land of Living Men*, p. 269. See too Horatio Dresser, *Voices of Hope* (Boston: George H. Ellis, 1898), p. 40.

32. James, "The Religion of Healthy-Mindedness," *The Varieties of Religious Experience*, p. 90.

33. Ernest Holmes, *New Thought Terms and Their Meanings* (New York: Dodd, Mead and Co., 1942), p. 126.

34. James Allen, *The Mastery of Destiny* (New York: G. P. Putnam's Sons, 1909), pp. iii–iv. See too John B. Anderson, *New Thought, Its Lights and Shadows: An Appreciation and a Criticism* (Boston: Sherman, French and Co., 1911), p. 10.

35. A. L. Allen, *op. cit.*, p. 3.

36. Dorothy Quigley, *Success Is For You* (New York: E. P. Dutton and Co., 1897), p. 165. For emphasis on harmony and wholeness, see Eugene Del Mar, *Spiritual and Material Attraction: A Conception of Unity* (Denver: The Smith-Brooks Printing Co., 1901), p. 5; Horatio Dresser, *The Perfect Whole: An Essay on the Conduct and Meaning of Life* (New York: G. P. Putnam's Sons, 1901), p. 206; and John H. Randall, *The Mastery of Life* (New York: Robert M. McBride Co., 1931), p. 41.

37. A. L. Allen, *op. cit.*, p. 204.

38. *Ibid.*

39. James Allen, *The Path of Prosperity* (New York: R. F. Fenno and Co., 1907), pp. 61–62.

40. Randall, "The Conquest of Fear and Worry," *A New Philosophy of Life*, p. 24.

41. *Ibid.* p. 32.

42. William James, "The Gospel of Relaxation," *Essays on Faith and Morals*, ed. Ralph Barton Perry (New York: Longmans, Green and Co., 1949), pp. 238–239.

43. *Ibid.*, p. 247.

44. *Ibid.*, p. 248.

45. *Ibid.*, p. 250.

46. *Ibid.*, p. 251. For Annie Payson Call's "gospel of relaxation," see her *Power Through Repose* (Boston: Roberts Bros., 1891); *Brain Power for Business Men* (Boston: Little, Brown and Co., 1911); and *How to Live Quietly* (Boston: Little, Brown and Co., 1914). See too Ralph Waldo Trine, *Character-Building Thought Power* (New York: Thos. Y. Crowell and Co., 1899), pp. 41–43.

47. James, "The Gospel of Relaxation," *Essays on Faith and Morals,* p. 255.

48. Wood, *op. cit.,* p. 31.

49. Joseph E. Tuttle, *Prosperity Through Thought Force* (Holyoke: The Elizabeth Towne Co., 1907), p. 79.

50. Towne, *op. cit.,* p. 119.

51. This was defined as "The principle that we attract that to which our thought is attuned." Holmes, *op. cit.,* p. 76.

52. Trine, *Character-Building Thought Power,* p. 27. See too F. W. Sears, *How to Attract Success* (New York: New Thought Publishers, 1914), p. 15.

53. Frederick Clifton Bond, *Success for You* (Los Angeles: The Catterlin Publishing Co., 1933), p. 14.

54. Orison Swett Marden, *The Young Man Entering Business* (New York: Thos. Y. Crowell Co., 1903), p. 279.

55. Randall, Foreword to *A New Philosophy of Life,* p. 34.

56. Hubbard, *The Book of Business,* p. 90. Hubbard belongs to a group of what might be called transitional inspirationalists, who in their writings combined the teachings of the Protestant ethic with those of New Thought. Other examples of this can be found in George H. Knox, *Ready Money* (Des Moines: Personal Help Publishing Co., 1905); Thomas Tapper, *Youth and Opportunity: Being Chapters on the Factors of Success* (New York: The Platt and Peck Co., 1912); and in Marden's *Success* magazine.

57. Marden, *Peace, Power and Plenty,* p. 38.

58. *Ibid.*

59. Wattles, *op. cit.,* pp. 133–134. See too Tuttle, *op. cit.,* p. 154, and Towne, *op. cit.,* p. 44.

60. Helen Post, *A Conquest of Poverty* (Seabreeze, Fla.: International Scientific Association, 1899), p. 10.

61. A. L. Allen, *op. cit.,* p. 223. See too Randall, "The Achievement of Character," *A New Philosophy of Life,* p. 74; Tapper, *op cit.,* pp. 9–16; Joseph E. Tuttle, *The Law of Success* (New York: R. F. Fenno and Co., 1916), p. 9; Ralph Waldo Trine, *What All the World's A-Seeking* (New York: Thos. Y. Crowell & Co., 1899), pp. 11, 58–64; and Frank Haddock, *The King's Achievement: or Power for Success* (Lynn, Mass.: Nichols Press, 1903), p. 191.

62. Stanton D. Kirkham, *Resources: An Interpretation of the Well-Rounded Life* (New York: G. P. Putnam's Sons, 1910), p. 17.

63. John Herman Randall, *The Philosophy of Power, or What to Live For* (New York: Dodge Publishing Co., 1917), pp. 40–41.

64. Trine, *In Tune With the Infinite,* p. 190.

65. Wattles, *op. cit.,* p. 49.

66. *Ibid.,* p. 50.

67. Sears, *op. cit.*, p. 28. See too Julia Seton, *The Science of Success* (New York: Edward J. Clode, 1914), p. 52.

68. Tuttle, *Law of Success*, pp. 107–108.

69. Emerson had written: "The compensations of calamity are made apparent to the understanding . . . after long intervals of time. A fever, a mutilation, a cruel disappointment, a loss of wealth, a loss of friends, seems at the moment unpaid loss, and unpayable. But the sure years reveal the deep remedial force that underlies all facts. The death of a dear friend, wife, brother, lover, which seemed nothing but privation, somewhat later assumes the aspect of a guide or genius; for it commonly operates revolutions in our way of life, terminates an epoch of infancy or of youth which was waiting to be closed, breaks up a wonted occupation, or a household, or style of living, and allows the formation of new ones more friendly to the growth of character. It permits or constrains the formation of new acquaintances and the reception of new influences that prove of the first importance to the next years; and the man or woman who would have remained a sunny garden-flower, with no room for its roots and too much sunshine for its head, by the falling of the walls and the neglect of the gardener is made the banian of the forest, yielding shade and fruit to wide neighborhoods of men." "Compensation," *The Selected Writings of Ralph Waldo Emerson,* ed. Brooks Atkinson (New York: Random House, 1950), pp. 188–189.

70. Wattles, *op. cit.*, p. 148.

71. Horatio Dresser, *Handbook of the New Thought* (New York: G. P. Putnam's Sons, 1917), p. 153.

72. Sears, *op. cit.*, pp. 182–184.

73. Wood, *op. cit.*, p. 94. See too Stanton D. Kirkham, *The Philosophy of Self-Help* (New York: G. P. Putnam's Sons, 1909), p. 266.

74. Dresser, *A Book of Secrets*, p. 7.

75. Dresser, *A History of the New Thought Movement* (New York: Thos. Y. Crowell Co., 1919), p. 331.

76. See *Good Housekeeping*, L, 470–473; LI, 73–77, 431–435. For critiques of New Thought by non-adherents, see "Pathological View of the New Thought As a Form of Mania," *Current Literature*, XLVI (January 1909), 97–99, and W. J. Ghent, "To the Seekers of Success," *The Independent*, LXIX (September 1910), 453–457.

77. See flyleaf of *Arena*, XXV (January 1901).

78. Paul Tyner, "The Metaphysical Movement," *American Monthly Review of Reviews*, XXV (March 1902), 316.

79. Hall dedicated one of his books to Jane Addams, "who is trying to destroy class distinctions through the practice of the Gospel of Love." Bolton Hall, *Things as They are* (New York: The Arcadia Press, 1909). For other of Hall's works relating to reform, see *Even As You and I*

(Boston: Small, Maynard and Co., 1900); *A Little Land and a Living* (New York: The Arcadia Press, 1908); *The Game of Life* (New York: M. M. Breslow Co., 1909); *Three Acres and Liberty* (New York: The Macmillan Co., 1908); and *Free America* (Chicago: L. S. Dickey and Co., 1904).

80. Towne, *op. cit.*, p. 58.

81. Trine, *The Land of Living Men* (New York: Thos. Y. Crowell and Co., 1910).

82. On this theme, see Sidney E. Mead, "American Protestantism Since the Civil War, I: From Denominationalism to Americanism," *The Journal of Religion*, XXXVI (January 1956), 12. See too Edward M. Burns, *The American Idea of Mission* (New Brunswick: Rutgers University Press, 1957).

83. On the importance of the ethic of individual responsibility in the reform mentality, see Richard Hofstadter, *The Age of Reform* (New York: Alfred A. Knopf, 1955), pp. 203 ff.

84. Charles Brodie Patterson, *Dominion and Power: or The Science of Life and Living* (New York: Funk and Wagnalls, 1910), p. 189.

85. Dresser, *A Book of Secrets*, p. 4.

86. Kirkham, *Resources*, p. 172.

87. See Marden, *Peace, Power and Plenty*, pp. 17 ff., and Trine, *In Tune With the Infinite*, p. 177.

88. A. L. Allen, *op. cit.*, p. 222.

89. Tuttle, *Law of Success*, p. 223.

90. Trine, *The Land of Living Men*, p. 15.

91. *Ibid.*, p. 39.

92. Robert H. Bremner, *From the Depths, The Discovery of Poverty in the United States* (New York: New York University Press, 1956), p. 131.

93. Dresser, *A Book of Secrets*, p. 98.

94. A. L. Allen, *op. cit.*, p. 242.

95. Charles G. Davis, *The Philosophy of Life* (Chicago: D. D. Publishing Co., 1910), p. 127. See too Charles Brodie Patterson, *What the New Thought Stands For* (New York: The Alliance Publishing Co., 1901), p. 13.

96. Randall, "The Law of Suggestion," *A New Philosophy of Life*, pp. 24–25.

97. James A. Edgerton, *Invading the Invisible* (New York: The New Age Press, 1931), p. 332.

98. Wood, *op. cit.*, p. 95. See too H. R. Sharman, *The Power of the Will, or Success* (Boston: Roberts Bros., 1894), pp. 45–46. Here, as in other aspects of their thinking, New Thoughters cited Emerson as authority. In this context, Emerson was quoted as follows: "It is easy to see that a great self-reliance, a new respect for the divinity in man, must work a revolution in all the offices and relations of men; in their religion; in

their education; in their pursuits; their modes of living; their associations; in their property; in their speculative views." Quoted in A. L. Allen, *op. cit.*, p. 222.

99. Trine, *The Land of Living Men*, pp. 28–34.

100. *Ibid.*, p. 42.

101. *Ibid.*, p. 69.

102. A. L. Allen, *op. cit.*, p. 237.

103. Frederick Winslow Taylor, *The Principles of Scientific Management* (New York: Hayes and Bros., 1942), pp. 9–10. The book first appeared in 1911.

104. Horatio Dresser, *Human Efficiency: A Psychological Study of Modern Problems* (New York: G. P. Putnam's Sons, 1912), p. v.

105. *Ibid.*, p. 2.

106. See, for example, Edward E. Purinton, *Efficient Living* (New York: Robert M. McBride and Co., 1915), and Luther H. Gulick, *The Efficient Life* (Buffalo: Corlis Co., 1907). An intensive examination of the efficiency cult in the Progressive era is provided in Samuel Haber, *Efficiency and Uplift, Scientific Management in the Progressive Era* (Chicago: University of Chicago Press, 1964).

107. Dresser, *Human Efficiency*, p. 44.

108. See Robert H. Wiebe, *The Search for Order* (New York: Hill and Wang, 1967), pp. 145–166.

109. William H. Whyte, Jr., *The Organization Man* (New York: Simon and Schuster, 1956), p. 29.

110. Trine, *The Land of Living Men*, p. 58.

111. Tuttle, *The Law of Success*, p. 169.

112. See Trine, *The Land of Living Men*, pp. 186–234. The chapter is entitled "Agencies Through Which We Shall Secure the Return of an Efficient People's Government—and the Return of Their Rights."

113. Dresser, *History of the New Thought Movement*, p. 330.

114. The gradual erosion of Calvinist theology in pre-Civil War America is the subject of Joseph Haroutunian's *Piety versus Moralism, The Passing of the New England Theology* (New York: Henry Holt and Co., 1932).

Chapter 7

The American Mystique
of the Mind

I

The ideology of success through mind-power is intimately bound up with the growth of psychotherapy in the present century. Both emerged simultaneousy, and the popularizers of the one were often practitioners of the other. Mental healers have become legion, ranging from students of psychoanalysis to disciples of positive thinking. My concern is not to evaluate these various schools of thought as therapies or sciences for understanding the human personality. The differences among them are glaring; somewhat less clear, but more significant in terms of this study, are their points of convergence. Psychotherapy, generically understood, is more than a development of medicine or science; it is a phenomenon of culture, an aspect of the *zeitgeist* of twentieth-century America. It is this dimension of the psychotherapeutic movement which commands our attention here.

Mind-power and popular psychotherapy have a common root in the mind-cure movement of the nineteenth century. Mind-cure was devoted to using psychological means in helping people suffering from physical illness—a situation in which individuals feel particularly powerless in the face of forces beyond their control. New Thought, an outgrowth of this movement was, as we have noted, a response to socially induced feelings of helplessness. It purported to teach the psychological techniques which empowered individuals to direct their own lives. Mind-power, both as therapy and inspiration, gained force through the crisis of American individualism which resulted from industrialization and related changes in our national life. The concern for buoying up individuals burdened beyond their ability to cope with life runs through the whole mentalistic self-help tradition. Inspirationalists of the old school sought to nurture conscience and instill virtue; inspirationalists of the new concentrate on the cultivation of personal power and self-mastery. By this important shift in emphasis, the new success ideology places the enhancement of ego rather than super-ego at the center of its message.

II

The mind-cure movement grew out of the work and thought of Phineas Parkhurst Quimby, born in Lebanon, New Hampshire, in 1802. His father, a blacksmith, moved to Maine when Quimby was two years old. Quimby grew to manhood and lived there until his death in 1866. He had very little formal schooling, became a clockmaker by trade, and, in his spare time, devised a number of mechanical appliances. His interest in mental healing began in the 1830s when Charles Poyen, a French mesmerist, visited and demonstrated in Belfast, Maine.[1] Shortly thereafter, Quimby embarked on his own career as a healer. His son relates that in the course of his work, Quimby became convinced that disease was psychogenic in origin, that the cause of illness was "an error of the mind." He did not deny the reality of sickness, "but the fact that pain might be a state of the mind, while apparent in the body, he did believe." Through his attempts at mesmeric treatment, he discovered that the hypnotic state was not essential to healing—a discovery later made by Freud—and soon abandoned it altogether. "Instead of putting the patient into a mesmeric sleep, Mr. Quimby would sit by him . . . he would simply converse with him, and explain the causes of the troubles, and thus change the mind of the patient, and disabuse it of its errors and establish the truth in its place; which, if done, was the cure." [2]

At the time of his death in 1866, Quimby was little known outside of Maine.[3] The subsequent spread of his ideas is attributable to several of his patients—Warren Felt Evans, sometimes referred to as the Paul of mental science, Julius and Annetta Dresser, and Mary Baker Eddy. All of these "pioneers of the mental-healing movement were restored invalids," [4] and the emphasis on therapeutics persisted even after the movement expanded its claims to include such things as financial success.

Mind-cure gained momentum in the 1880s and its popularity was quickly felt in the medical profession. Fear was expressed that unless physicians began to study the new therapeutic techniques, the public would depend increasingly on mental healers rather than doctors for the treatment of illness. On the whole, the profession scorned the suggestive therapy used by popular healers. One worried physician pointed out that this only encouraged "the constant exercise of . . . superstitious creeds . . . which proudly show their wonderful, even miraculous, cures, and scoff at the blind and conceited medical profession." [5]

With characteristic tolerance, William James also urged doctors to look seriously at mind-cure and learn what it had to offer. He perceived that the science of psychology was changing and that the therapeutic implications of the new psychology were scarcely realized. Contrasting the "classic academic and the romantic type of imagination," he wrote in 1901:

> The former has a fondness for clear pure lines and noble simplicity in its constructions. It explains things by as few principles as possible and is intolerant of either nondescript facts or clumsy formulas. . . . Until quite recently all psychology was written on classic-academic lines. . . . But of late years the terrace has been overrun by romantic improvers, and to pass to their work is like going from classic to gothic architecture, where few outlines are pure and where uncouth forms lurk in the shadows. . . . The world of mind is shown as something infinitely more complex than was suspected; and whatever beauties it may still possess, it has lost at any rate the beauty of academic neatness.[6]

Important among the "romantic improvers" were mind-curers, and in the 1890s James opposed licensing attempts in Massachusetts which were partially aimed at preventing them from practicing. He objected on the grounds that whole new areas of study in the realm of nervous and mental diseases were opening up. This began in Europe, "when the medical world so tardily admitted the facts of hypnotism to be true; and in this country they have been carried on in a much bolder and more radical fashion by all those 'mind-curers' and 'Christian Scientists' with whose results the public . . . are growing familiar." James held no brief for these healers and their theories. "But," he declared, "their *facts* are patent and startling; and anything that interferes with the multiplication of such facts, and with our freest opportunity of observing and studying them, [would], I believe, be a public calamity." [7] The real interests of medicine required "that mental therapeutics . . . *not* be stamped out, but studied, and its laws ascertained." [8]

When the licensing bill came up again in 1898, he appeared before the Massachusetts legislature and berated the medicos for pushing the measure.

> One would suppose that any set of sane persons interested in the growth of medical truth would rejoice if other persons were found willing to push out their experiences in the mental-healing direction, and provide a mass of material out of which the conditions and limits of such therapeutic methods may at last become clear. One would suppose that our orthodox medical brethren might so rejoice; but instead of rejoicing, they adopt the fiercely partisan attitude of a powerful trades-union, demanding legislation against the competition of the "scabs." . . . The mind-curers and their public return the scorn of the regular profession with an equal scorn, and will never come up for examination. Their movement is a religious or quasi-religious movement; personality is one condition of success there, and impressions and intuitions seem to accomplish more than chemical, anatomical or physiological information. [9]

Though licensing was in fact instituted, doctors were forced to take cognizance of the new therapeutics. A decade after James's eloquent plea, Dr. Richard Cabot—a prominent Boston physician and teacher of clinical medicine at Harvard—acknowledged "that a great deal which the physicians have now taken into their practice they really owe to Quimby and to Christian Science." [10] Psychosomatic medicine in America received its first impulse outside the medical profession.

III

Established religious denominations also felt the impact of the mental healers. Their influence was dramatically witnessed by the formation of the Emmanuel Movement, initiated by the ministers of the largest Episcopal church in Boston. Already known for its extensive social settlement activities, the Emmanuel Church, in 1906, embarked on a "new healing mission." Mental healing joined the social gospel as a means of enhancing the appeal of the established churches.[11]

The leaders of Emmanuel declared that the church had been remiss in abdicating the healing mission of Christ. If she continued to do so, "she must expect to find herself forsaken for strange cults which with all their absurdities aim at supplying present strength for present needs." [12] When criticized for compromising the spiritual ideal of the Gospel, they responded that their healing work had enabled them "to communicate spiritual life and a living faith in God and Christ to hundreds of persons who had remained untouched by religion and whom we could have reached in no other way." [13]

The movement caught on quickly. In a few years, it had branches in several cities outside of Boston, and was represented in most of the major religious denominations.[14] Cautious in their claims, the leaders of Emmanuel emphasized that "although a sound physical and moral method is a valuable adjunct in every branch of medicine, yet viewed as an

independent remedial agent the legitimate sphere of psychotherapy is strictly limited." [15] From its inception, the movement enlisted the cooperation of physicians, and stands as
one of the earliest examples of joint efforts by ministers and
doctors to handle human problems, presaging the large-scale
development of pastoral counseling that has come to pass in
America. Hugo Munsterberg, head of the psychological laboratory at Harvard, praised the movement as deserving "the
highest credit for bringing about a systematic contact between religious faith cure and scientific medicine. . . ." He
hoped that the role of the church would become narrower in
the future, but noted that if "physicians will at last make use
of psychical factors in their regular practice, they ought not
to forget . . . that the important step forward was taken
under the pressure of popular religious movements." [16]

Mind-power inspirationalists were pleased to find "the
control of thought . . . to bring about health, happiness,
and success," being "more and more studied and understood." [17] Mentalism was achieving an acceptance in the most
respectable circles. Furthermore, there was growing recognition that psychological techniques had a much broader area
of application than the cure of disease. Psychotherapy became directed, in a more general way, to the total enhancement of living. Josiah Royce, perhaps the foremost philosophical idealist of his generation, saw the new psychology as
part of a larger movement—"a movement closely connected
with all that is most vital in recent civilization."

Human life has been complicated by so many new personal
and social problems, that man has needed to aim, by whatever
means are possible, towards a much more elaborate knowledge
of his fellow man than was even possible before. . . . The
psychological movement means then something that far tran-

scends the interests of the group of sciences to which the name psychology now applies.[18]

Indeed, psychology was changing from a discipline of study into a way of life. Health, always the aim of therapy, began to take on vastly expanded meaning. In this connection, Royce declared: "Health comes to its fullness . . . when we learn . . . to know better the business of the loyal soul, and better to disregard everything that hinders our devotion to our cause. Our cause, I repeat, is, in one form or another, the progressive incarnation of the divine will in the social order. When we are absorbed in that cause, we are healthy." [19] In a similar vein, an inspirationalist remarked that mental healing, "far from lying wholly within the domain of Psychology," rested on a "foundation of metaphysics and ethics." [20] Here lies the vital connection between psychotherapy and the new success ideology. Both were expressions of a common world-view, of a renascent idealism, committed to a humanistic conception of the individual.

IV

In the early years of this century, psychotherapy was defined broadly enough to include mind-power cultists, ministers, and doctors. Their common ground was "the practice of treating the sick by influencing mental life." [21] This kind of treatment also encompassed the use of "moral and spiritual methods." [22] Little distinction was made between psychological and moral or spiritual counseling. Dr. Richard Cabot of Harvard, expressed the prevalent conviction that it was "unwise . . . to try to distinguish a person's 'mind' from his 'soul' or his 'intellect' from his 'moral life' by any hard-and-fast lines." Successful psychotherapy required treatment of the "whole personality." This breadth of approach made "the American type of psychotherapy . . . distinguishable," and in Cabot's opinion, "in many respects superior to any other type now existing." [23]

This orientation was certainly characteristic of New Thought and related cults, which produced the largest body of psychotherapeutic literature.[24] Munsterberg, of the Harvard psychological laboratory, examining popular treatises, noted that chapters dealing with the medical uses of psychotherapy generally began with a discussion "of the 'mental and moral' factors" involved in illness.[25] This same linkage was maintained by the ministerial leaders of the new healing mission at Emmanuel. They emphasized that numerous nervous disorders had "their main root in the moral region." For example, "selfishness . . . leads to worry, and worry is one of the most prolific causes of neurasthenia and allied troubles." Similarly, "the sense of some moral fault unpurged by penitence creates a dissociation of consciousness which in turn may lead to hysteria, and hysteria . . . can simulate almost any disease and turn life into a prolonged wretchedness." And finally, but most important, "wrong conceptions of God and of His relations to his creatures depress the soul, sink it into melancholy delusions and thereby set up all sorts of functional nervous disturbances." [26] This last point raised a critical question for theologians. Did not the insights of psychotherapy require a reconsideration of doctrine? Ministers, themselves, began to ask whether their religious messages might not be "reconstructed so as to place more emphasis upon hopefulness, cheerfulness, and the joy of being of service to others rather than upon intellectual problems of doctrine, or upon the distressing aspects of the problem of evil, or . . . upon an uncompromising ideal of duty." [27] This was precisely the kind of theological reorientation New Thought had been asking for.

The therapeutic concerns of ministers were often matched by the moral concerns of psychologists. Any science of the human personality must perforce encounter questions of morality. Because the pursuit of knowledge has become so professionalized and fragmented in recent years, this relationship is frequently sloughed over, if not ignored altogether. Early in the century, however, psychology was still being taught in departments of philosophy, and was closely associated with the study of ethics. The kinship between psychologist and moralist is revealed in the following remarks on preventive psychotherapy by the head of one of the nation's leading psychological laboratories in 1909.

> The saloon and its humiliating indecency must disappear and every temptation to intemperance should be removed. Above all, from early childhood the self-control has to be strengthened, the child has to learn from the beginning to know the limits to the gratification of his desires and abstain from reckless over-indulgence. With such a training later on even the temptations of alcoholic beverages would lose their danger. Not less injurious than the strong drinks are the cards. All gambling from the child's play to the stock exchange is ruinous for the psycho-physical equilibrium. The same is true of any overuse of coffee and tea and tobacco, and as a matter of course still more the habitual use of drugs like the popular headache powders and sleeping medicines. The life at home and in public ought to be manifold and expansive but ought to avoid over-excitement and over-anxiety. A good conscience, a congenial home, and a serious purpose are after all the safest conditions for a healthy mind, and the community works in

preventive psychotherapy whenever it facilitates the securing of these three factors.[28]

So conceived, the healthy life and the good life were virtually identical. Psychotherapy applied the terms health and disease to problems that had conventionally been thought of only in moral terms. In consequence, the distinction between sin and sickness has become increasingly vague. The drunkard of the nineteenth century has become the alcoholic of the twentieth; the one was the victim of Satan, the other is the victim of psychic disorder; the drunkard was sick of soul, the alcoholic is mentally ill. The parallels might be extended. Suffice it to say that mind and soul are much less distinguishable today than a century ago.

In inspirational writing, the distinction disappears altogether and healing by mental therapeutics takes on the aspect of spiritual regeneration. Early in the century, New Thoughters welcomed scientific verifications of psychogenic factors in disease as proof of man's "non-material" nature. They predicted that the role of mental therapeutics in medicine would continue to expand and that doctors would become physicians of the soul. In this way science would reinforce faith and the healing message of the gospel would be revived.[29] To one inspirationalist, the spread of psychotherapy made it seem "as if Religion, Medicine, and Psychology had joined hands in forming a New Religion . . . sweeping this country from end to end." [30] A new moral creation—the mind-body-soul complex—had come into being.

This blending of the mental, the physical, and the spiritual was not confined to inspirational advocates of mental healing. There was, even among prominent medical advocates of psychotherapy, the feeling that a proper religious and philosophical orientation was necessary for personal well-being.

Perhaps the foremost medical spokesman for this point of view was James Jackson Putnam, teacher of neuropathology at Harvard and among the leading figures in the profession of his day. In 1909, he wrote two articles emphasizing the importance of philosophical considerations for the future of medicine. He noted that while various types of idealism were in the air, there were still educated persons who clung to a materialistic world-view. This was especially true of scientists who, carried away with admiration for the marvelous mechanisms they helped to discover, "feel themselves under bonds of loyalty to maintain against all comers the eternal validity of the laws of physics." More unfortunate was the fact that this mental set characterized physicians as well. While it might be a matter of small concern to the community how the scientists viewed these questions, the physician's attitudes were of vital importance.

For their work calls on them to deal with persons thrilling with hopes and fears and doubts, brought face to face with the problems of the meaning of sickness and death, of the apparent unfairness in the distribution of changes in this world and of the possibility of life beyond it. How shall they encourage their patients to meet these problems? . . . If the doctrine of free will is, in every sense, a mockery . . . if spontaneity, the conscious choice of "purposes" and conscious effort to attain them are but dreams; if "adaptation" to an environment which in the last analysis is a physical environment is the principle by which we are finally governed; if we have not the right to consider it—I will not say proved, but possible that the universe is, in some sense the expression of a purpose, of the will of a moral personality, then the lot of those on whom the stress of life falls heavily is indeed harder than, in my judgment, it should be held. And, therefore, if there are solid arguments by which some portion of these pessimistic doctrines can be con-

troverted and their opposites established, it is the duty of physicians to know them, in their practical and their theoretical
bearings, and to make them known. . . .[31]

Hence, Putnam felt obliged "to reinforce the doctrine—
which common sense inclines already to accept—that the
world is demonstrably a world of rationality and order and
presumably of goodness, and that it rests with each person
who desires to find the elements of rationality in the universe
to seek them in himself."[32] The physician's concern over
problems of pessimism and free will is a measure of how far
beyond the inspirational realm the reverberations of the new
success ideology had traveled.

V

Against this backdrop of concern over materialism and idealism, the new psychology brought forth one of its most pregnant discoveries—the existence in man of a "subconscious"
mind. No one was able to define this dimension of the psyche
very precisely. Nonetheless, the new awareness of psychic
processes beyond normal consciousness had an immediate impact in both medical[33] and inspirational circles.[34] Self-help
popularizers seized upon the discovery and invested it with
the most far-reaching implications. One described "the great
subconscious mind" as "an infinite storehouse of intelligence
and power . . ." Once man learned its laws, he would be
able to "draw from its inexhaustible depths at will to supply
his needs and wants."[35] Here was further proof that men
could remake themselves at will.

The new transcendentalists conceived of each person as a partial incarnation of the universal essence. Each individual was, in a manner of speaking, a fragment of the Universal Soul. The discovery of the subconscious was used as verification of this notion. Mind-power advocates declared "that the newer psychology which recognizes the subconscious mind, and admits its powers, undreamed of heretofore, is proving to us most clearly that this subconscious mind, resident in all, is of the same essence as the Universal Mind." [36] Eager to stamp their teachings with the impress of science, inspirationalists emphasized that the discovery of this dimension of psychic activity came from science, not religion. It was science which had finally "come forward to affirm that in his deeper self, in his subconscious or subliminal being, man possesses the qualities that relate him vitally and essentially to the Infinite Mind of the Universe." [37] Thus, in the popular idiom, the idea of the subconscious was transmuted into a metaphysical concept and used to enhance the belief in individual power. Science, once again, was made to support the claims of faith.

VI

The theories of Sigmund Freud entered the American thought stream amidst the eddies of ideas we have described. At least two decades of intensive interest in various kinds of mental healing had prepared the public mind for the new discipline. Initially, both the medical and psychological professions received Freud's insights with skepticism and even hostility.[38] On the other hand, mind-power advocates welcomed

Freud as a distinguished addition to the growing galaxy of mental healers. In 1899, before Freud was much known in America, one inspirationalist described the curative theories of New Thought in terms which illuminate its later affinity for psychoanalysis. He stated that the subconscious was frequently a repository for disturbing thoughts which the individual was not conscious of, and that an awareness of these thoughts must be achieved if their disruptive force was to be eliminated. "Accordingly," he wrote, "real entrance into the precincts of the New Thought world means that one shall pass through a long period of self-revelation, or coming to consciousness of that which has hampered, oppressed, sickened, and enslaved the spirit. In other words, the process is the search for freedom." [39] When Freud became known in America, New Thoughters embraced him as one of their own. "The psychologist," one inspirationalist declared, "who . . . like Dr. Freud, can diagnose from the symptoms of the body their causes in the soul, and can compel his patient to set to work to counteract his suppressed hallucinations, or dissolve his *ideés fixes*, or discuss his phobia, is in reality applying a spiritual power to disease . . ." [40] Critics, too, viewed psychoanalysis as a variant of spiritual healing and attacked it as a new form of mysticism. One such wrote that anyone claiming cure through psychoanalysis placed himself in the company of devotees of hypnotism, divine healing, and Christian Science, and attributed the rise of the new therapy to the "general mystic tendency in the modern world." [41]

Arguments of science or mysticism apart, certain similarities between psychoanalysis and popular mind-cure did exist. Religious healers, for example, were aware of the importance of the therapist-patient relationship, and of the value of catharsis in the therapeutic process. Describing the techniques of the Emmanuel group, Ray Stannard Baker observed that before successful treatment could take place, the patient "must unburden his soul, must let the minister who is treating him understand to the depths all the sources of his troubles." Without this, cure was impossible but "the very fact that a sufferer can thus unburden himself . . . often starts him on his way towards better living." [42] Even on the level of theory, inspirationalists, in some ways, anticipated Freud. In 1914, one New Thoughter articulated a notion strikingly similar to the pleasure-pain principle.

> There exist in man two opposite forces or principles. . . . The one has positive, constructive, and upbuilding tendencies; the other negative, destructive, and tearing-down tendencies; the one constructs and builds, and is the basis of all life and growth; the other dissolves, disintegrates, and tears down, and is the cause of all weakness, dissolution, and decay. The one is active and directs the life-forces to build; the other is inactive and negatives the same forces. The one produces unfoldment, development, and growth; the other, arrested strength, stagnation, and decay. [43]

This appeared six years before Freud published *Beyond the Pleasure Principle*. To be sure, the similarities between Freudianism and the theory and technique of popular mind-cure movements are only superficial. Their importance lies in illuminating the remarkable receptivity of Americans to psychoanalysis, a fact which is quite inexplicable without an awareness of the role of mentalism in American culture before Freud became known. Notions resembling his ideas were in the air, so to speak, and provided a cultural atmosphere into which psychoanalysis could enter and flourish with relatively little resistance.

The prior existence of a large-scale psychotherapeutic

movement also significantly conditioned the way in which Freud's ideas were interpreted. The philosophical bias of mind-cure required that certain aspects of psychoanalytic theory be played down, and inspirationalists entirely ignored whatever pessimism resided in Freud's thought. For them, psychoanalysis was not something new so much as a confirmation of what they already believed. One inspirationalist declared that all psychic researchers, even those not aware of the fact, were "really seeking for the assurance that man is a spiritual being, living in a spiritual universe, whose true ideals belong not to time but to eternity." He went on:

> As the Freudian school of psychoanalysis would explain it, the age in which we have been living has tended to suppress the instinctive, natural desires of man to experience a spiritual freedom, to attain a moral stability and to realize a sense of something permanent and of infinite value within himself. The practical philosophy, the low ideals and the selfish motives that dominate the age have all tended to limit the normal satisfaction of these instinctive human needs, that are as deep as life itself, and to stultify man's expression of his natural moral aims and spiritual aspirations. And in this field of psychic research there are many who honestly think they have found an outlet for what has been suppressed in them for so long.[44]

Freud would scarcely have given any such explanation for human ills, but men agitated by such concerns were drawn to his theory. Furthermore, this was not confined to inspirationalists, but was true of physicians as well. Among Freud's early converts in the medical profession, many shared the broader philosophical orientation of the mind-cure movement. Dr. Isador Coriat, co-author of *Mind and Medicine*, the bible of the Emmanuel movement, was among the earliest and most prominent American physicians to endorse psycho-analysis.[45] James Jackson Putnam, the first president of the American Psychoanalytic Association, was also a representative of this tendency. Discussing the qualities requisite in a good psychoanalyst, he wrote:

> That a thorough student of psychoanalysis, earnestly desiring to learn all that can be learned about the nature of mental phenomena, should be contented to assume that he can neglect that portion of knowledge of the mind which he can get only by philosophic methods, would be equivalent to his assuming that from observing the symptoms of a psychoneurosis he could learn to understand the real conditions of which the symptoms are but symbols. The mind contains a real, permanently abiding energy of which the life of the universe itself is made. From the standpoint of the nature of his mind, a man belongs to the eternal and immortal realities of the universe. In order to realize this he must learn to believe that he speaks the truth when he talks of the world of spirit, and says that the things which are unseen are eternal.[46]

Freud himself expressed gratitude for Putnam's efforts in behalf of the psychoanalytic movement, but was disturbed by his insistence on placing it in the service of a particular philosophy. Combining appreciation with criticism, Freud wrote:

> The most noteworthy personal relationship which resulted at Worcester [during Freud's trip to Clark University in 1909], was that established with James J. Putnam, teacher of neuropathology at Harvard University. . . . Yielding too much to the great ethical and philosophical bent of his nature, Putnam later required of psychoanalysis what, to me, seems an impossible demand. He wished that it should be pressed into the service of a certain moral, philosophical conception of the

universe; but Putnam has remained the chief prop of the psychoanalytic movement in his native land.[47]

Putnam, however, was only a representative of an endemic American idealism. The same quality of mind which molded psychoanalytic theory to philosophic purposes also made possible its widespread acceptance. As we noted with New Thought, this idealistic world-view fit in well with the Progressive temper. Putnam and other early medical converts to Freud's theories were generally liberals in other areas as well,[48] and "the Progressive hope that man could improve himself and his environment was the keynote of pre-war psychoanalysis." [49] This commitment to the individual has remained an enduring aspect of the psychoanalytic movement in America. William Alanson White—founder of the psychoanalytic institute that bears his name—gave eloquent expression to the reconciliation between humanism and science that psychotherapeutics had to offer. In words that might well have come from a New Thought manual, he wrote:

Man has had to repeatedly renounce cherished convictions of his own importance and significance in the universe. His self-regard has been wounded by each dethronement forced upon him by the advances in science. But as compensation for being forced to a recognition of his own insignificance he has gradually become, not merely an inhabitant of the universe, organically separate, distinct and apart from its operations except as he may control small bits of it in his immediate neighborhood, but a part of this gigantic affair, infinite in time and space, and a medium through which it is focused and in accordance with the laws of which he has his being and finds his ways of self-expression. While he has contracted on the one hand he has infinitely expanded on the other, and instead of just losing his importance he has been reinstated and re-enthroned as the central figure in the universe, by and through which the cosmos must, in the last analysis, be interpreted and receive its meaning.[50]

One, of course, may not generalize about the whole psychoanalytic movement from the idealism of certain of its leaders. No doubt, there are within the profession representatives of widely differing philosophical orientations. This should not obscure the fact that a broad current of idealism characterizes the American psychotherapeutic movement as a whole. Among those attracted to mental healing—psychoanalysts, pastoral healers, and mind-curers—there were common concerns extending beyond the cure of disease. These included: an awareness of the need to apply balm to the bruises sustained by the human ego in the nineteenth century; a desire to restore man to a position of pre-eminence in the cosmic scheme of things; and a felt need to preserve the notion that the individual was free in a universe that was rational, ordered, and just.

VII

Around the turn of the century, devotees of mind-power expanded their claims to include the achievement of material success.[51] It was logical that the new defenders of individualism should become the popularizers of its greatest symbol. As the classic rags-to-riches literature waned, a mentalistic success literature arose to take its place. The new teachers of "how-to-succeed" drew more from psychology than from religion, and techniques of healthy habit formation replaced the earlier moralists' exhortatory calls to virtue. The aim of the new gospelers of success was the achievement of self-mastery. Through control of the self, the individual could master, even in large measure determine, his external environment.

One of the first popularizers of psychological techniques for getting ahead in the world was Frank Channing Haddock, whose work stands as something of a bridge between New Thought and the more secular inspiration of the 1920s. Haddock, the son of a minister, was a lawyer and a popular lecturer on ethics and psychology. He was the author of the Power Book Library, a series of seven self-help books. The first of these, *Power of Will*, appeared in 1907. Over a twenty-year period, it had sales of upwards of three quarters of a million copies, surpassing those of any other turn-of-the-century success book.[52] Haddock stressed the volitional power of the individual in a manner which clearly marks his affinity for the new transcendentalism. He wrote:

> The Will is God, the Will is Man,
> The Will is power loosed in thought;
> In Will th'unfathomed self began,
> In Will the lesser mind is wrought;
> Nothing is will-less entity:
> All one—to act, to will, to be.
> He only is who wills to live
> The best his nature prophesies:
> Master of fate, executive
> Of Self—a sovereign strong and wise.
> Art thou a pigmy? Courage, soul!
> For thee, as all, the Kingly goal.[53]

Along with discussions of "will-culture," Haddock provided exercises for developing the senses, improving powers of attention and memory, enlarging the imagination—in short, for training the various mental faculties.[54] The development of "mind-power" occupied the same position in the new literature of self-help that the development of character had in the old.

Introducing *Business Power, A Practical Manual in Financial Ability*, a later work in the Power Book series, Haddock explained that he was not offering advice on specific business techniques. His purpose was not "instruction in the conduct of . . . business, but suggestion on the practical psychology of business power." [55] "The foundation and edifice of business," he instructed his readers, "are first of all psychic. . . ." [56] This held for other aspects of living as well. The new success cultists were offering a comprehensive approach to life rather than advice on the particulars of making a living. This links them to the nineteenth-century inspirational tradition, and distinguishes their work from guides such as Dale Carnegie's *How to Win Friends and Influence People*, which offer direction, in a more practical vein, on such matters as writing business letters, conversing over the telephone, or winning the cooperation of business associates.[57]

Mind-power, of course, needed to address itself to problems which the earlier rags-to-riches popularizers had not troubled about. The need for restraint had motivated much of the older inspirational writing; the need for confidence motivated much of the new. "However it may have been in the era of wooden shoes," wrote Haddock, "to-day the test requires the very utmost of two indispensable qualities, the quality of courage and the quality of confidence." It was no longer enough "to have the old-time plodding merchant's faith . . ." Success now required a faith "electric enough to travel a discovered highway against a universe." [58] Haddock's answer for building such faith was tantamount to the will to believe. "If you long enough assume . . . that you are full of sound, red-blooded courage and are vitally confident in yourself and your business, you will in the end actually possess these splendid qualities." [59]

The belief in the power to assume or to will what one wished was not, as it appears, simply a pre-emption of attributes previously considered divine. Rather, it was faith transliterated into the modern idiom. As old structures of belief crumbled, man's need to believe in a power beyond himself required a new means of expression. Psychology and the new transcendentalism combined to provide that means. Man's link to the Infinite was the subconscious which could be controlled and made to serve the individual's ends. As Haddock explained:

> We may train the subjective mind, that which connects the individual mind with the Infinite, to use its telepathic ability and to draw on the larger Infinite Reservoir, for new ideas and greater intuitional knowledge of even practical affairs. So, by insisting to yourself, say, at stated times—morning or night— "I, IN MY DYNAMIC POWER AS A THINKER, COMMAND THAT PHASE OF MYSELF WHICH RESTS ON AND NEAREST THE INFINITE . . . TO DRAW FORTH FROM THE DEPTH AND THE VASTNESS OF LIFE, NEW POWER, NEW THOUGHT, NEW PLANS AND METHODS FOR MY BUSINESS AND MY SUCCESS." Sooner or later the subjective self will hear, obey, and report. [60]

Thus, by repeated affirmation or suggestion, man could make or unmake himself and his fortune. In this context, suggestion takes on the quality of prayer. Praying to God for the realization of one's desires gives way to suggesting their fulfillment to the subconscious. Both are really appeals to a supernatural agency, with the difference that the latter has a "scientific" ring attuned to the modern ear.

"Health, wealth, and happiness" through suggestion was popularized in a more secular form in the 1920s under the heading of "applied psychology." With a touch of exasperation, one commentator at the beginning of the decade noted the "rampant systems of so-called 'applied psychology,' which profess to teach everything—from curing gall-stones to the secret of perpetual happiness, fame, and prosperity." [61] Among these systems was Swoboda's "Subtle Principle of Success . . . destined to revolutionize the human race by raising it . . . to a new and higher plane . . . of Happiness, Superiority, Prosperity, Supremacy, Pleasure, Freedom and Liberty." [62] Another was Pelmanism, which received the support of George Creel, an old Progressive who had headed the Committee of Public Information—the government's chief propaganda agency—during World War I. In one advertisement, Creel gave the following endorsement: "Talk of quick and large salary raises suggests quackery, but with my own eyes I saw bundles of letters telling how Pelmanism had increased earning capacity from 20 to 200 per cent.—I say deliberately and with deepest conviction, that Pelmanism will do what it promises to do." [63] The most popular apostle of the powers of suggestion was, ironically enough, a foreign import—Emil Coué, who arrived in this country in 1923. Creel, forgetting his association with Pelmanism, ridiculed the enthusiastic welcome accorded the healer of Nancy. "Instead of being laughed out of the country, M. Coué was hailed as the prophet of a new order, and thousands gibbered his formula for happiness and prosperity: 'Day by day, in every way, I am getting better and better.' " [64] Coué, himself, found "Americans in general more responsive . . . than the French or English." [65] Even certain of the clergy were pleased by Coué's appearance. Here was mind-cure without threat of competing denominations. To one Baptist minister, it seemed that Coué offered "everything that was ever of any good in Christian Science." Yet he gave it "without the bunk and junk that have made Christian Science neither scientific nor Christian." [66]

To be sure, Coué offered nothing strikingly new. Like his inspirational counterparts in America, he placed the center of man's power in the subconscious. There, he claimed, "is the source of creation and inspiration; it is the mysterious power that germinates ideas and affects their materialization in the conscious form of action." [67] In the 1920s, anything which referred to that "mysterious power" found a receptive audience. Inspirationalists, themselves, were aware of the public's fascination. Warren Hilton—founder of an organization called the Society for Applied Psychology and author of an inspirational series of books—remarked that the "fad of the hour" was the subconscious mind. "It is the chief topic of discussion in religious circles, health resorts and women's clubs . . . [and] is employed by the unlettered with as much easy assurance as by the scientific." [68] Commenting on this phenomenon, Dr. Adolf Meyer, one of the country's most prominent psychiatrists, wrote:

> The recent wave of uncritical popularization of psychoanalysis has undoubtedly added to the inflammability of popular imagination and to the widespread notion that plausability and desirability are sufficient evidence of truth and actuality. Everybody seems to be perfectly ready to think of the "unconscious self" as if its existence, in whatever form you might want to imagine it, could no longer be disputed.
>
> The concept of the "subconscious" is a convenient one because you can make it out to consist of what suits your theory

or wish. Freud makes it one thing, Morton Prince another, and Coué yet another. . . .

Turning specifically to Coué, Meyer expressed the opinion that "this enthusiastic and thoroughly sincere man . . . who did a lot of good in his sphere" could not avoid doing a certain disservice to the cause of science. "With all his good will and efforts . . . Coué will never be able to eradicate from his patients a certain attitude of mysticism, which is apt to oppose itself to what is scientifically verifiable and commendable. . . ." [69]

Advocates of Couéism steadfastly denied the charge. While admitting that autosuggestion was nothing "more nor less than simply 'thinking' ourselves well," one defender hastened to add that it contained nothing of faith healing but rested "on rational grounds for belief—belief, in other words, based on reason." [70] This was typical of purveyors of "applied psychology." Mysticism was not respectable to engineers, technicians, and bureaucrats, and inspirationalists had to disguise their potions. Warren Hilton, for example, took pains to point out that his books had nothing to do with "telepathy, spiritism, clairvoyance, animal magnetism . . . astrology or witchcraft . . ." On the contrary, he contended, "applied psychology" by revealing mental processes was "laying a scientific basis for a highly differentiated type of efficiency engineering." [71] New Thought had looked forward to a reconciliation with science, but in the more secular atmosphere of the 1920s, inspirationalists found it necessary to eschew any connection with the avowed supernaturalism of their predecessors.

To move from the bottle's label to its contents, however, is to find that "applied psychology" and New Thought were composed of identical ingredients. "Scientific" inspirationalists also found the classic equation—industry, frugality, and temperance equals success—inadequate.[72] They offered surer nostrums based on scientific discoveries which revealed "beyond the world of the senses and beyond the domain of consciousness, a wide and hitherto hidden realm of human energies and resources." [73] They promised to plumb "the depths of this reservoir of mental power," and to teach "the means of tapping its resources." In this way, they could provide anyone "the master key to achievement" and teach them "to use it with confidence and with the positive assurance of success." [74] Like New Thoughters, "applied psychologists" made boundless claims. In this vein, Coué wrote: "I hope to show . . . that the domain of auto-suggestion is practically unlimited. Not only are we able to control and modify our physical functions, but we can develop in any desired direction our moral and mental faculties merely by the proper exercise of suggestion. . . ." [75]

Similarities between religious and secular inspirationalists extended to their specific techniques as well. "Applied psychologists" advised practicing the affirmation of desires during periods of extreme relaxation—states of reverie or half-wakefulness—when the mind was most receptive to suggestion.[76] In New Thought, this was designated as "entering the silence." Likewise both purported to teach "how to make hard tasks easy . . . how to accomplish things with a minimum of effort and nerve expenditure." [77] In the terminology of "applied psychology," the principle involved here was labeled the law of reversed effort; in the lexicon of New Thought, it was called the law of non-resistance. Both groups, then, encouraged the passive rather than the active mood, receptivity rather than struggle. Further similarities might be enumerated. Suffice it to say that, allowing for differences in terminology, "applied psychologists" continued to popularize the ideology of success as it had been reformulated by the idealistic defenders of individualism early in the century.

The mystique of mind-power in the 1920s was enhanced, from outside the inspirational sphere, by the emergence of the behaviorist school of psychology under the leadership of John B. Watson. While behaviorism was deterministic, and hence philosophically at odds with the mind-power movement, it encouraged the notion that, through mental manipulation, individuals could be developed in any direction desired. This was expressed in Watson's famous dictum: "Give me a dozen healthy infants, well-formed, and my own specified world to bring them up in and I'll guarantee to take any one at random and train him to become any type of specialist I might select—doctor, lawyer, artist . . . regardless of his talents, penchants, tendencies, abilities, vocations, and race of ancestors." [78] Thus, like the new inspiration, Watson proffered a doctrine of limitless possibilities for the individual. Inherent limitation was dismissed as an illusion. There was no such thing "as an inheritance of *capacity, talent, temperament, mental constitution,* and *characteristics.* These things . . . depend on training that goes on mainly in the cradle." [79] The hope behaviorism held forth took on millennial proportions. "For the universe will change," Watson declared, "if you bring up your children, not in the freedom of the libertine, but in behavioristic freedom—a freedom which we cannot even picture in words, so little do we know of it. Will not these children in turn, with their better ways of living and thinking, replace us as society and in turn bring up their children in a still more scientific way, until the world finally becomes a place fit for human habitation?" [80] Thus did behaviorism hold the promise of perfection for both man and society. The promise was an appealing one. "More than any interpretation of psychology, with the exception of the psychoanalytic theory," one student has noted, "behaviorism has awakened popular interest in the United States." [81] Though behaviorism and the success ideology ultimately rested on different premises, their teachings bore important similarities. Both were boundlessly optimistic about human potentialities and offered easy and "fool-proof" techniques for developing them; both regarded their methods, very democratically, as effective for *all* people; and finally, both placed man's strength and salvation in the realm of psychological manipulation. Thus behaviorism added another stream to the swelling waters of mentalism in twentieth-century America.

VIII

The most recent popularization of success through mind-power comes as part of Norman Vincent Peale's gospel of "positive thinking." A few figures concerning his popularity may serve as some indication of the quantitative dimension of this kind of inspiration in contemporary America.

In 1957, Peale reached an estimated audience of thirty million a week.[82] In 1954, 150 newspapers carried his syndicated column, "Confident Living"; his radio show, "The Art of Living," was broadcast into a million homes; his television show was shown over 140 stations; and his magazine *Guideposts* had a circulation of 650,000. Peale also puts out long-playing inspirational records, does extensive lecturing, and has a column in *Look* entitled "Norman Vincent Peale Answers Your Questions." [83] His *Power of Positive Thinking*

(1952) had sales of two million by 1955 and was only surpassed in the non-fiction best-seller category during these years by the *Revised Standard Version of the Bible*.[84]

As a popularizer of the mentalistic self-help tradition, Peale is without peer, past or present. He markets his inspiration with all the flair of a top-notch entrepreneur. "Like thousands of other clergymen," notes one admirer, "Dr. Peale takes his texts from the Old and New Testaments but, unlike most of them, he interprets Christianity as a highly useful scientific and modern commodity for modern people, and dispenses it with the same kind of skill that astute corporation executives use in selling shoes, stoves or automobiles. . . ." [85] Part of his appeal, too, is his complete lack of pretension. The son of a Methodist minister, Peale was raised in Ohio in a strict prohibitionist household. His teaching, he explains, is intended "for the plain people of this world, of whom certainly I am one. I was born and reared in humble midwestern circumstances, in a dedicated home. The everyday people of this land are my own kind whom I know and love and believe in with great faith." [86]

Early in his son's career, the elder Peale criticized Norman for overdressing his sermons. "The job of a preacher is to simplify, not to complicate . . . There's no subject on earth that can't be put simply, if you will just think clearly and logically about it, and use plain instead of fancy language . . . In your desire to impress people with your own profundity, you seem to have forgotten that the way to the human heart is through simplicity." [87] Peale heeded the lesson well, and left scholarly preaching and serious theology to others. "He was not an intellectual," his biographer tells us, "he had never pretended to be one." [88] Peale assures his readers that academic excellence is not necessary for a successful life. "Just because somebody gets an A in college doesn't make him the greatest man in the United States, because maybe his A's will stop when he gets his diploma, and the fellow who got C's in school will go on later to get the real A's in life." [89] There is, then, a populistic anti-intellectualism in Peale's work. This reflects the democratic quality of his appeal, which is directed to ordinary people and pays homage to the common sense of "plain folk."

Carrying the functional defense of faith to its ultimate extreme, Peale contends that *"Christianity is entirely practical."* [90] Introducing his *Power of Positive Thinking,* he writes: "This book teaches applied Christianity; a simple yet scientific system of practical techniques of successful living that works." [91] As illustration, he tells of one of the "most remarkable people" he ever met, a saleswoman who was having business difficulties until she learned to have faith. Now she declares, "God helps me sell vacuum cleaners." [92]

Peale's most striking story of faith and monetary success is the one of Maurice and Alice Flint. In a time of trouble, they consulted Peale, who advised them to repeat the following New Testament injunction whenever they felt despondent: "If ye have faith as a grain of mustard seed . . . nothing shall be impossible unto you." Flint asked his wife for a mustard seed to carry as a reminder, and she obliged with one from the family pickle jar. One day, feeling low, he reached into his pocket for the seed, but it was gone. To guard against losing it again, he hit upon the idea of placing it in a plastic container. He then began to make costume jewelry out of mustard seeds in plastic containers. The jewelry was advertised as "Symbol of faith—a genuine mustard seed enclosed in sparkling glass, makes a bracelet with real meaning." According to Peale, "these articles sold like hot cakes." Now the Flints own a mustard seed plant in the Midwest and have become quite prosperous. Peale concludes the story, urging his readers to take heart, for through faith "perhaps you, too, will get an idea that will rebuild not only your life but your business as well." [93] Will Herberg, in his study of contemporary American religion, remarks: "Of course, religious Americans speak of God and Christ, but what they seem to regard as really redemptive is primarily religion, the 'positive' attitude of *believing*. It is this faith in faith, this religion that makes religion its own object, that is the outstanding characteristic of contemporary American religiosity." [94] This cast of mind, however, extends well beyond the avowedly religious. Among secularists, the "faith in faith" or the will to believe, finds its outlet in popular psychotherapeutics. Thus the belief in the realizable wish is one of those pervasive assumptions, transcending particular groups, which define the common culture of an era.

In a manner reminiscent of the efficiency cult of the Progressive period, Peale urges that devotional expressions be studied "from an efficiency point of view," [95] and considers it "a mistake to think that laws of efficiency do not apply to prayer." [96] He emphasizes that God "is as real as your wife, or your business partner, or your closest friend," [97] and recommends imitating him and his wife, who "have the policy of taking God into working partnership in all our problems and activities." [98] Peale has rejected the orthodoxy of his background and is a liberal in theological terms. The just God has been replaced by the benevolent father. Peale insists that "God never meant us to carry around our necks the millstones of old misdeeds. We can be free of a sense of guilt about them." [99] Similarly the concept of original sin has given way to a benign view of man. "One element in the adventure of self-discovery is to become aware of our innate goodness. Whether you are prepared to admit it or not, you *are* a good person basically." [100]

Thus Peale continues in the inspirational tradition initiated by New Thoughters. Like them, he de-emphasizes struggle in the quest for success. "Americans," he writes, "are inheritors of the Horatio Alger tradition: 'strive and succeed.' The author is an apostle of hard work, of the good old American principle of creating your own wealth and position by means of your own abilities and efforts. But there is a sense in which it is a mistake to try too hard. Effortless ease is the procedure best designed to achieve superior results with the least strain." [101] Similarly, injunctions to be honest, prudent, and frugal have been replaced with admonitions to "flush out your thoughts." [102] Peale tells us we require "a mind emptying at least twice a day, more often if necessary." [103] Like his inspirational predecessors, he uses suggestion as the chief means of filling the mind with wholesome thoughts. The formula for getting what you want out of life is "(1) PRAYERIZE, (2) PICTURIZE, (3) ACTUALIZE." [104] The force of the Protestant ethic has clearly diminished. The virtues which the Puritans extolled, which Franklin immortalized, and which Alger tried to preserve, have taken second place to the "powers of mind" in the success cult of the twentieth century.

"Positive thinking," the most recent variant of this cult, combines the religious and secular inspirationalism of New Thought and popular psychotherapeutics into a single system. The religio-psychiatric clinic created under Peale's auspices stands as a symbol of this fusion. Established in 1937 with the cooperation of Dr. Smiley Blanton, a psychoanalyst, the clinic began as a free service of the Marble Collegiate Church. In 1953, it was organized on an independent basis as the American Foundation of Religion and Psychiatry. Cooperation between ministers and doctors urged in the early years of the century has become increasingly widespread and has achieved a large measure of respectability in both medical and religious circles.[105] Doctors are more willing to discuss morals and the therapeutic value of religious faith. Clergymen, on the other hand, devote more time to learning psychiatric theories and techniques for use in pastoral counseling. Remarking on this phenomenon, one contemporary inspirationalist notes "how shrewdly psychiatry documents religion and how, in turn, religion elevates and universalizes the findings of psychiatry. To those most familiar with these mutually complementary aspects of reality, it would seem that religion and psychiatry were twin angels, bending in unison to lift up ailing and bewildered man." [106] The cooperation of religion and psychiatry in the amelioration of human problems is symptomatic of the merging of concepts of sin and sickness which characterizes our age. Faith and science can find such a common meeting ground because of the close identity which has developed between mind and soul in the American cosmology. This amalgam of supernaturalism and secular psychology marks one of the major ideational creations of the twentieth century.

Blanton, the psychoanalyst, and Peale, the minister, can be seen as archetypes of this new creation. "It is my belief," Blanton writes, "that the psychiatrist has a substantial contribution to make to the religious life of the normal man or woman." [107] He also contends that psychiatry seeks "to renew faith where faith has been lost; faith in self, faith in fellow men, and faith in God." [108] Peale, in turn, acknowledges "the practical working unity between religion and psychiatry." [109] More than that, he believes "in being truly and completely scientific and rational in religious faith and practice." [110] "Christianity . . ." he declares, "is itself a science," [111] and the New Testament a textbook of spiritual laws "as specific as the laws of physics and chemistry." [112] Carrying the comparison further, Peale explains that the minister uses "group therapy"[113] on his congregation and "should be looked upon in the community as a skilled, well-trained scientific man—a shepherd of human souls, a physician of personality."[114] Thus have the ideas of Quimby and New Thought penetrated the mainstream of American Christianity and beyond.

Like early mind-power advocates, Peale addresses himself to the need to build the individual ego. "Every normal person," he writes, "wants power over circumstances; power over situations; power over fear; power over weakness; power over themselves."[115] Having stated the desire, Peale offers the assurance that "everyone can have that power,"[116] —an assurance that rests on the belief in the omnipotence of thought.[117] Peale's biographer relates the minister's encounter with this notion. "In his delving into psychiatric literature, Norman came across a sentence that seems to state the principle even more explicitly than the biblical saying, 'As a man thinketh, so is he': 'In physics, the basic factor is force, in psychology, the basic factor is the realizable wish.' . . . It was around this concept that Norman built the new book, *The Power of Positive Thinking.*"[118] Peale's message in this and his other inspirational writings was little more than a re-statement of what mentalistic self-helpers had been saying for more than half a century. To think defeat was to court it. Men who would achieve success and happiness must think positively. The victorious "train the mind to think victory" and as a result gain it.[119] Mind-training, once mastered, can "regenerate a person, bring him into touch with his own creative forces and, in turn, with the infinite forces of the universe."[120] The notion of mind as somehow relating man to supernatural forces remains the key to individual power. Whatever its promise of material rewards, the success ideology is rooted in the idealistic tradition.

A major strain in American idealism, from Emerson onward, has been an emphasis on psychological self-manipulation as a means of effecting reality. In New Thought and its inspirational offspring, the often poetic exaggerations of the Concord Sage have become quite literal. The result has been the widespread popularization of notions of mental omnipotence.[121] These find expression in such success formulas as Peale's "prayerize, visualize, actualize." The metamorphosis of the self-help ideology from "rags to riches" to "think your way to success" was, as we have noted, a response to the crisis of individualism that accompanied America's emergence as a modern industrial state. As men became cogs in complex organizational structures, their sense of personal significance diminished. The increasing concern for individual power reflected anxiety over the loss of it.

Discussing the meaning of success, and the individual's quest for power, in our society, psychoanalyst Karen Horney notes: "The striving for power serves in the first place as a protection against helplessness, which . . . is one of the basic elements in anxiety. . . . The weaker he factually becomes, the more anxiously he has to avoid anything that has a faint resemblance to weakness." [122] Furthermore, she observes: "Protection against helplessness and insignificance or humiliation can be had, in our culture, by striving for possession, inasmuch as wealth gives both power and prestige." [123] In this light, it seems reasonable to suggest that the assurance of material success in the cult of mind-power is merely a reflection of its more compelling concern with preserving a view of man as free and prepotent.

As a phenomenon of American culture, the ideology of success through mind-power seems destined for indefinite extension. Short of a radical shift in values along cooperative lines, the myth of success will continue to serve an important function. This has little to do with our purported attachment to material gain *per se*. The cult of success must be understood in terms of its symbolic significance. What gives it force is its confirmation of the individual's power over his destiny, rather than its promise of material goods. So long as the ideal of individualism continues to command devotion, some means of obscuring contradicting realities is likely to remain. Actual social conditions, of course, force compromises with the ideal. Ideology, however, is suceptible of the distortion which permits perception to conform to the purity of desire. Mentalism allows what reality often denies.

IX

While the ideational content of the mentalistic success cult has remained relatively static since the beginning of the century, its position vis-à-vis reform politics has varied. Trine, the most popular mind-power inspirationalist of his day, was an ardent sympathizer of the Progressive movement;[124] Peale, the most popular mind-power inspirationalist of our day is quite hostile to reform as this came to be defined in the 1930s. Initially, he was heartened by Roosevelt's inaugural statement that the only thing the country had to fear was fear itself. This seemed to confirm Peale's own view of the depression. His biographer tells us:

> He did not wish to minimize the difficulties; no one in his right mind in the autumn of 1932 was inclined to do that. But he believed with all his unshakeable Ohio optimism that the country was basically sound, that the qualities that had made it great still existed under the paralysis of panic, and that if

people could just regain their faith in God and in themselves the downward trend would be reversed.[125]

With the first hundred days, however, disillusionment came fast. The spate of legislation which poured from the nation's capitol seemed to Peale to be undermining the values of his America. "He did not always fully reason these things out. He was a firm believer in the validity of intuition—the surest road to truth, Bergson had called it. His intuition told him that while the pump-priming and other forms of social legislation might have a short-term remedial effect, the underlying philosophy of the New Deal was implacably anti-individualistic." [126] Individualism, a cardinal tenet of one of the main streams of Progressivism, was not a prominent New Deal theme. This may go some way toward explaining why the most prominent advocates of mind-power in different periods reacted so differently toward the reform movements of their times. Peale's conviction that the New Deal and individualism were entirely antithetical led him into the conservative camp, where he has remained.

He enjoys considerable popularity in the business community, as is illustrated by the fact "pointed out by *Fortune* in 1953 that U.S. Steel had spent $150,000 to subscribe to . . . *Guideposts* for 125,000 employees. . . ." [127] In 1961, another commentator noted that this magazine was "bought by 762 business firms for their employees . . ." [128] The favor business shows for Peale, he returns in full measure. Christianity, he believes, "has a considerable stake in the survival of capitalism." This derives from the fact that in Peale's view both capitalism and Christianity attach supremely important value to the individual. All the other "isms," whether of the right or left, "put the state where Christianity puts the person." In such societies, the Church and the social order are divided in aim, but in America "the social order [capitalism] was fashioned to express the belief, preached by the Church, of man's importance and his unlimited abilities." [129] Peale sees no threat to individualism in the large-scale organization of industry. This is a measure of how successful corporate enterprise has been in identifying itself with the individualistic ideal.

The political implications of "positive thinking," however, should not be measured solely in terms of Peale's own leanings. Since the 1948 presidential campaign, Peale has become more cautious in making statements on public policy, indicating an awareness on his part that not all who like his "positive thinking" like his politics. His biographer notes: "Slowly it began to be apparent to him that such partisan activities on the part of a minister were divisive," and he quotes Peale as saying, "I've done my ministry a lot of harm by getting mixed up in political activities." [130]

To be sure, mind-power, by giving exclusive emphasis to the importance of subjective psychic factors in the cause and cure of human problems, may be said to carry conservative political implications. Furthermore by promoting the illusion of limitless individual power, the ideology of success obscures certain social realities, and thereby serves a stabilizing function for the established order. On the other hand, certain of its teachings may encourage reformist tendencies as well. It is entirely democratic, denies the existence of natural elites of any kind, and exalts all individuals equally as the chosen creatures of God. Condemning human suffering as wrong and unnecessary, it does not offer the rewards of an after-life as a *douceur* for present miseries. On the contrary, it holds that all men can and should experience fulfillment, happiness, and success here on earth. In short, it is a humanistic doctrine. And in a century where war, the complexity and consequent depersonalization of economic relationships, and the increasing bureaucratization of life at every level combine to reduce man's sense of his unique value and importance, it is mentalism's commitment to the individual that provides its greatest appeal.

NOTES

1. See Horatio W. Dresser, *Health and the Inner Life* (New York: G. P. Putnam's Sons, 1906), p. 24.

2. George A. Quimby, quoted in Dresser, *ibid.*, p. 28.

3. Quimby's writings were in private hands and were not published until 1921. For the most recent edition, see P. P. Quimby, *The Quimby Manuscripts*, ed. Horatio W. Dresser (New York: The Julian Press, 1961).

4. Dresser, *Health and the Inner Life*, p. 13.

5. Frederik Van Eden, "How Mind Can Heal the Body," *American Magazine*, LXVI (October 1908), 534.

6. William James, "Frederic Myers' Service to Psychology," *Memories and Studies* (New York: Longmans, Green and Co., 1912), pp. 148–149.

7. William James, *The Letters of William James*, ed. Henry James (Boston: Little, Brown and Co., 1926), I, 68–69.

8. *Ibid.*, p. 70.

9. *Ibid.*, p. 7.

10. Richard C. Cabot, *Psychotherapy and Its Relation to Religion* (New York: Moffat, Yard and Co., 1908), p. 12. For other expressions and discussions of the medical debt to mental healing cults, see Hugo Munsterberg, *Psychotherapy* (New York: Moffat, Yard and Co., 1909), p. 62; Richard Dewey, "Mental Therapeutics in Nervous and Mental Diseases," *American Journal of Insanity*, LVII (April 1901), 663–664; R. M. Phelps, "Hopeful Faith and Curative Agency," *Journal of Nervous and Mental Diseases*, XXIII (1896), 275–277; and Stefan Zweig, *Mental Healers*, trans. Eden and Cedar Paul (New York: The Viking Press, 1932).

11. Ray Stannard Baker, *New Ideals in Healing* (New York: Frederick A. Stokes Co., 1909), p. 8.

12. Elwood Worcester, Samuel McComb, and Isador H. Coriat, *Religion and Medicine: The Moral Control of Nervous Disorders* (New York: Moffat, Yard and Co., 1908), p. 6. See too Raymond J. Cunningham, "The

Emmanuel Movement: A Variety of American Religious Experience," *American Quarterly*, XIV (Spring 1962), 57.

13. Worcester, McComb, and Coriat, *op. cit.*, p. 383.

14. Cunningham, *op. cit.*, p. 57.

15. Worcester, McComb, and Coriat, *op. cit.*, pp. 3–4.

16. Munsterberg, *op. cit.*, p. 345.

17. Orison Swett Marden, *Every Man a King, or Might in Mind-Mastery* (New York: Thos. Y. Crowell Co., 1906), p. 5.

18. Josiah Royce, "William James and the Philosophy of Life," *William James and Other Essays on the Philosophy of Life* (New York: The Macmillan Co., 1911), pp. 14–15.

19. Josiah Royce, "The Recent Psychotherapeutic Movement in America," *Psychotherapy: A Course of Reading on Sound Psychology, Sound Medicine, and Sound Religion*, I (1909), 34. This journal will hereafter be referred to as *Psychotherapy*.

20. Stanton D. Kirkham, *The Philosophy of Self-Help* (New York: G. P. Putnam's Sons, 1909), p. 6.

21. Munsterberg, *op. cit.*, p. 1.

22. Richard C. Cabot, "The American Type of Psychotherapy," *Psychotherapy*, I (1909), 5.

23. *Ibid.*, p. 7.

24. Richard C. Cabot, "The Literature of Psychotherapy," *Psychotherapy*, III (1909), 18 ff.

25. Munsterberg, *op. cit.*, p. 55.

26. Worcester, McComb, and Coriat, *op. cit.*, p. 351.

27. Irving King, "The Religious Significance of the Psycho-Therapeutic Movement," *The American Journal of Theology*, XIV (October 1910), p. 541.

28. Munsterberg, *op. cit.*, p. 395. See too Mary W. Calkins, *The Good Man and the Good* (New York: The Macmillan Co., 1918), p. vii. Miss Calkins was a professor of philosophy and psychology at Wellesley.

29. John Herman Randall, *The New Light on Immortality, or The Significance of Psychic Research* (New York: The Macmillan Co., 1921), pp. 146–147.

30. John Herman Randall, "Mind and Medicine," *A New Philosophy of Life* (New York: Dodge Publishing Co., 1911), p. 3.

31. James Jackson Putnam, "The Philosophy of Psychotherapy—I," *Psychotherapy*, III (1909), 15–16.

32. James Jackson Putnam, "The Philosophy of Psychotherapy—II," *Psychotherapy*, III (1909), 32.

33. See John C. Burnham, "Psychoanalysis in American Civilization Before 1918" (unpublished Ph.D. dissertation, Department of History, Stanford University, 1958), p. 124.

34. See Worcester, McComb, and Coriat, *op. cit.*, p. 14, and Dresser, *Health and the Inner Life*, p. 72.

35. A. L. Allen, *The Message of New Thought* (New York: Thos. Y. Crowell & Co., 1914), pp. 104–105. See too Henry Wood, *The New Thought Simplified: How to Gain Harmony and Health* (Boston: Lee and Shepard, 1904), pp. 42–52, and Elizabeth Towne, *15 Lessons in New Thought, or Lessons in Living* (Holyoke: The Elizabeth Towne Co., 1921), p. 77.

36. Randall, "The Divinity of Man," *A New Philosophy of Life*, p. 48.

37. *Ibid.*, p. 49. On the more general belief that science and religion eventually teach the same lesson as a "necessary consequence of the unity of truth," see Sidney E. Mead, "American Protestantism Since the Civil War, I. From Denominationalism to Americanism," *The Journal of Religion*, XXXVI (January 1956), 11.

38. See Burnham, *op. cit.*, p. 105. See too David Shakow and David Rapaport, "The Influence of Freud on American Psychology," *Psychological Issues*, IV (1964), 55 ff.

39. Horatio Dresser, "What is New Thought," *Arena*, XXI (January 1899), p. 40.

40. Horatio Dresser, *Handbook of the New Thought* (New York: G. P. Putnam's Sons, 1917), p. 178. See too Dresser, *A History of the New Thought Movement* (New York: Thos. Y. Crowell Co., 1919), p. 306.

41. F. X. Dercum, "An Evaluation of the Psychogenic Factors in the Etiology of Mental Disease," *Journal of the American Medical Association*, LXII (1914), p. 756. See too Knight Dunlap, *Mysticism, Freudianism, and Scientific Psychology* (St. Louis: C. V. Mosby Co., 1920), and James R. Angell, "Psychoanalysis and the Practice of Medicine," *Journal of the American Medical Association*, LXVII (1917), 1657–1658.

42. Baker, *op. cit.*, p. 44.

43. A. L. Allen, *op. cit.*, p. 173.

44. Randall, *The New Light on Immortality*, p. 127.

45. Burnham, *op. cit.*, p. 132.

46. James J. Putnam, "A Plea for the Study of Philosophic Methods in Preparation of Psycho-Analytic Work," *Journal of Abnormal Psychology*, VI (October–November 1911), 253.

47. Sigmund Freud, *A History of the Psychoanalytic Movement* (New York: The Nervous and Mental Disease Publishing Co., 1917), p. 25.

48. Burnham, *op. cit.*, p. 169.

49. *Ibid.*, p. 377.

50. William A. White, *Twentieth Century Psychiatry, Its Contribution to Man's Knowledge of Himself* (New York: W. W. Norton and Co., 1936), p. 183.

51. Dresser, *Health and the Inner Life*, p. 94.

52. Frank Luther Mott, *Golden Multitudes: the Story of Best Sellers in the United States* (New York: The Macmillan Co., 1947), p. 260.

53. Frank Channing Haddock, *Power of Will* (Meriden, Conn.: The Pelton Publishing Co., 1916), p. 14.

54. *Ibid., passim.*

55. Frank Channing Haddock, *Business Power, A Practical Manual in Financial Ability* (Alhambra, Calif.: The Power Book Library, 1911), p. vi.

56. *Ibid.*

57. See Dale Carnegie, *How To Win Friends and Influence People* (New York: Pocket Books, 1964), *passim.*

58. Haddock, *Business Power*, p. 21.

59. *Ibid.*, p. 25.

60. *Ibid.*, p. 275.

61. Henry Foster Adams, "Psychology Goldbricks" (Part I), *Scribner's Magazine*, LXIX (June 1921), 656.

62. Advertisement in *Current Opinion*, LXX (April 1921), vii–ix.

63. *Current Opinion*, LXX (June 1921), i.

64. George Creel, *Rebel At Large: Recollections of Fifty Crowded Years* (New York: G. P. Putnam's Sons, 1947), p. 262.

65. Emil Coué, *My Method: Including American Impressions* (Garden City: Doubleday, Page and Co., 1923), p. 112; see also p. 128. Coué's work on autosuggestion was reprinted in 1961. See Coué, *Better and Better Every Day* (New York: Barnes and Noble, 1961).

66. Quoted in *New York World*, January 1, 1923, p. 13. See too DeWitt L. Pelton, "M. Coué and the Church," *The Forum* LXIX (April 1923), 1393–1398.

67. Coué, *My Method*, p. 7.

68. Warren Hilton, *Mind Mechanism*, Vol. VIII of *Psychology and Achievement* (New York: Literary Digest, 1920), p. 6. There were twelve volumes in this series.

69. Adolf Meyer, "Shall Couéism Spell Progress or Regression?" *The Collected Papers of Adolf Meyer*, ed. Eunice E. Winters (Baltimore: Johns Hopkins Press, 1952), IV, 407–408. This first appeared in *The Open Court* XXXVII (1923), 473–477.

70. J. Herbert Duckworth, *Autosuggestion and Its Personal Application* (New York: James A. McCann Co., 1922), p. xi.

71. Warren Hilton, *Driving Power of Thought*, Vol. III of *Psychology and Achievement*, pp. 52–53.

72. Warren Hilton, *Techniques of Success*, Vol. X of *Psychology and Achievement*, pp. 3–4.

73. Warren Hilton, *Psychology and Achievement*, Vol. I of *Psychology and Achievement*, p. 5. See too *Pelmanism on Your Subconscious Mind*,

No. 11 in the *Pelmanism* series (New York: The Pelman Institute of America, 1924), *passim*. There were twelve pamphlets in this series.

74. Hilton, *ibid.*, p. 120. See too *Pelmanism in Action*, No. 12 in the *Pelmanism* series, p. 14.

75. Coué, *My Method*, p. 5.

76. See Hilton, *Techniques of Success*, p. 65, and *Pelmanism on Will and Effort*, No. 3 in the *Pelmanism* series, p. 15.

77. Coué, *My Method*, p. 173.

78. John B. Watson, *Behaviorism* (New York: W. W. Norton and Co., 1925), p. 82.

79. *Ibid.*, p. 74.

80. *Ibid.*, p. 348.

81. Edna Heidbreder, *Seven Psychologies* (New York: D. Appleton-Century Co., 1933), p. 261. See too Grace Adams, "The Rise and Fall of Psychology," *Atlantic Monthly*, CLIII (January 1934), 88.

82. "Tranquilizers in Print," *Time*, LXIX (March 25, 1957), 112.

83. Chester Morrison, "Religion Reaches Out," *Look*, XVII (December 14, 1954), 41–47.

84. Alice Payne Hackett, *60 Years of Best Sellers, 1895–1955* (New York: R. R. Bowker Co., 1956), pp. 15, 84. One salesman from Prentice-Hall has estimated that "in a good inspirational year these books account for 25 per cent or more of our total bookstore sales." Quoted in "Tranquilizers in Print," *Time*, LXIX, 116.

85. Clarence Woodbury, "God's Salesman," *The American Magazine*, CXLVII (June 1949), 37.

86. Norman Vincent Peale, *The Power of Positive Thinking* (Englewood Cliffs, N.J.: Prentice-Hall, 1952), p. vi.

87. Quoted in Arthur Gordon, *Norman Vincent Peale: Minister to Millions* (Englewood Cliffs, N.J.: Prentice-Hall, 1958), p. 82.

88. *Ibid.*, p. 173.

89. Peale, *op. cit.*, p. 6.

90. Norman Vincent Peale, *A Guide to Confident Living* (New York: Prentice-Hall, 1948), p. 55.

91. Peale, *The Power of Positive Thinking*, p. ix.

92. *Ibid.*, p. 120.

93. *Ibid.*, pp. 166–169.

94. Will Herberg, *Protestant, Catholic, Jew* (Garden City, Doubleday and Co., 1960), p. 265. This is the central theme of Smiley Blanton and Norman Vincent Peale, *Faith Is the Answer* (New York: Abingdon-Cokesbury Press, 1940), in which Peale assures his readers (p. 214) of "the great fact that for your every problem faith is the answer."

95. Peale, *The Power of Positive Thinking*, p. 53.

96. Peale, *A Guide to Confident Living*, p. 98.

97. Peale, *The Power of Positive Thinking*, p. 160.

98. *Ibid.*, p. v.

99. Smiley Blanton and Norman Vincent Peale, *The Art of Real Happiness* (New York: Prentice-Hall, 1950), p. 73.

100. Blanton and Peale, *Faith Is the Answer*, p. 54.

101. Peale, *A Guide to Confident Living*, pp. 67–68.

102. Peale, *The Power of Positive Thinking*, p. 134.

103. *Ibid.*, p. 22.

104. *Ibid.*, p. 55. Contemporary commentators have remarked the similarity to Coué. "He takes Dr. Coué's famous autosuggestion jingle and puts it in 3-D. The added dimensions: religion and psychology." "Dynamo in the Vineyard," *Time*, LXIV (November 1, 1954), 68. See too Edmund Fuller, "Pitchman in the Pulpit," *Saturday Review*, XL (March 9, 1957), 28.

105. For an examination of relations between psychiatrists and ministers in the American Foundation of Religion and Psychiatry, see Samuel H. Klausner, *Psychiatry and Religion* (New York: The Free Press, 1964). For a discussion of the tremendous increase in pastoral counseling after World War II, see C. P. Oberndorf, *Psychoanalysis in America* (New York: Grune and Stratton, 1953), pp. 238–241.

106. Joshua Loth Liebman, *Peace of Mind* (New York: Bantam Books, 1955), p. 139.

107. Blanton and Peale, *Faith Is the Answer*, p. 7.

108. *Ibid.*, p. 11. For an interesting discussion of the importance of "ethical world-views" for the psychoanalyst, see Erik Erikson, "The Golden Rule in the Light of New Insight," *Insight and Responsibility* (New York: W. W. Norton and Co., 1964), pp. 219–243.

109. Blanton and Peale, *Faith Is the Answer*, p. 9.

110. Peale, *A Guide to Confident Living*, p. 11.

111. *Ibid.*

112. Blanton and Peale, *The Art of Real Happiness*, p. 13.

113. Peale, *A Guide to Confident Living*, pp. 5–6.

114. *Ibid.*, pp. 28–29.

115. *Ibid.*, p. 147.

116. *Ibid.*

117. Sigmund Freud used the phrase "omnipotence of thought" to describe "the over-valuation of mental processes as compared with reality," common among neurotic patients. He regarded this psychic pattern as a survival from primitive modes of thought, most clearly visible in cases of "obsessional neuroses." Freud, *Totem and Taboo*, trans. James Strachey (New York: W. W. Norton and Co., 1952), pp. 85 ff.

118. Gordon, *op. cit.*, p. 228.

119. Peale, *A Guide to Confident Living*, p. 47.

120. Blanton and Peale, *The Art of Real Happiness*, p. 6.

121. In psychoanalytic terminology, the belief in the omnipotence of thought is defined as "an exaggerated conviction that mere wishes are and must be followed by results or changes in the external world." Howard C. Warren, ed., *Dictionary of Psychology* (Cambridge, Mass.: The Riverside Press, 1934), p. 186.

122. Karen Horney, *The Neurotic Personality of Our Time* (New York: W. W. Norton and Co., 1937), p. 166.

123. *Ibid.*, pp. 172–173.

124. See Chapter 6.

125. Gordon, *op. cit.*, p. 157.

126. *Ibid.*, pp. 161–162.

127. "Norman Vincent Peale, Minister to Millions," *Look*, XVII (September 22, 1953), 86.

128. Meg Greenfield, "The Great American Morality Play," *The Reporter*, June 8, 1961, p. 16.

129. Norman Vincent Peale, "Let the Church Speak Up for Capitalism," *Reader's Digest*, LVII (September 1950), 126–130.

130. Gordon, *op. cit.*, pp. 226–227.

Selected Bibliography

DISSERTATIONS AND THESES

Burnham, John C. *Psychoanalysis in American Civilization Before 1918*. Unpublished doctoral dissertation, Department of History, Stanford University, 1958.
Griswold, Alfred Whitney. *The American Gospel of Success*. Unpublished doctoral dissertation, Department of History, Yale University, 1934.
Huber, Richard M. *The Idea of Success in America, 1865–1929: A History of the Puritan Ethic*. Unpublished doctoral dissertation, Yale University, 1953.
McLachlan, James Stuart. *The Genteel Reformers: 1865-1884*. Unpublished Master's thesis, Department of History, Columbia University, 1958.
Teener, James W. *Unity School of Christianity*. Unpublished doctoral dissertation, Divinity School, University of Chicago, 1939.
Wishy, Bernard W. *Images of the American Child in the Nineteenth Century*. Unpublished doctoral dissertation, Department of History, Columbia University, 1958.

BOOKS AND ARTICLES

Abbott, Jacob. *Caleb in the Country*. Boston: Crocker and Brewster, 1839.
———. *Caleb in Town*. Boston: Crocker and Brewster, 1839.
———. *The Corner Stone, or A Familiar Exhibition of the Elementary Principles of Religious Truth*. Boston: William Pierce, 1834.

———. *The Rollo Code of Morals: or The Rules of Duty for Children*. Boston: Crocker and Brewster, 1841.

Abbott, Lyman (ed.). *How to Succeed*. New York: G. P. Putnam's Sons, 1882.

Abraham, Karl. "Psycho-analytical Notes on Coué's Method of Self-Mastery," *The International Journal of Psycho-Analysis*, VII, 1926.

Adams, Grace. "The Rise and Fall of Psychology," *Atlantic Monthly*, CLIII (January 1934), 82–92.

Adams, Henry Foster. "Psychology Goldbricks," *Scribner's Magazine*. LXIX (June 1921), Part I, 655–664; LXX (July 1921), Part II, 94–101.

Alcott, William A. *Familiar Letters to Young Men*. Buffalo: Geo. H. Derby, 1850.

———. *The Young Men's Guide*. Boston: Perkins and Marvin, 1838.

Alger, Horatio, Jr. *A Cousin's Conspiracy*. Chicago: M. A. Donohue and Co., no date.

———. *Herbert Carter's Legacy*. New York: A. L. Burt, no date.

———. *Mark, the Match Boy*. Philadelphia: Porter and Coates, 1869.

———. *Only an Irish Boy, or Andy Burke's Fortunes*. New York: Hurst and Co., no date.

———. *Risen from the Ranks*. Philadelphia: Porter and Coates, 1874.

———. *Strive and Succeed: the Story of Walter Conrad's Success*. New York: A. L. Burt, no date.

———. *Strong and Steady, or Paddle Your Own Canoe*. New York: New York Book Co., 1910.

———. *Struggling Upward and Other Works*. Edited, with an Introduction, by Russel Crouse. New York: Crown Publishers, 1945. Works included are: *Struggling Upward; Ragged Dick; Phil, the Fiddler; Jed, the Poorhouse Boy*.

———. *The Telegraph Boy*. Boston: A. K. Loring, 1879.

———. *Wait and Hope*. New York: New York Book Co., 1908.

———. *The Young Acrobat*. New York: American Publishers Corp., 1890.

Allen, Abel Leighton. *The Message of New Thought*. New York: Thos. Y. Crowell Co., 1914.

Allen, James. *The Mastery of Destiny*. New York: G. P. Putnam's Sons, 1909.

———. *Men and Systems*. New York: Dodge Publishing Co., 1914.

———. *The Path of Prosperity*. New York: R. F. Fenno and Co., 1907.

Anderson, John Benjamin. *New Thought, Its Lights and Shadows: An Appreciation and a Criticism*. Boston: Sherman, French and Co., 1911.

Arnot, William. *The Race for Riches*. Philadelphia: Lippincott, Grambo and Co., 1853.

Arthur, T. S. *Advice to Young Men*. Boston: N. C. Barton, 1849.

———. *Lessons in Life, for All Who Will Read Them*. Philadelphia: Lippincott, Grambo and Co., 1851.

———. *Rising in the World: or A Tale for the Rich and Poor*. New York: Baker and Scribner, 1850.

Ayer, Mary A. (ed.). *Keep Up Your Courage: Keynotes to Success*. Boston: Lothrop, Lee and Shepard Co., 1908.

Baker, Ray Stannard. *New Ideals in Healing*. New York: Frederick A. Stokes Co., 1909. Original copyright by Phillips Publishing Co., 1908.

Barton, Bruce. *The Man Nobody Knows: A Discovery of the Real Jesus*. Indianapolis: Bobbs-Merrill, 1925.

Berthoff, Werner. "The Art of Jewett's Pointed Firs," *New England Quarterly*, XXXIII (March 1959), 31–53.

Beveridge, Albert J. *The Young Man and the World*. New York: D. Appleton and Co., 1906.

Bierbower, Austin. *How to Succeed*. New York: R. F. Fenno and Co., 1900.

Björkman, Frances M. "The Literature of 'New Thoughters,' " *The World's Work*, XIX (January 1910), 12471–12475.

Blackmar, Frank W. "Charles M. Sheldon, A Man with a Mission," *Harper's Weekly*, XLIII (August 5, 1899), 769–772.

Blanton, Smiley, and Peale, Norman Vincent. *The Art of Real Happiness*. New York: Prentice-Hall, 1950.

———. *Faith Is the Answer*. New York: Abingdon-Cokesbury Press, 1940.

Bok, Edward. *The Keys to Success*. Philadelphia: John D. Morris and Co., 1898.

———. *The Young Man In Business*. Boston: L. C. Page and Co., 1900.

Bond, Frederick Clifton. *Success for You*. Los Angeles: The Catterlin Publishing Co., 1933.

Selected Bibliography

Bourne, Randolph S. "The Two Generations," *Atlantic Monthly*, CVII (May 1911), 591–598.

Brace, Charles Loring. *The Dangerous Classes of New York and Twenty Years' Work Among Them.* New York: Wynkoop and Hallenbeck, 1872.

Braden, Samuel Charles. *These Also Believe: A Study of Modern American Cults and Minority Religious Movements.* New York: The Macmillan Co., 1949.

Brill, A. A. "The Introduction and Development of Freud's Work in the United States," *American Journal of Sociology*, XLV (November 1939), 318–325.

Bromberg, Walter. *The Mind of Man: A History of Psychotherapy and Psychoanalysis.* New York: Harper and Bros., 1959.

Brooks, C. Harry. *The Practice of Autosuggestion by the Method of Emile Coué.* London: George Allen & Unwin, 1922.

Brown, Archer. *Top or Bottom—Which?: A Study of the Factors Which Most Contribute to the Success of Young Men.* New York: Post and Davis, 1902.

Brown, Grace M. *Mental Harmony, Its Influence on Life.* New York: Edward J. Clode, 1916.

———. *Think Right for Health and Success.* New York: Edward J. Clode, 1916.

Bruce, H. Addington. "Masters of the Mind," *American Magazine*, LXXI (November 1910), 71–81.

Burnham, John C. "Psychiatry, Psychology and the Progressive Movement," *American Quarterly*, XII (Winter 1960), 457–465.

Butler, Charles. *The American Gentleman.* Philadelphia: Hogan and Thompson, 1836.

Cabot, Richard C. *Psychotherapy and Its Relation to Religion.* New York: Moffat, Yard and Co., 1908.

Calkins, Mary Whiton. *A First Book in Psychology.* New York: The Macmillan Co., 1910.

———. *The Good Man and the Good: An Introduction to Ethics.* New York: The Macmillan Co., 1918.

———. *An Introduction to Psychology.* New York: The Macmillan Co., 1908.

———. *Sharing the Profits.* Boston: Ginn and Co., 1888.

Call, Annie Payson. *As a Matter of Course.* Boston: Roberts Brothers, 1894.

————. *Every Day Living.* New York: F. A. Stokes Co., 1906.

————. *The Freedom of Life.* Boston: Little, Brown and Co., 1911.

————. *How to Live Quietly.* Boston: Little, Brown and Co., 1914.

————. *Nerves and Common Sense.* Boston: Little, Brown and Co., 1909.

————. *Power Through Repose.* Boston: Roberts Brothers, 1891.

Carman, Bliss. *The Making of Personality.* Boston: L. C. Page and Co., 1908.

Carnegie, Andrew. *The Gospel of Wealth.* New York: Century Co., 1900.

————. *The Empire of Business.* Garden City: Doubleday, Page and Co., 1902.

Carpenter, Frederic I. "William James and Emerson," *American Literature,* II (March 1939), 39–57.

Cawelti, John G. *Apostles of the Self-Made Man.* Chicago: University of Chicago Press, 1965.

Chamberlain, J. S. *Makers of Millions: or The Marvelous Success of America's Self-Made Man.* Chicago: George M. Hill Co., 1899.

Chapin, E. H. *Duties of Young Men.* Boston: Putnam and Brother, 1856.

Clark, F. E. *Danger Signals: the Enemies of Youth from the Business Man's Standpoint.* Boston: D. Lothrop Co., 1885.

————. *The Gospel of Out of Doors.* New York: Association Press, 1920.

————. *The Great Secret: Health, Beauty, Happiness, Friendmaking, Common Sense, Success.* Boston: United Society of Christian Endeavor, 1897.

————. *Memories of Many Men in Many Lands: An Autobiography.* Boston: United Society of Christian Endeavor, 1922.

————. *Our Business Boys.* Boston: D. Lothrop and Co., 1884.

Clarke, Dorus. *Lectures to Young People in Manufacturing Villages.* Boston: Perkins and Marvin, 1836.

Cochran, Thomas C. "The Social Scientists," *American Perspectives: The National Self-Image in the Twentieth Century.* Edited by Robert E. Spiller and Eric Larrabee, *et al.* Cambridge, Mass.: Harvard University Press, 1961.

Connolly, Margaret. *The Life Story of Orison Swett Marden: A Man Who Benefited Men.* New York: Thomas Y. Crowell Co., 1925.

Selected Bibliography

Conwell, Russell H. *Acres of Diamonds*, and Shackleton, Robert, *His Life and Achievements*. New York: Harper and Bros., 1915.

———. *The New Day or, Fresh Opportunities*. Philadelphia: The Griffith and Rowland Press, 1904.

Cottingham, Walter H. *Business Success*. New York: Dodge Publishing Co., 1907.

Coué, Emile. *My Method: Including American Impressions*. Garden City, N.Y.: Doubleday, Page and Co., 1923.

Crafts, Wilbur F. *Familiar Talks on That Boy and Girl of Yours: Sociology from the Viewpoint of the Family*. New York: Baker and Taylor Co., 1922.

———. *National Perils and Hopes: A Study Based on Current Statistics and the Observations of a Cheerful Reformer*. Cleveland: F. M. Barton Co., 1910.

———. *Practical Christian Sociology*. New York: Funk and Wagnalls, 1907.

———. *Successful Men of To-day and What They Say of Success*. New York: Funk and Wagnalls, 1883.

Crane, Aaron Martin. *Right and Wrong Thinking and Their Results: the Undreamed of Possibilities Which Man May Achieve Through His Own Mental Control*. Boston: Lothrop, Lee and Shepard Co., 1905.

Crewdson, Charles N. *Building Business*. New York: D. Appleton and Co., 1907.

Crosby, Howard. *A Sermon to Young Men*. New York: B. Stradley, 1876.

Crosby, W. C. "Acres of Diamonds," *The American Mercury*, XIV (May 1928), 104–113.

Cunningham, Raymond J. "The Emmanuel Movement: A Variety of American Religious Experience," *American Quarterly*, XIV (Spring 1962), 48–63.

Dale, John T. *The Secret of Success: or Finger Posts on the Highway of Life*. Chicago: Fleming H. Revell, 1889.

———. *The Way to Win: Showing How to Succeed in Life*. Chicago: Hammond Publishing Co., 1891.

Davidson, John T. *Sure to Succeed*. New York: A. C. Armstrong and Son, 1889.

Davis, Charles Gilbert. *The Philosophy of Life*. Chicago: D. D. Publishing Co., 1910.

Denney, Reuel. "The Discovery of the Popular Culture," *American Perspectives: The National Self-Image in the Twentieth Century*. Edited by Robert E. Spiller and Eric Larrabee, *et al*. Cambridge, Mass.: Harvard University Press, 1961. Pp. 154–177.

Derby, J. C. *Fifty Years Among Authors, Books and Publishers*. New York: G. W. Carleton and Co., 1884.

Dewey, John. *Democracy and Education*. New York: The Macmillan Co., 1916.

Dewey, Richard. "Mental Therapeutics in Nervous and Mental Diseases," *American Journal of Insanity*, LVII (April 1901), 661–687.

Diamond, Sigmund. *The Reputation of the American Businessman*. Cambridge, Mass.: Harvard University Press, 1955.

Dresser, Horatio W. *A Book of Secrets: With Studies in the Art of Self-Control*. New York: G. P. Putnam's Sons, 1907.

———. *Handbook of the New Thought*. New York: G. P. Putnam's Sons, 1917.

———. "The Harmony of Life," *Arena*, XXI (May 1899), 612–628.

———. "Has Life a Meaning," *Arena*, XXI (February 1899), 162–182.

———. *Health and the Inner Life*. New York: G. P. Putnams' Sons, 1906.

———. *A History of the New Thought Movement*. New York: Thomas Y. Crowell Co., 1919.

———. *Human Efficiency: A Psychological Study of Modern Problems*. New York: G. P. Putnam's Sons, 1912.

———. *The Perfect Whole: An Essay on the Conduct and Meaning of Life*. New York: G. P. Putnam's Sons, 1901.

———. *The Philosophy of the Spirit: A Study of the Spiritual Nature of Man and the Presence of God, with a Supplementary Essay on the Logic of Hegel*. New York: G. P. Putnam's Sons, 1908.

———. *Voices of Freedom: and Studies on the Philosophy of Individuality*. New York: G. P. Putnam's Sons, 1899.

———. *Voices of Hope*. Boston: Geo. H. Ellis, 1898.

———. "What Is the New Thought?" *Arena*, XXI (January 1899), 29–50.

Dubbs, Joseph Henry. *Conditions of Success in Life*. Philadelphia: Reformed Church Publication Board, 1870.

Duckworth, J. Herbert. *Autosuggestion and Its Personal Application.* New York: The James A. McCann Co., 1922.

Dudden, Arthur P. "Nostalgia and the American," *Journal of the History of Ideas,* XXII, No. 4 (October-December 1961), 515–530.

Dumont, Theron O. *The Master Mind or the Key to Mental Power.* Chicago: Advanced Thought Publishing Co., 1918.

Dunlap, Knight. *Mysticism, Freudianism and Scientific Psychology.* St. Louis: C. V. Mosby Co., 1920.

Eckhardt, A. Roy. *The Surge of Piety in America.* New York: Association Press, 1958.

Edgerton, James Arthur. *Invading the Invisible.* New York: The New Age Press, 1931.

———. *Poems.* Marietta, Ohio: E. R. Alderman and Sons, 1889.

———. *Voices of the Morning.* Chicago: Charles H. Kerr and Co., 1898.

Elliott, James W. *The Wail of the Quitter.* New York: The Man Message Corporation, 1921.

Ellsworth, Paul. *Direct Healing.* Holyoke: The Elizabeth Towne Co., 1926.

Emerson, Ralph Waldo. *The Conduct of Life.* Garden City, N.Y.: The Masterworks Program, no date [1860].

Evans, Augusta J. *Beulah.* New York: Derby and Jackson, 1859.

———. *St. Elmo.* New York: Carleton Publishers, 1867.

Fall, Frank A. *Little Stories of Progress.* New York: The Platt and Peck Co., 1914.

———. *Working for the Boss.* New York: The Platt and Peck Co., 1913.

Faris, John T. *How It Was Done in Harmony.* Cincinnati: The Standard Publishing Co., 1916.

———. *Making Good: Pointers for the Man of Tomorrow.* New York: Fleming H. Revell Co., 1911.

———. *Men Who Made Good.* New York: Fleming H. Revell Co., 1912.

Fidler, William Perry. *Augusta Evans Wilson, 1835–1909.* University, Ala.: University of Alabama Press, 1951.

Fowler, Nathaniel C., Jr. *The Boy: How to Help Him Succeed.* Boston: Oakwood Publishing Co., 1902.

———. *Getting a Start: First Aids to Success.* New York: Sully and Kleinteich, 1915.

————. *How to Get and Keep a Job*. Boston: The Oakwood Co., 1907.

————. *Starting in Life*. Boston: Little, Brown and Co., 1906.

Frank, Henry. *The Mastery of Mind in the Making of a Man*. New York: R. F. Fenno and Co., 1908.

Freedley, E. T. *Opportunities for Industry and the Safe Investment of Capital, or A Thousand Chances to Make Money*. Philadelphia: J. B. Lippincott and Co., 1859.

————. *A Practical Treatise on Business: or How to Get, Save, Spend, Give, Lend and Bequeath Money: with an Inquiry into the Chances of Success and Causes of Failure in Business*. Philadelphia: Lippincott, Grambo and Co., 1855.

Freud, Sigmund. *A History of the Psychoanalytic Movement*. New York: The Nervous and Mental Disease Publishing Co., 1917.

————. *Totem and Taboo*. James Strachey, trans. New York: W. W. Norton and Co., 1952.

Frost, John. *The Book of Good Examples; Drawn from Authentic History and Biography; Designed to Illustrate the Beneficial Effects of Virtuous Conduct*. New York: D. Appleton and Co., 1846.

————. *The Young Merchant*. Philadelphia: R. W. Pomeroy, 1839.

Gardner, Ralph D. *Horatio Alger, or the American Hero Era*. Mendota, Ill.: The Wayside Press, 1964.

Ghent, W. J. *Socialism and Success: Some Uninvited Messages*. New York: John Lane Co., 1910.

————. "To the Seekers of Success," *The Independent*, LXIX (September 1910), 453–457.

Gillis, James M. "Couéism and Catholicism," *The Catholic World*, CXVI (March 1923), 790–803.

Gladden, Washington. *Straight Shots at Young Men*. New York: Thomas Y. Crowell Co., 1900.

Gordon, Arthur. *Norman Vincent Peale: Minister to Millions*. Englewood Cliffs, N. J.: Prentice-Hall, 1958.

Greenfield, Meg. "The Great American Morality Play," *The Reporter*, XXIV (June 8, 1961), 13–18.

Grenside, Dorothy. *Little Builders: New Thought Talks to Children*. New York: Dodge Publishing Co., 1916.

Griswold, Alfred Whitney. "New Thought: A Cult of Success," *The American Journal of Sociology*, XL (November 1934), 309–318.

Selected Bibliography

Gruber, Frank. *Horatio Alger, Jr.* Los Angeles: Grover Jones Press, 1961.

Gulick, Luther H. *The Efficient Life.* Buffalo: Corlis Co., 1907.

Hackett, Alice Payne. *60 Years of Best Sellers, 1895–1955.* New York: R. R. Bowker Co., 1956.

Haddock, Frank Channing. *Business Power, A Practical Manual in Financial Ability.* Alhambra, Calif.: The Power-Book Library, 1911.

————. *The King's Achievements, or Power for Success.* Lynn, Mass.: Nichols Press, 1903.

————. *Power of Will.* Meriden, Conn.: The Pelton Publishing Co., 1916.

Hall, Bolton. *Even As You and I.* Boston: Small, Maynard and Co., 1900.

————. *The Game of Life.* New York: M. M. Breslow Co., 1909.

————. *A Little Land and a Living.* New York: The Arcadia Press, 1908.

————. *Money Making in Free America: Short Chapters on Prosperity.* New York: The Arcadia Press, 1909.

————. *Things As They Are.* New York: The Arcadia Press, 1909.

————. *Three Acres and Liberty.* New York: The Macmillan Co., 1908.

————. *Thrift.* New York: B. W. Huebsch, 1916.

Haller, William. *The Rise of Puritanism, or the Way to the New Jerusalem as Set Forth in Pulpit and Press from Thomas Cartwright to John Lolbarne and John Milton (1570–1643).* New York: Columbia University Press, 1938.

Hardwicke, Henry. *The Art of Getting Rich.* New York: The Useful Knowledge Publishing Co., 1897.

Haroutunian, Joseph. *Piety versus Moralism, the Passing of the New England Theology.* New York: Henry Holt and Co., 1932.

Harrison, Jonathan Baxter. *Certain Dangerous Tendencies in American Life, and Other Papers.* Boston: Houghton, Osgood and Co., 1880.

Hart, James D. *The Popular Book: A History of America's Literary Taste.* New York: Oxford University Press, 1950.

Heidbreder, Edna. *Seven Psychologies.* New York: D. Appleton-Century Co., 1933.

Herberg, Will. *Protestant, Catholic, Jew.* Garden City: Doubleday and Co., 1960.

Hesseltine, William B. "Four American Traditions," *Journal of Southern History*, XXVII (February 1961), 3–32.

Hill, Napoleon. *Think and Grow Rich*. Greenwich: Fawcett Publications, 1960.

Hilton, Warren. *Psychology and Achievement*. 12 vols. New York: Literary Digest, 1920. Vol. I, *Psychology and Achievement;* Vol. II, *Making Your Own World;* Vol. III, *Driving Power of Thought;* Vol. IV, *The Trained Memory;* Vol. V, *Power of Mental Imagery;* Vol. VI, *Initiative Psychic Energy;* Vol. VII, *Processes and Personality;* Vol. VIII, *Mind Mechanism;* Vol. IX, *Mind Mastery;* Vol. X, *Techniques of Success;* Vol. XI, *External Efficiency Factors;* Vol. XII, *Specific Applications*.

Holmes, Ernest. *New Thought Terms and Their Meanings*. New York: Dodd, Mead and Co., 1942.

Holmes, Ernest, and Lathem, Maude A. (eds.). *Mind Remakes Your World*. New York: Dodd, Mead and Co., 1941.

Holmes, Fenwicke L. *The Twenty Secrets of Success*. New York: Robert McBride and Co., 1927.

Horney, Karen. *The Neurotic Personality of Our Time*. New York: W. W. Norton and Co., 1937.

Horton, Robert F. *Success and Failure*. New York: Dodd, Mead and Co., 1897.

Hubbard, Elbert. *The Book of Business*. New York: The Roycrofters, 1913.

Hunt, Freeman. *Lives of American Merchants*. 2 vols. New York: Derby and Jackson, 1858.

———. *Worth and Wealth: A Collection of Maxims, Morals and Miscellanies for Merchants and Men of Business*. New York: Stringer and Townsend, 1856.

Hunter, William C. *Dollars and Sense*. Chicago: The Reilly and Britton Co., 1911.

Hyslop, James H. *Democracy, A Study of Government*. New York: Charles Scribner's and Sons, 1899.

James, William. *Essays in Pragmatism*. Edited by Alburney Castell. New York: Hafner Publishing Co., 1948.

———. *Essays on Faith and Morals*. Edited by Ralph Barton Perry. New York: Longmans, Green and Co., 1949.

———. *Human Immortality: Two Supposed Objections to the Doctrine*. Boston: Houghton Mifflin and Co., 1898.

Selected Bibliography

————. *The Letters of William James.* 2 vols. Edited by his son, Henry James. Boston: Little, Brown and Co., 1926.

————. *Memories and Studies.* New York: Longmans, Green and Co., 1912.

————. "The Powers of Men," *The American Magazine,* LXV (November 1907), 57–65.

————. *Talks to Teachers on Psychology: and to Students on Some of Life's Ideals.* New York: Henry Holt and Co., 1925. First published 1899.

————. *The Varieties of Religious Experience.* New York: Random House, 1929.

————. *The Will to Believe and Other Essays in Popular Philosophy.* New York: Longmans, Green and Co., 1909.

Johannsen, Albert. *The House of Beadle and Adams: and Its Dime and Nickel Series: the Story of a Vanished Literature.* Norman, Okla.: University of Oklahoma Press, 1950.

Johns, Alfred E. *Scientific Autosuggestion: For Personality Adjustment and Development.* New York: Alfred E. Johns, 1952.

Jones, Ham. *About Money: A Lively Tract for the Present Time.* Boston: New England News Co., 1872.

Jordan, Alice M. *From Rollo to Tom Sawyer and Other Papers.* Boston: The Horn Book, 1948.

Jordan, David Starr. *The Call of the Twentieth Century: An Address to Young Men.* Boston: American Unitarian Association, 1903.

————. *Life's Enthusiasms.* Boston: American Unitarian Association, 1906.

Kent, Charles H. *How to Achieve Success: A Manual for Young People.* New York: The Christian Herald, 1897.

Keys, C. M. "How Men Get Rich Now," *The World's Work,* XI (January 1906), 7066–7071.

King, Irving. "The Religious Significance of the Psychotherapeutic Movement," *The American Journal of Theology,* XIV (October 1910), 533–551.

Kirkham, Stanton Davis. *The Philosophy of Self-Help: An Application of Practical Psychology to Daily Life.* New York: G. P. Putnam's Sons, 1909.

————. *Resources: An Interpretation of the Well-Rounded Life.* New York: G. P. Putnam's Sons, 1909.

————. *Where Dwells the Soul Serene.* San Francisco: Paul Elder and Co., 1904.

Kirkland, Edward Chase. *Dream and Thought in the Business Community, 1860–1900.* Chicago: Quadrangle Books, 1964.

Klausner, Samuel Z. *Psychiatry and Religion.* New York: The Free Press, 1964.

Knox, George H. *Ready Money.* Des Moines: Personal Help Publishing Co., 1905.

Landone, Brown. *Powers That Turn Failure Into Success: A New Discovery in Truth and a New Method of Using Your Powers.* Holyoke: The Elizabeth Towne Co., 1933.

Legge, Arthur E. "Mental Healing," *Quarterly Review,* CCXXXVIII (October 1922), 252–264.

Lewis, Alexander. *Manhood-Making: Studies in the Elemental Principles of Success.* Boston: The Pilgrim Press, 1902.

Lewis, H. A. *Hidden Treasures: or Why Some Succeed While Others Fail.* New York: A. W. Richardson, 1887.

Liebman, Joshua Loth. *Peace of Mind.* New York: Bantam Books, 1955. First published by Simon and Schuster, 1946.

Lister, J. B. *How to Succeed: A Book for the Young.* Philadelphia: American Baptist Publication Society, 1856.

Lowenthal, Leo. "Biographies in Popular Magazines," *American Social Patterns.* Edited by William Petersen. Garden City: Doubleday Anchor Books, 1956. Pp. 63–118.

Lynn, Kenneth S. *The Dream of Success: A Study of the Modern American Imagination.* Boston: Little, Brown and Co., 1955.

Lyon, Ida. *The Wonders of Life.* New York: R. F. Fenno and Co., 1910.

Macdonald, Dwight. *Against the American Grain: Essays on the Effects of Mass Culture.* New York: Random House, 1962.

McGuffey, William H. *The Eclectic Fourth Reader,* 2nd edn. Cincinnati: Truman and Smith, 1837.

————. *McGuffey's Eclectic Primer.* Cincinnati: Sargent, Wilson and Hinkle, 1844.

————. *McGuffey's Newly Revised Eclectic Fourth Reader.* Cincinnati: Sargent, Wilson and Hinkle, 1853.

————. *McGuffey's Newly Revised Eclectic Third Reader.* Cincinnati: Winthrop B. Smith, 1843.

———. *McGuffey's Newly Revised Rhetorical Guide or Fifth Reader.* Cincinnati: Winthrop B. Smith and Co., 1853.

Marden, Orison Swett (ed.). *The Consolidated Library.* 15 Vols. Revised edn. New York and Washington: Bureau of National Literature and Art, 1907.

———. *Every Man a King, or Might in Mind-Mastery.* New York: Thomas Y. Crowell Co., 1906.

———. *Not the Salary but the Opportunity.* New York: Thomas Y. Crowell Co., no date.

———. *Peace, Power and Plenty.* New York: Thomas Y. Crowell Co., 1909.

———. *The Young Man Entering Business.* New York: Thomas Y. Crowell Co., 1903.

Martin, Alfred W. *Psychic Tendencies of To-day.* New York: D. Appleton and Co., 1918.

Martin, Edward S. "Too Much Success," *North American Review,* CLXXXVIII (July 1908), 62–70.

Mather, Cotton. *The Angel of Bethesda, Visiting the Invalids of a Miserable World . . . by a Fellow of the Royal Society.* New London: Timothy Green, 1722.

———. *Bonifacius: Essays to Do Good.* Boston: B. Green, 1710.

Mathews, William. *Getting On In the World: or, Hints on Success in Life.* Chicago: S. C. Griggs and Co., 1883.

Mathison, Richard R. *Faiths, Cults and Sects of America: From Atheism to Zen.* Indianapolis: Bobbs-Merrill, 1960.

Matthiessen, F. O. *American Renaissance: Art and Expression in the Age of Emerson and Whitman.* New York: Oxford University Press, 1941.

Maurice, Arthur B. "Best Sellers of Yesterday: I—Augusta Jane Evans' St. Elmo," *Bookman,* XXXI (March 1910), 35–42.

May, Henry F. *The End of American Innocence: A Study of the First Years of Our Own Time, 1912–1917.* New York: Alfred A. Knopf, 1959.

———. *Protestant Churches and Industrial America.* New York: Harper and Bros., 1949.

Mayes, Herbert R. *Alger: A Biography Without a Hero.* New York: Macy-Mesius, 1928.

Mead, Sidney E. "American Protestantism since the Civil War. I. From Denominationalism to Americanism," *The Journal of Religion,* XXXVI (January 1956), 1–16.

———. "American Protestantism since the Civil War. II. From Americanism to Christianity," *The Journal of Religion,* XXXVI (April 1956), 67–89.

———. *The Lively Experiment, the Shaping of Christianity in America.* New York: Harper and Row, 1963.

Meehan, Jeannette Porter. *The Lady of the Limberlost: the Life and Letters of Gene Stratton-Porter.* New York: Doubleday, Doran and Co., 1928.

Meigs, Cornelia, *et al.* (eds.). *A Critical History of Children's Literature.* New York : The Macmillan Co., 1953.

Merton, Robert K. *Mass Persuasion: the Social Psychology of a War Bond Drive.* New York: Harper and Bros., 1946.

———. *Social Theory and Social Structure: Toward the Codification of Theory and Research.* Glencoe: The Free Press, 1949.

Meyer, Donald. *The Positive Thinkers.* Garden City: Doubleday and Co., 1965.

Meyers, Marvin. *The Jacksonian Persuasion: Politics and Belief.* New York: Vintage Books, 1960.

Millard, Bailey. "The Personality of Harold Bell Wright," *The Bookman,* XLIV (January 1917), 463–469.

Miller, Joseph Dana. "Apostles of Autolatry," *Arena,* XXIV (December 1900), 608–617.

Miller, William. "American Historians and the Business Elite," *Journal of Economic History* (November 1949), pp. 184–208.

———. "The Gospel of Norman Vincent Peale," *Union Seminary Quarterly Review,* X (January 1955), 15–22.

———. "The Recruitment of the American Business Elite," *Quarterly Journal of Economics* (May 1950), pp. 242–253.

———. "Some Negative Thinking About Norman Vincent Peale," *The Reporter* (January 13, 1955), pp. 19–24.

Mills, C. Wright. "The Professional Ideology of Social Pathologists," *Power, Politics, and People.* Edited by I. L. Horowitz. New York: Oxford University Press, 1963. Pp. 525–552.

———. *White Collar: The American Middle Class.* New York: Oxford University Press, 1951.

Mills, James D. *The Art of Money Making or the Road to Fortune: A Universal Guide for Honest Success.* New York: International Publishing Co., 1872.

Minnich, Harvey C. *William Holmes McGuffey and His Readers.* New York: American Book Co., 1936.

Modern Achievement. 10 vols. Edited by Edward Everett Hale. New York: The University Society, 1902. Vol. I, *Science of Business;* Vol. II, *Business and Professional Life;* Vol. III, *Health and Recreation;* Vol. IV, *Reading and Home Study;* Vol. V, *Modern Home Life;* Vol. VI, *Leaders of Men—Biographies;* Vol. VII, *Men of Achievement—Inventors and Scientists;* Vol. VIII, *Men of Achievement—Travelers and Explorers;* Vol. IX, *Heroes and Heroism;* Vol. X, *Patriotism and Citizenship.*

Morrison, Chester. "Religion Reaches Out," *Look* (December 14, 1954), pp. 41–47.

Mosier, Richard D. *Making the American Mind: Social and Moral Ideas in the McGuffey Readers.* New York: King's Crown Press, 1947.

Mott, Frank Luther. *Golden Multitudes: the Story of Best Sellers in the United States.* New York: The Macmillan Co., 1947.

———. *A History of American Magazines,* Vol. IV. Cambridge, Mass.: Harvard University Press, 1957.

Munsterberg, Hugo. *Psychotherapy.* New York: Moffat, Yard and Co., 1909.

Niebuhr, H. Richard. *The Social Success of Denominationalism.* New York: Henry Holt and Co., 1929.

Oberndorf, C. P. *A History of Psychoanalysis in America.* New York: Grune and Stratton, 1953.

Oliver, M. P. *Success Preparedness.* New York: Thomas Y. Crowell Co., 1916.

Orton, J. Louis. *Emile Coué: The Man and His Work.* London: The Francis Mott Co., 1935.

Owen, William D. *Success in Life and How to Secure It.* Chicago: Howe Watts and Co., 1882. First published in 1878.

Parker, W. B. (ed.). *Psychotherapy: A Course of Reading in Sound Psychology, Sound Medicine, and Sound Religion.* 3 vols. New York: The Centre Publishing Co., 1909.

Parsons, Talcott. *The Structure of Social Action.* Glencoe: The Free Press, 1949.

Patterson, Charles Brodie. *Dominion and Power: or The Science of Life and Living.* New York: Funk and Wagnalls, 1910.

———. *What the New Thought Stands For.* New York: The Alliance Publishing Co., 1901.

Peale, Norman Vincent. *A Guide to Confident Living.* New York: Prentice-Hall, 1948.

———. "Let the Church Speak Up for Capitalism," *Reader's Digest,* LVII (September 1950), 126–130.

———. *The Power of Positive Thinking.* Englewood Cliffs, N.J.: Prentice-Hall, 1952.

Pelmanism. New York: The Pelman Institute of America, 1924. 12 pamphlets: *The First Principles of Pelmanism; Purpose, or What Is Your Aim?; Knowledge and the Senses; Will and Effort; Concentration; The Pelman Principles of Mental Connection; Imagination and Originality; The Pursuit of Truth; Pelmanism on Personality; How to Organize Your Mental Life; Pelmanism on Your Subconscious Mind; Pelmanism in Action.*

Pelton, DeWitt L., D.D. "M. Coué and the Church," *The Forum,* LXIX (April 1923), 1393–1398.

Penniman, James H. *Practical Suggestions.* Syracuse: C.W. Bardeen, 1905.

Phelps, R. M. "Hopeful Faith, a Curative Agency," *Journal of Nervous and Mental Disease,* XXIII (1896), 274–277.

Pitkin, Walter B. *The Psychology of Achievement.* New York: Simon and Schuster, 1930.

———. *The Psychology of Happiness.* New York: Simon and Schuster, 1929.

Porter, Gene Stratton. *Freckles.* New York: Grosset and Dunlap, 1904.

———. *A Girl of the Limberlost.* New York: Doubleday, Page and Co., 1910.

———. *The Harvester.* New York: Doubleday, Page and Co., 1911.

———. *Michael O'Halloran.* New York: Doubleday, Page and Co., 1915.

Post, Helen. *A Conquest of Poverty.* Seabreeze, Fla.: International Scientific Association, 1899.

Post, Louis F. *Ethics of Democracy: A Series of Optimistic Essays on the Natural Laws of Human Society.* Indianapolis: Bobbs-Merrill, 1916. Originally published in 1903.

———. *Success in Life.* New York: The Civic Publishing Co., 1902.

The Problem of Success for Young Men and How to Solve It: An Educational Symposium by Successful Men and Leaders of Thought. New York: W. R. Hearst, 1903.

Prothro, James Warren. *The Dollar Decade: Business Ideas in the 1920's.* Baton Rouge: Louisiana State University Press, 1954.

Purinton, Edward Earle. *Efficient Living*. New York: Robert M. McBride and Co., 1915.

Putnam, James J. "A Plea for the Study of Philosophic Methods in Preparation for Psycho-Analytical Work," *Journal of Abnormal Psychology*, VI (October-November 1911), 249–264.

Quigley, Dorothy. *Success Is for You*. New York: E. P. Dutton and Co., 1897.

Quimby, P. P. *The Quimby Manuscripts*. Edited by Horatio W. Dresser. Introduction by Ervin Seale. New York: The Julian Press, 1961. Originally published in 1921.

———. *The Science of Health and Happiness*. Edited by E. S. Collie, 1939. On mimeograph in Columbia University Library.

Randall, John Herman. *The Culture of Personality*. New York: H. M. Caldwell Co., 1912.

———. *The Mastery of Life*. New York: Robert M. McBride and Co., 1931.

———. *The New Light on Immortality, or The Significance of Psychic Research*. New York: The Macmillan Co., 1921.

———. *A New Philosophy of Life*. New York: Dodge Publishing Co., 1911.

———. *The Philosophy of Power, or What to Live For*. New York: Dodge Publishing Co., 1917.

Reich, Emil. *Success in Life*. New York: Duffield and Co., 1907.

Roe, Edward P. *Barriers Burned Away*. New York: Dodd, Mead and Co., 1872.

———. *Driven Back to Eden*. New York: P. F. Collier and Son, 1885.

———. *"Miss Lou."* New York: P. F. Collier and Son, 1888.

———. *Opening a Chestnut Burr*. New York: Dodd, Mead and Co., 1874.

———. *Taken Alive and Other Stories: with an Autobiography*. New York: P. F. Collier and Son, 1902.

Roe, Mary A. *E. P. Roe: Reminiscences of His Life by His Sister*. New York: Dodd, Mead and Co., 1899.

Roosevelt, Theodore. "The Conditions of Success," *African and European Addresses*. New York: G. P. Putnam's Sons, 1910.

Royce, Josiah. *Outlines of Psychology*. New York: The Macmillan Co., 1903.

———. *William James and Other Essays on the Philosophy of Life*. New York: The Macmillan Co., 1911.

Samuelsson, Kurt. *Religion and Economic Action.* Translated by E. Geoffrey French. New York: Harper and Row, 1961.

Santayana, George. *Winds of Doctrine: Studies in Contemporary Civilization.* New York: Charles Scribner's Sons, 1913.

Schneider, Herbert Wallace. *Religion in Twentieth Century America.* Cambridge, Mass.: Harvard University Press, 1952.

Schneider, Louis. *The Freudian Psychology and Veblen's Social Theory.* New York: King's Crown Press, 1948.

Schneider, Louis, and Dornbusch, Sanford M. *Popular Religion: Inspirational Books in America.* Chicago: University of Chicago Press, 1958.

Scott, Frank Lincoln. *Autosuggestion and Salesmanship, or Imagination in Business.* Preface by Orison Swett Marden. New York: American Library Service, 1923.

Sears, F. W. *How to Attract Success.* New York: New Thought Publishers, 1914.

Seton, Julia. *Destiny: A New Thought Novel.* New York: Edward J. Clode, 1917.

———. *The Science of Success.* New York: Edward J. Clode, 1914.

Shakow, David, and Rapaport, David. "The Influence of Freud on American Psychology," *Psychological Issues,* Vol. IV. Monograph No. 13.

Sharman, H. R. *The Power of the Will, or Success.* Boston: Roberts Bros., 1894.

Shaw, Albert. *The Outlook for the Average Man.* New York: The Macmillan Co., 1907.

Sheldon, Charles M. *His Brother's Keeper, or Christian Stewardship.* Chicago: Advance Publishing Co., 1898.

———. *The History of "In His Steps" by Its Author.* Privately printed, 1938.

———. *In His Steps.* New York: Hurst and Co., no date.

———. *Malcolm Kirk: A Tale of Moral Heroism in Overcoming the World.* Chicago: The Church Press, 1898.

———. *The Mere Man and His Problems.* Chicago: Fleming H. Revell Co., 1924.

———. *The Reformer.* Chicago: Advance Publishing Co., 1902.

Sheldon, Henry C. *Theosophy and New Thought.* New York: The Abingdon Press, 1916.

Sherin, Henry. *Individual Mastery or How to Make the Most of Yourself.* New York: The Trow Press, 1915.

Selected Bibliography

Sherman, John Carleton. *The Stunted Saplings*. Boston: Sherman, French and Co., 1911.

Sizer, Nelson. *The Royal Road to Wealth: How to Find and Follow It*. San Francisco: J. Dewing and Co., 1883.

Smiles, Samuel. *The Autobiography of Samuel Smiles*. Edited by Thomas Mackay. New York: E. P. Dutton and Co., 1905.

―――. *Self-Help*. Boston: Ticknor and Fields, 1860.

Smith, Timothy L. *Revivalism and Social Reform in Mid-Nineteenth Century America*. New York: The Abingdon Press, 1957.

Spiller, Robert E., and Larrabee, Eric, *et al.* (eds.). *American Perspectives: The National Self-Image in the Twentieth Century*. Cambridge, Mass.: Harvard University Press, 1961.

Starke, D. *Character: How to Strengthen It*. New York: Funk and Wagnalls, 1916.

―――. *Poise: How to Attain It*. New York: Funk and Wagnalls, 1916.

Steele, Richard. *The Religious Tradesman*. Charlestown: Samuel Etheridge, 1804.

Stevens, Walter B. *Eleven Roads to Success: Charted by St. Louisans Who Have Traveled Them*. St. Louis, 1914.

Stockwell, H. G. *Essential Elements of Business Character*. New York: Fleming H. Revell Co., 1911.

Strong, Josiah. *Our Country: Its Possible Future and Its Present Crisis*. New York: The Baker and Taylor Co., 1891.

―――. *The Problem of Tainted Money*. New York: Funk and Wagnalls, 1905.

―――. *The Times and Young Men*. New York: The Baker and Taylor Co., 1901.

Success. Edited by Orison Swett Marden. Vols. I–XIV (1897–1911).

Sweet, William Warren. *The Story of Religions in America*. New York: Harper and Bros., 1930.

Tansley, A. G. *The New Psychology and Its Relation to Life*. New York: Dodd, Mead and Co., 1922.

Tapper, Thomas. *Efficiency: Its Spiritual Source*. New York: The Platt and Peck Co., 1911.

―――. *How to Build a Fortune*. New York: The Platt and Peck Co., 1913.

―――. *Youth and Opportunity: Being Chapters on the Factors of Success*. New York: The Platt and Peck Co., 1912.

Taylor, Frederick Winslow. *The Principles of Scientific Manage-*

ment. New York, Harper and Bros., 1942. Original copyright, 1911.

Taylor, Walter Fuller. *The Economic Novel in America*. Chapel Hill: University of North Carolina Press, 1942.

Tebbel, John. *From Rags to Riches: Horatio Alger, Jr., and the American Dream*. New York: The Macmillan Co., 1963.

Thayer, Wm. M. *Aim High: Hints and Helps for Young Men*. New York: Thomas Whittaker, 1895.

——. *The Bobbin Boy: or How Nat Got His Learning: An Example for Youth*. Boston: J. E. Tilton and Co., 1860.

——. *Domestic Wine: a Foe of Temperance*. New York: National Temperance Society, 1864.

——. *Ethics of Success*. Boston: Silver, Burdett and Co., 1894.

——. *Nelson: or, How a Country Boy Made His Way in the City*. New York: T. Y. Crowell, 1878.

——. *New Cider, A Dangerous Beverage*. New York: National Temperance Society, 1870.

——. *Onward to Fame and Fortune: or Climbing Life's Ladder*. New York: The Christian Herald, 1897.

——. *Turning Points in Successful Careers*. New York: Thos. Y. Crowell and Co., 1895.

Tilley, William James. *Masters of the Situation: or Some Secrets of Success and Power*. New York: N. D. Thompson Publishing Co., 1890.

Todd, John. *The Student's Manual*. Northampton: Hopkins, Bridgman and Co., 1859.

——. *The Young Man: Hints Addressed to the Young Men of the United States*. Northampton: Hopkins, Bridgman and Co., 1856.

Towne, Elizabeth. *15 Lessons in New Thought, or Lessons in Living*. Holyoke: The Elizabeth Towne Co., 1921. Original copyright, 1910.

Townsend, Charles. *Forty Witnesses to Success*. New York: Anson D. F. Randolph and Co., 1894.

Trine, Ralph Waldo. *Character-Building Thought Power*. New York: Thos. Y. Crowell and Co., 1899.

——. *In Tune with the Infinite*. New York: Dodd, Mead and Co., 1921. Originally published in 1897.

——. *The Land of Living Men*. New York: Thos. Y. Crowell and Co., 1910.

——. *On the Open Road: Being Some Thoughts and a Little Creed of Wholesome Living.* New York: Thomas Y. Crowell and Co., 1928.

———. *The Power That Wins.* Indianapolis: Bobbs-Merrill, 1928.

———. *What All the World's A-Seeking.* New York: Thos. Y. Crowell and Co., 1899.

Troward, T. *The Creative Process in the Individual.* New York: McBride, Nast and Co., 1915.

Tuthill, L. C. *Success in Life: the Mechanic.* New York: George P. Putnam, 1850.

———. *Success in Life: the Merchant.* New York: George P. Putnam, 1850.

Tuttle, Joseph. *The Law of Success.* New York: R. F. Fenno and Co., 1916.

———. *Prosperity Through Thought Force.* Holyoke: The Elizabeth Towne Co., 1907.

Tyler, Thomas P. *The Elements of Success in Life. A Sermon.* Hartford: Case, Tiffany and Co., 1856.

Tyner, Paul. "The Metaphysical Movement," *The American Monthly Review of Reviews,* XXV (March 1902), 312–320.

Vail, Henry J. *A History of the McGuffey Readers.* Cleveland: privately printed, 1910.

Van Doren, William Howard. *Mercantile Morals.* New York: Charles Scribner, 1852.

Van Eden, Frederik. "How Mind Can Heal the Body," *The American Magazine,* LXVI (October 1908), 531–538.

Wade, J. M. *How to Command Money.* Boston: M. Gifford Publishing Co., 1903.

Walsh, Chad. *Stop Looking and Listen: An Invitation to the Christian Life.* New York: Harper and Bros., 1947.

Ward, Lester F. *Dynamic Sociology.* 2 vols. New York: D. Appleton and Co., 1883.

Warner, W. Lloyd, and Abegglen, James C. *Big Business Leaders in America.* New York: Harper and Bros., 1955.

———. *Occupational Mobility in American Business and Industry.* Minneapolis: University of Minnesota Press, 1955.

Waters, Robert. *Intellectual Pursuits or Culture by Self-Help.* New York: The Humboldt Publishing Co., 1892.

Watson, John B. *Behaviorism.* New York: W. W. Norton and Co., 1925.

Wattles, Wallace D. *Financial Success Through Creative Thought: or the Science of Getting Rich*. Holyoke: The Elizabeth Towne Co., 1927.

Weaver, G. S. *The Ways of Life*. New York: Fowles and Wells, 1855.

Webb, C. H. *St. Twelv'mo, or the Cuneiform Encyclopedist of Chattanooga*. New York: C. H. Webb, 1868.

Weisberger, Bernard A. *They Gathered at the River*. Boston: Little, Brown and Co., 1958.

West, Nathaniel. *A Cool Million*. New York: Berkley Publishing Corp., 1961. First published in 1934.

Westgard, Gilbert K., II (ed.). *Alger Street, the Poetry of Horatio Alger, Jr*. Boston: J. S. Canner and Co., 1964.

Whipple, Edwin P. *Success and Its Conditions*. Boston: James R. Osgood and Co., 1871.

White, William A. *Twentieth Century Psychiatry, Its Contribution to Man's Knowledge of Himself*. New York: W. W. Norton and Co., 1936.

Whyte, William H., Jr. *The Organization Man*. New York: Simon and Schuster, 1956.

Wilcox, Ella Wheeler. *New Thought Common Sense and What Life Means to Me*. Chicago: W. B. Conkey Co., 1908.

Williams, James Watson. *The Passion for Riches; and Its Influence upon Our Social, Literary and Political Character*. Utica: Eli Maynard, 1838.

Williams, Robin M., Jr. *American Society: A Sociological Interpretation*. New York: Alfred A. Knopf, 1960.

Wilson, Bryan R. *Sects and Society*. Berkeley: University of California Press, 1961.

Wilson, Floyd B. *Paths to Power*. New York: R. F. Fenno and Co., 1901.

Wiman, Erastus. *Chances of Success: Episodes and Observations in the Life of a Busy Man*. New York: American News Co., 1893.

Winston, Carl. *How to Run a Million into a Shoestring and Other Shortcuts to Success*. New York: G. P. Putnam's Sons, 1960.

Wise, Daniel. *The Young Man's Counsellor*. New York: Carlton and Phillips, 1853.

Wood, Benjamin. *The Successful Man of Business*. New York: Brentano's, 1899.

Selected Bibliography

Wood, Henry. *The New Thought Simplified: How to Gain Harmony and Health*. Boston: Lee and Shepard, 1904.

Worcester, Elwood; McComb, Samuel; and Coriat, Isador H. *Religion and Medicine: the Moral Control of Nervous Disorders*. New York: Moffat, Yard and Co., 1908.

Wright, Harold Bell. *The Calling of Dan Matthews*. Chicago: The Book Supply Co., 1909.

———. *The Eyes of the World*. New York: A. L. Burt, 1914.

———. *That Printer of Udell's: A Story of the Middle West (A Story of Practical Christianity)*. Chicago: The Book Supply Co., 1903.

———. *The Shepherd of the Hills*. New York: A. L. Burt, 1907.

———. *Their Yesterdays*. Chicago: The Book Supply Co., 1912.

———. *To My Sons*. New York: Harper and Bros., 1934.

———. *When a Man's a Man*. Chicago: The Book Supply Co., 1916.

———. *The Winning of Barbara Worth (The Ministry of Capital)*. Chicago: The Book Supply Co., 1911.

Wright, Louis B. "Franklin's Legacy to the Gilded Age," *The Virginia Quarterly Review*, XXII (1946), 268–279.

———. *Middle-Class Culture in Elizabethan England*. Chapel Hill: University of North Carolina Press, 1935.

Wyllie, Irvin G. *The Self-Made Man in America: the Myth of Rags to Riches*. New Brunswick: Rutgers University Press, 1954.

The Young Man's Own Book. Philadelphia: Key, Mielke and Biddle, 1832.

Young, Vash. *A Fortune to Share*. New York: Blue Ribbon Books, 1931.

———. *Let's Start Over Again*. New York: Blue Ribbon Books, 1932.

Zweig, Stefan. *Mental Healers: Franz Anton Mesmer, Mary Baker Eddy, Sigmund Freud*. Translated by Eden and Cedar Paul. New York: The Viking Press, 1932.

INDEX

Abbott, Jacob, on ethics for children, 21
Abbott, Lyman, 33; on E. P. Roe's novels, 69
academic excellence, 224–225
Adams, Henry, 51, 154
Addams, Jane, 177
agrarian radicalism, 111
alcoholic vs. drunkard, 205
Alger, Horatio, Jr., 64, 68, 79, 90, 91, 173, 227; and Children's Aid Society, 55; on city vs. country, 57–58; early life and education of, 49–52; emphasis on luck, 53–54; Freudian interpretation of works of, 49 n, 58, 60; as genteel reformer, 54–56; and the Gilded Age, 59–60; and hereditary determinism, 56–57; on Marlborough, Massachusetts, 49; and merchants as benefactors, 58; middle-class orientation of, 49, 55, 58–60; and mill owner as villain, 50; and Newsboys' Lodging House, 55; and orphan heroes, 57–58; and *padrone* system, 54; pastorate of, 51; and plots of Christian novels, 78–79; present reputation of, 52–53; and rags-to-riches theme, 52, 56; sales of his books, 53, 60; and social mobility, 55, 56, 91;
as spokesman for traditional virtues, 53; as symbol of an era, 48–49; and wealth, 57, 59, 91
Alger, Horatio, Sr., 49
Alger, Olive Augusta, 55
American Foundation of Religion and Psychiatry, 227
American Psychoanalytic Association, 212
anti-evolution crusade, 120
anxiety and New Thought, 167–168
applied psychology, *see* psychology, applied
Arena magazine, 155, 177
aristocratic values vs. capitalism, 23–24
"Art of Living," 223
asceticism, practical, 20–23
autosuggestion: and Coué, 221–222; vs. prayer, 217

Baker, Ray Stannard, on psychotherapy, 211
Barriers Burned Away, 67–68
Beecher, Henry Ward, on theology, 115
behaviorism, 222–223
Bellamy, Edward, 178
Belmont, Perry, 107
Bergson, Henri, 161, 232

Index

Beyond the Pleasure Principle, 210

Blackmar, Frank, on social gospel, 72

Blanton, Smiley: and Norman Vincent Peale, 227; on psychiatry and religion, 228

Bonifacius: Essays to Do Good, 25, 26

Bourne, Randolph, on diminishing opportunity for success, 128

Brace, Charles Loring, 57, 70

Bremner, Robert, on poverty, 180

Bryan, William Jennings, 107, 121

Business Power, A Practical Manual in Financial Ability, 216

Cabot, Richard: on psychosomatic medicine, 199–200; on psychotherapy, 202–203

Caleb in the Country, 29

Call, Annie Payson, 168

Calvinism, 21, 115, 144, 162, 168, 178

capitalism: vs. aristocratic values, 23–24; and ascetic Protestantism, 18, 20–23; and Christianity, 232–233; and economic individualism, 9; and individual freedom, 13–14; in McGuffey's readers, 33–36; and Protestant ethic, 8, 18–23; in self-help literature, 35–36; and success literature, 116–117; and success myth, 7–8

Carnegie, Andrew, 110 *n*, 118 *n*

Carnegie, Dale, 216

Carpenter, Frederic, on William James, 137–138

Castiglione, Baldasarre, 16

Century Dictionary, 98

child-rearing: and behaviorism, 222; and New Thought, 145–148

Children's Aid Society, 52, 55

children's literature, authors of: Jacob Abbott, 30–32; Horatio Alger, Jr., 48–62; William H. McGuffey, 32–36; E. P. Roe, 69–70

Christ: healing mission of, 200, 205; and social reform, 182, 186

Christian Endeavor Union, 110

Christian novel, 65; and Alger pattern, 78–79; and city, 69–70, 90; Augusta Jane Evans, 65–67, 92; and hereditary determinism, 78–79; and immigrants, 79, 81, 90, 116; and industrial conflict, 73–74; and industrialism, 88, 90; and middle class, 78, 81; and New Thought, 155–156; nostalgic tone of, 88–89; orphan heroes in, 66, 68, 79, 84; plots of, 88–89; Gene Stratton Porter, 76, 79–83, 90, 92; rags-to-riches theme, 78–79, 83; vs. realism, 89–92, 156; E. P. Roe, 64, 67–71, 74; Charles M. Sheldon, 64, 71–76; and social reform, 71–76; and wealth, 79–83, 91–92; Harold Bell Wright, 76, 83–88, 90; *see also* conduct-of-life literature; self-help literature; success literature

Christian Science, 130, 134, 159, 198, 200, 209, 219

Christianity: and capitalism, 232–233; as commodity, 224; and divinity of man, 148–149; and earning living, 129; muscular, 159; vs. naturalistic universe, 113; and positive thinking, 228–229; practical, 225–226

city: in Christian novels, 69–70, 90; vs. country, 8, 41, 57–59, 70–71, 79, 89, 90, 102–104, 110–111; and slums, 108–109

civil liberty vs. natural liberty, 29

Clark, Francis E., on city vs. country, 110–111

clergy: and business community, 113 *n*, and Couéism, 219; and medical profession, 200–201, 203, 227–228

compensation, idea of, in New Thought, 174–175

competition, in New Thought, 171–172

Comstock, Anthony, 83

conduct-of-life literature: in Gilded Age, 97–121; in Jacksonian period, 29–32, 43–44; Josiah Strong, 114; *see also* Christian novel; self-help literature; success literature

"Confident Living," 223

Coriat, Isador, and psychoanalysis, 211–212

corporation vs. individualism, 9, 119

corporation employee and success literature, 118

Cortegiano, Il, 16

Coué, Emil, 218–221; on autosuggestion, 221; and clergy, 219

Courtier, 16

covenant, Puritan, 6–7

Crafts, Wilbur: on business vs. Christian principles, 112; on 13 American evils, 111 *n*

Creel, George: on Emil Coué, 218; on Pelmanism, 218

Dale, John T., on city vs. country, 103–104

Darwinism, 10, 114, 163; and idealism, 161; and individualism, 162–164; social, 54, 116; Spencerian, 162–163

determinism: vs. mind power cult, 12; vs. New Thought, 163–164

Dewey, John, 147

divinity of man in New Thought, 148–149

Dreiser, Theodore, 89–91

Dresser, Annetta, 197

Dresser, Horatio, 168; and *Good Housekeeping* magazine, 176

Dresser, Julius, 197

Driven Back to Eden, 70–71

drunkard vs. alcoholic, 205

Eddy, Mary Baker, 130, 197

Edgerton, James Arthur, 177

education and New Thought, 147

ego, 196; power of, 229

élan vital, 161

Emerson, Ralph Waldo, 13, 14, 137, 148, 174 *n,* 229; on transcendental idealism, 134–136

Emerson, Ralph Waldo, 98

Emmanuel Movement, 200–201, 203, 210, 211

Enlightenment, 32

"entering the silence" in New Thought, 221

entrepreneur, independent, 185

Evans, Augusta Jane, 65–67, 92; *St. Elmo,* 66–67

Evans, Warren Felt, 197

evil, 204; and New Thought, 164–165

Eyes of the World, 86–88

extravagance vs. simplicity, 105–107

failure in New Thought, 170

faith: in faith, 226; vs. reality, 139–140; and salesmanship, 225–226; vs. science, 138–139, 208, 228; and will-to-believe, 217

Fletcher, Horace, 168

Flower, Benjamin O., on materialism, 155–156

Fortune magazine, 232

Franck, Sebastian, 20

Index

Franklin, Benjamin, 37, 227; and rags-to-riches theme, 4; and success literature, 28–29; on social mobility, 28–29
Freckles, 77–78
free-will, 207
Freedley, Edwin, 37; on city vs. country, 41; on wealth, 38, 40
Freud, Sigmund, 197, 208, 210, 220; and James Jackson Putnam, 212–213
Freudianism: and Horatio Alger, Jr., 49 *n,* 58, 60; and mind-cure, 208–211; and New Thought, 209, 210; reception, in U.S., 208–212; *see also* psychoanalysis
Fuller, Margaret, 33
fundamentalism, religious, 111

Gates Academy, 50, 51
general welfare and individual responsibility, 178–183
Getting on in the World, 101
Gilded Age, 8, 9–11, 51, 79, 108, 111, 114, 120, 121; and Alger myth, 53; and Alger novels, 59–60; and conduct-of-life literature, 97–121; and Harvard College, 51; and number of millionaires, 99–101
Gladden, Washington, 33
God: and divinity of man, 148–149; in mind-power cult, 14, 226; and nervous disturbances, 203; New Thought concept of, 160
Golden Rule, 74, 117, 172
Good Housekeeping magazine, 176
gospel of efficiency, 183–185
Gospel of Out of Doors, 110
gospel of relaxation, 168, 188
gospel of success, 131
group therapy, 229
Guideposts magazine, 223

Haddock, Frank Channing: on business power, 216; on power of individual, 215–216; on subconscious, 217; on will-to-believe, 216–217
Hall, Bolton, 177; on older success literature, 131–133
Hammond, Bray, 34
Harmony, 130
Harvard College, in Gilded Age, 51
Harvester, 81–82
Hawthorne, Julian, on E. P. Roe's novels, 69
health: and the good life, 205; and virtue, 14
Hegel, G. W. F., 13, 161
Herberg, Will, on faith in faith, 226
hereditary determinism: in Alger novels, 56–57; in Christian novels, 78–79
Herrick, Robert, 90, 91
higher criticism, Biblical, 10, 114
Hilton, Warren: on applied psychology, 220; on subconscious mind, 219
His Brother's Keeper, 73–74
historical materialism, 18
"holding the thought" in New Thought, 175–176
Holmes, Oliver Wendell, on success, 98
Horney, Karen, on striving for power, 230
How to Win Friends and Influence People, 216
Hubbard, Elbert, on success as natural, 170, 170 *n*
Hunt, Freeman: on money, 41; and nostalgia for past, 41–42; on worth vs. wealth, 37, 39
Hunter, Robert, 180
hypnotism, 196, 197, 198, 209

Hyslop, James, on immortality, 141–143

idea, Hegelian, 161
idealism, 170, 207; and Darwinism, 161; and gospel of efficiency, 185; and individualism, 229–231; vs. industrialism, 128–131; and New Thought, 134–136; vs. pessimism, 155, 169–170; practical, 136–137, 173; and pragmatism, 137–138; and psychoanalytic movement, 213–214; transcendental, 134–136
illness: as mental error, 197; mental and moral factors in, 203; and sin, 14, 205, 228
immigrants, 50, 56; and Christian novel, 79, 81, 90; in New Thought, 132–133; in success literature, 116
immortality: in New Thought, 140–143; and science, 140–141, 142–143; and social reform, 142–143
individual: and power of self-direction, 140; and quest for power, 230–231; and Universal Soul, 208
individual freedom under capitalism, 13–14
individual responsibility and general welfare, 178–179, 180–183
individualism: vs. corporation, 9, 119; vs. industrialism, 196, 229–231; and mind-power cult, 13–14, 196; and New Deal, 232; and social Darwinism, 162–164; vs. social regulation, 108
industrial conflict: in Christian novel, 73–74; and New Thought, 183–185; and success literature, 117, 117 *n*
industrialism, 71; and Christian novel, 88, 90; vs. idealism, 128–131; vs. individualism, 196, 229–231; in self-help literature, 9–11
In His Steps, 74–75
International New Thought Alliance, 177
In Tune with the Infinite, 12

Jackson, Andrew, 29, 30
Jacksonian era, 6, 49, 159; conduct-of-life literature in, 29–32, 43–44
James, William, 147, 161 *n;* on anxiety, 167–168; on emotion, 166; on evolution, 163; on gospel of relaxation, 168; on immortality, 140–141; on licensing of mental healers, 198–199; on mind power, 159; and New Thought movement, 133–134, 137–141; on therapeutic implications of new psychology, 198–199
James-Lange theory, 166
Jed, the Poorhouse Boy, 56
Jefferson, Thomas, 32, 158
Jones, "Golden Rule," 171, 177

Ku Klux Klan, 120

La Follette's Weekly Magazine, 120
Land of Living Men, 178
law of attraction, 169
law of non-resistance, 168–169, 221
law of reversed effort, 221
liberalism, economic, and Puritanism, 23–25
licensing of mental healers, 198–199
Lindsey, Ben, 158 *n*
liquor in success literature, 108–110

Index

London, Jack, 91
luck: in Alger novels, 53–54; in Protestant ethic, 53–54
Lutheranism, 21, 168
Lynn, Kenneth, on success myth, 90–91

McGuffey, William H.: on education, 35; on luxury and wealth, 36; on morality vs. success, 33–34; on open road to success, 33; profile of, 32
McGuffey's readers, 32–36
manual labor in success literature, 101–102
Marden, Orison Swett, 119, 156; on city vs. country, 103; on competition, 171; early life of, 156–157; on optimism, 158; on pessimism vs. success, 169–170
Marx, Karl, 18
Marxism, 116
materialism, 12, 207; vs. New Thought, 133–136, 155
Mather, Cotton, 25–28
Matthews, William, 101; on cities, 110
medical profession: and clergy, 200–201, 203, 227–228; and mind-cure movement, 197–199, 201, 205, 206; reception of Freudianism, 208–209, 211–212; and will to do good, 25
medicine and philosophy, 205–207
Mencken, H. L., on rural origins vs. success, 52
mental error and illness, 197
mental healers, see mind-cure movement
Mental Science, 130
mentalism in American culture, 14
merchants in Alger novels, 59
mesmerism, 196, 197

messianic tradition, 178–179
Metaphysical Healing, 130, 159
Meyer, Adolf: on Coué, 220; on subconscious mind, 219–220
Michael O'Halloran, 79–81
middle class: and Alger novels, 49, 55, 58–60; and Christian novels, 79, 81; and New Thought, 131, 134; and success literature, 107, 115–116
mill owner in Alger novels, 50
Miller, Perry, on free will, 6
millionaires, 50, 59, 79, 91, 179; in Gilded Age, 99–101
Mills, C. Wright, on changing patterns of success, 128
Mind, 130
Mind and Medicine, 211
mind-cure movement, 130, 168; effect on churches, 200–201; and Emmanuel Movement, 200–201; and Freudianism, 208–211; and medical profession, 197–199, 201, 205, 206; origin and spread of, 195–200; and psychoanalysis, 209–210; Phineas Parkhurst Quimby, 196–197, 199, 229; *see also* psychotherapy
mind-power cult, 133, 137; and behaviorism; 222–223; Emil Coué, 218–221; and determinism, 12; Frank Channing Haddock, 215–218; as humanistic doctrine, 233–234; and idea of God, 14, 226; and individualism, 13–14, 196; and Norman Vincent Peale, 223–233; Pelmanism, 218; and Protestant ethic, 15; and psychology vs. religion, 214–215; and psychotherapy, 195; vs. rags-to-riches theme, 11–12, 14; and social reform, 231–234; and subconscious mind, 207–208, 217, 218, 220–221; and success, 195,

270

214–231; Swoboda, 218; *see also* New Thought

money, love of, 104–105, 108, 172–173

moral problems and psychology, 204–205

motherhood, 106 *n*

Mulford, Prentice, 168

Munsterberg, Hugo, on Emmanuel Movement, 201; on preventive psychotherapy, 204–205; on psychotherapy, 203

mysticism, 220

National New Thought Alliance, 177

natural liberty vs. civil liberty, 29

natural man, 29

Nature, 137

Nautilus magazine, 177

New Deal, 232

New England, 4, 23, 24, 32, 50

New Thought movement, 130, 215, 229; and anxiety, 167–168; and applied psychology, 220–222; Bergson, 161, 232; and childrearing, 145–148; and competitive struggle, 171–172; and concept of God, 160; and definition of success, 172; vs. determinism, 163–164; and divinity of man, 148–149; and education, 147; Emerson, 134–136; and "entering the silence," 221; and failure, 170; Benjamin O. Flower, 155; and Freudianism, 209, 210; and gospel of efficiency, 183–185; and gospel of relaxation, 168, 188; and gospel of success, 131; Hegel, 161; and "holding the thought," 175–176; and idea of compensation, 174–175; and idealism vs. materialism, 134–136; and idealism and pragmatism, 137–138; and immigrants, 132–133; and immortality, 140–143; and individual's quest for power, 230–231; and industrial conflict, 183–185; William James, 133–134, 137–141; and law of attraction, 169; and law of nonresistance, 168–169, 221; and licensing of mental healers, 198–199; Orison Swett Marden, 156–158; vs. materialism, 133–136, 155; and messianic tradition, 178–179; and middle class, 131, 134; and muscular Christianity, 159; and organization man, 185–186; origin of, 196; and original sin, 144–145, 226; optimism in, 154–156, 158, 165–167, 169–170, 186; and other mind-power groups, 134; Norman Vincent Peale, 227; and political reform, 186; and poverty, 179–183; and practical idealism, 136–137; vs. priesthood, 144; and Progressive movement, 155, 156, 213; and prosperity, 149; and Protestant ethic, 187; and psychical research, 134, 141–143, 211; and psychotherapy, 203; vs. radical social change, 171–172, 181; vs. rags-to-riches theme, 131; and religion, 130–131, 200–201; and San Francisco earthquake, 175; and science, 161–164; and sin, 164–165; and social Darwinism, 162–164; and social reform, 154–156, 177–183; and Spanish-American war, 175; and success through mind power, 132–133, 169–170; as theology, 143–145; vs. theology, 203–204; and transcendentalism, 134–135; urban orientation of, 131; and wealth, 172–176; vs. wealthy, 179; and

New Thought movement (*cont'd*)
work, 144–145, 169, 172–174; *see also* mind-power cult
Newsboys' Lodging House, 55
Norris, Frank, 91
nostalgia: in Christian novels, 88–89; in self-help literature, 41–42

optimism in New Thought, 154–156, 158, 165–167, 169–170, 186
organization man, 185–186
original sin, 144–145, 226
orphan hero: in Alger novels, 57, 58; in Christian novels, 66, 68, 79, 84
Oxford English Dictionary, 98

padrone system, 54
Parsons, Talcott, 17
pastoral counseling, 201, 228
Patterson, Charles Brodie, 177
Peale, Norman Vincent, 12; on academic excellence, 224–225; and ego building, 229; on group therapy, 229; on nature of Christianity, 228–229; on nature of God, 226; and New Thought, 227; popularity of, 223–224, 232; on practical Christianity, 225–226; and religio-psychiatric clinic, 227–228; and social reform, 231–234
Pelmanism, 218
pessimism, 207; vs. idealism, 155, 169–170; in post-Civil War period, 154–156, 158
Phil, the Fiddler, 54, 56
Phillips, David Graham, 89, 91
philosophy and medicine, 205–207
political corruption and success literature, 112–113
political reform and New Thought, 186
Porter, Gene Stratton, 76, 79–83,

90, 92; and critics, 82; as crusader for righteousness, 82–83; *Freckles*, 77–78; *The Harvester*, 81–82; *Michael O'Halloran*, 79–81; *The Song of the Cardinal*, 77
positive thinking, 12, 195, 223, 227–229
positivism: and immortality, 141; vs. supernaturalism, 139, 140
Post, Louis, on rewards of industriousness, 118–119
poverty, 158; in New Thought, 179–183; in success literature, 108–110; vs. virtue, 57
Power Book Library, 215, 216
Power of Positive Thinking, 223, 225, 229
Power of Will, 215
Poyen, Charles, 196–197
pragmatism and idealism, 137–138
prayer vs. autosuggestion, 217
predestination, 6–7
prescriptive literature and Protestant ethic, 17
priesthood and New Thought, 144
Prince, Morton, 220
Principles of Scientific Management, 184
Progressive movement, 9, 56, 60, 80, 81, 177, 178, 180, 183, 186, 218, 226, 231; and New Thought, 155, 156, 213; and success literature, 118–119
prohibition movement, 120
prosperity: in New Thought, 149; vs. virtue, 112–113, 129
Protestant ethic, 41, 102, 120, 133, 227; and capitalism, 8, 18–23; and desire for wealth, 38–39; and luck, 53–54; and mind-power cult, 15; and New Thought, 187; and personal gain,

24–25; and prescriptive literature, 17; and rags-to-riches theme, 5–6; and success, 16–18, 27

Protestant Ethic and the Spirit of Capitalism, 17, 18

Protestantism: in American culture, 17; vs. Darwinism and higher criticism, 113; and development of capitalism, 18, 20–23

psychiatry: and New Thought, 134, 141–143, 211; and religion, 227–228

psychoanalysis, 195, 223; and idealism, 213–214; and mind-cure, 209–210, 212

psychology, 217; behaviorism, 222–223; and mind-power cult, 214–215; and moral problems, 204–205; and psychotherapy, 201–202; and reception of Freudianism, 208–209; and subconscious mind, 207–208; and supernaturalism, 228; therapeutic, 198; *see also* psychology, applied

psychology, applied: 218–222

Psychology, 147

psychosomatic medicine, 200

psychotherapy: early development of, 195–196; and New Thought, 203; preventive, 204–205; and psychology, 201–202; and spiritual regeneration, 205–207; and theology, 203–204

public ownership, 119–120

Puritanism, 4–5, 17, 134, 144, 147, 149, 227; vs. economic liberalism, 23–25; and idea of salvation, 54; messianic tradition of, 178; moderation vs. social regulation, 108; predestination vs. covenant, 6–7; and social mobility, 28–29; as reform influence, 24–25

Pushing to the Front, 157

Putnam, James Jackson: and Freud, 212–213; on philosophy and medicine, 206–207; on psychoanalysis, 212

Quimby, Phineas Parkhurst, life and influence of, 196–197, 199, 229

Ragged Dick, 51, 58

rags-to-riches theme, 17, 43, 90, 101, 111, 120, 121, 140, 216, 230; in Alger novels, 52, 56; in Christian novels, 78–79, 83; in Augusta Jane Evans novels, 65–67; Benjamin Franklin, 4; vs. mind power, 11–12, 14; vs. New Thought, 131; and Protestant ethic, 5–6; rural bias of, 8; and social reform, 7–9; virtue vs. sin, 6–7; wane of, 118, 214

Ralph Waldo Emerson, 98

realism, literary, vs. Christian novel, 89–92, 156

religion: fundamental, 111; and mind-power cult, 214–215; and New Thought, 130–131, 200–201; and psychiatry, 227–228; vs. science, 11, 114, 115, 161–162; utility of, 136–137

revivalism, religious, and success literature, 115

Rockefeller, John D., 9

Roe, E. P., 64, 67–71, 74; *Barriers Burned Away,* 67–68; children's novel, 67–70; on city vs. rural living, 69–70; *Driven Back to Eden,* 69–71

Roosevelt, Franklin D., 231

Roosevelt, Theodore, 81, 159

Royce, Josiah, 138, 161 *n;* on definition of psychology, 201–202; on health, 202

Index

St. Elmo, 66–68

salvation, 54, 149, 165; and evolution, 163

Salvation Army, 85

Samuelson, Kurt, 23

Santayana, George, 138; on moral confusion, 130

Schiller, F. C. S., 138

science, 129, 130, 133, 138–140, 187, 206, 220; vs. faith, 138–139, 208, 228; and immortality, 140–143; and New Thought, 161–164; vs. religion, 11, 114, 115, 161–162

Science and Health, 130

scientific determinism, 135

Secret of Achievement, 156

self-help literature, 4, 5; ancestral virtues in, 43; and capitalism, 35–36; city vs. country in, 41; Edwin Freedley, 37, 38, 40, 41; and industrialism, 9–11; McGuffey's readers, 32–36; nostalgic tone of, 41–42; and social reform, 40; on wealth vs. worth, 37–41; and yeoman myth, 41–42; *see also* Christian novel; conduct-of-life literature; success literature

self-made man, 29, 32

self-mastery, 215

Sheldon, Charles M., 64, 71–76; *His Brother's Keeper*, 73–74; on industrial conflict, 73–74; *In His Steps*, 74–75; and social gospel, 71–76

simplicity vs. extravagance, 105–107

sin: and illness, 14, 205, 228; in New Thought, 164–165; original, 144–145, 226; vs. success, 6–7

social change, radical, and New Thought, 171–172, 181

social gospel: in Sheldon novels, 71–76; Harold Bell Wright, 84

social mobility, 3, 5–7, 91; in Alger novels, 55, 56, 91; changing patterns of, 128; vs. hereditary determinism, 78–79; vs. Puritanism, 28–29; and success literature, 100–101

social protest and success literature, 111, 115–116, 120–121

social reform, 17, 111; in Christian novels, 71–76; and immortality, 142–143; and mind-power cult, 231–234; and New Thought, 154–156, 177–183; and Puritanism, 24–25; and rags-to-riches theme, 7–9; and self-help literature, 40

social regulation vs. individualism, 108

socialism, 181

Society for Applied Psychology, 219

Song of the Cardinal, 77

Spencer, Herbert, 162

Spiritualism, 134

Strong, Josiah, on breakup of traditional beliefs and values, 10–11, 113–114

subconscious mind: in Couéism, 219; in mind-power cult, 207–208, 217, 218, 220–221; as Universal Mind, 208

success: definitions of, 15, 97–99, 172; gospel of, 131; entrepreneurial vs. white-collar, 128–129; internal impediments to, 169–170; by power of mind, 132–133, 169–170, 195, 214–231; in Protestant ethic, 16–18, 27; vs. sin, 6–7; vs. virtue, 112; vs. wealth, 104, 172–174

success literature, 4; and city vs.

rural living, 102–104, 108–111; and corporation employee, 118; definition of success, 15, 97–99; Benjamin Franklin, 28–29; and immigrants, 116; and increase in millionaire class, 99–101; and individual freedom vs. social regulation, 108; vs. industrial capitalism, 116–117; and industrial conflict, 117, 117 *n;* and love of money, 104–105, 108; and manual labor, 101–102; Cotton Mather, 25–27; middle-class appeal of, 107, 115–116; and motherhood, 106 *n;* on political corruption, 112–113; and poverty, 108–110; and Progressive movement, 118–119; Puritan, 4–5; and religious revivalism, 115; and simplicity vs. extravagance, 105–107; and social mobility, 101–110; as social protest, 111, 115–116, 120–121; and temperance, 108–110; on wealth vs. success, 97–100, 104; *see also* Christian novel; conduct-of-life literature; self-help literature
Success magazine, 103; on political corruption, 112–113; on public ownership, 119–120; on ten-dollar political banquets, 107
success myth, 3, 65, 66, 91–92, 207; and capitalism, 7–8; defined, 3–4; and ego vs. super-ego, 196; vs. mass society, 13–14; vs. materialism and determinism, 12; and Protestant ethic, 16–18, 27; vs. success dream, 90–92; as world-view, 111
Sumner, Charles, on city, 41
super-ego, 196
supernaturalism, 113, 139, 228
Swedenborg, Emanuel, 138 *n*

Swoboda, 218

Taylor, Frederick W., on scientific management, 184
temperance and success literature, 108–110
That Printer of Udell's, 84–85
theology: and psychotherapy, 203–204; in New Thought, 143–145
Theosophy, 134, 168
Thrift, 131
Tom, the Bootblack, 52, 56
Towne, Elizabeth, 177
transcendentalism, 208, 215, 217; and New Thought, 134–135
Transcendentalist, 134
Trine, Ralph Waldo, 11–12, 168, 177, 231; on drawing power of mind, 169; on money, 173; on poverty, 180; on social ills, 182–183; on utility of religion, 136–137
Twentieth Century Magazine, 155

Universal Mind and subconscious mind, 208
Universal Soul and individual, 208

Veblen, Thorstein, 24
virtue: and happiness, 67; as health, 14; vs. poverty, 57; and prosperity, 112–113, 129; rural, 57–58; and success, 6–7, 9–11; vs. wealth, 40

Wallace, Henry A., on American middle class, 59
Watson, John B., on childrearing, 222
"Way to Wealth," 28
wealth: in Alger novels, 57–59, 91; in Christian novels, 79–83, 91–

wealth (*con't*)
92; and mind power, 172–176, 230; vs. social harmony, 74; and social position, 39; from speculation, 37–41; and success, 97–100, 104; from work, 37–41; in Harold Bell Wright's novels, 84–86; vs. virtue, 40

wealthy men in New Thought, 179

Weber, Max, 17, 23; on ethical maxims of early capitalism, 19; influence on study of success myth, 17–18; on Protestantism and capitalism, 18–23, 23–25

Webster's *International Dictionary of the English Language*, 98

welfare, general, and individual responsibility, 178–183

Wesley, John, on riches and religion, 22

White, William Alanson, on psychotherapeutics, 213–214

Whitney, William Dwight, 98

Whyte, William, on organization man, 185

will-culture, 215

will-to-believe, 140, 217, 226

Williams, James Watson, on greed for wealth, 42, 43

Winning of Barbara Worth, 85–86

work in New Thought, 144–145, 169, 172–174

Worth and Wealth, 37

Wright, Harold Bell, 74, 83–88, 90; attitude toward wealth, 84–86; *The Eyes of the World*, 86–88; *That Printer of Udell's*, 84–85; on West vs. East, 86; *The Winning of Barbara Worth*, 85–86

Wyllie, Irvin, on clergy vs. business community, 113 *n*

yeoman, myth of, 41–42, 111, 111 *n*, 118, 185